Can we know God exists
when he can't be seen, touched, heard, or tasted?

SIGNALS OF TRANSCENDENCE

One Man's Story

FRANK SHAW

PRESS
APOPKA
FLORIDA

Published by
DC Press
2422 Ridgeside Road
Apopka, Florida

Publisher's Cataloging-in-Publication Data
Shaw, Frank, 1957–
    Signals of transcendence : one man's story / Frank Shaw. –
    Apopka, FL : DC Press, 2018.

    p. ; cm.

    ISBN13: 978-1-932021-87-5

    1. Shaw, Frank. 2. Shaw (Family : Shaw, Frank)
    3. Christian biography—Louisiana—New Orleans.
    4. Christian life—Louisiana—New Orleans.
    5. Lawyers—Louisiana—New Orleans—Biography. I. Title.

BR1725.S438 2018
209.2—dc23   2017956407

Project coordination by Jenkins Group, Inc.
www.BookPublishing.com

Interior design by Yvonne Fetig Roehler

Printed in the United States of America
22 21 20 19 18 • 5 4 3 2 1

I dedicate this book to God, for I am nothing without Him, and to my son, Fletcher Glen Shaw. I also wish to express my love and thanks to my wife Lee for putting up with me, and my sons, Nicholas, Spencer, Sam, Jackson, Ross, and Mason for their understanding and support.

This book would not have been possible without the support of so many, including my family, law partner, Walter Leger, publisher, Dennis McClellan, without whose encouragement, guidance, and support this book would not have been written, Leah Nicholson and the Jenkins Group team, and the great people at World Vision for showing the love of Jesus Christ throughout the world. And to all those not mentioned who have reflected God's light and love in even the darkest of times, you have my sincere gratitude.

Acknowledgments and Permissions

I acknowledge and thank the following authors, artists, and publishers without reference to which this book would not have come about. Everything I know I learned from someone else.

* * * * * * * * * *

All Scripture verses are taken from *The Holy Bible*, English Standard Version. ESV® Permanent Text Edition® (2016). © 2001 by Crossway Bibles, a publishing ministry of Good News Publishers.

* * * * * * * * * *

Saint Augustine of Hippo, *The Confessions*. AD 401. Translated by Edward Bouveire Pusey, e-Book.

Peter L. Berger, *A Rumor of Angels: Modern Society and the Rediscovery of the Supernatural*. © 1969. (Open Road Integrated Media, e-book, 2011). Used by Permission.

Fyodor Dostoyevsky, *The Brothers Karamazov*, trans. Constance Garnett (New York: Lowell, 1912).

Os Guiness, *Fool's Talk: Recovering the Art of Christian Persuasion*. © 2015 by Os Guiness. InterVarsity Press, P.O. Box 1400, Downers Grove, IL 60515, USA. www.ivpress.com. Used by Permission.

C.S. Lewis, *Mere Christianity*. © C.S. Lewis Pte Ltd. 1942, 1943, 1944, 1952. Used by Permission.

M. Scott Peck, M.D., *The Road Less Traveled*. © 1978 M. Scott Peck. Reprinted with the Permission of Touchstone, a division of Simon & Schuster, Inc. All Rights Reserved.

Bill W. [William G. Wilson], *Alcoholics Anonymous: The Story of How Many Thousands of Men and Women Have Recovered from Alcoholism*, [The "Big Book"] 4th ed. (New York City, Alcoholics Anonymous World Services, Inc., 1976).

John Calvin, *Institutes of the Christian Religion*, 2 vols., ed. John T. McNeill, trans. Ford Lewis Battles (Philadelphia: Westminster, 1960). Used by permission of the publisher, Westminster John Knox Press.

Billy Graham. Twitter @BillyGraham, Apr. 4, 2015, 12:10 pm, available at https://twitter.com/billygraham/status/584432845600468995?lang=en.

* * * * * * * * * *

"After the Hangover's Over" by Vaughn Horton and Sammy Mysels. © 1963, 1964 by Southern Music Publishing Co., Inc. Copyright Renewed. Used by Permission. All Rights Reserved.

(Acknowledgments and Permissions continued)

"Signs" Words and Music by Les Emmerson. © 1970 Sony/ATV Music Publishing LLC, Unichappell Music Inc. and Galeneye Music. Copyright Renewed. All Rights on behalf of Sony/ATV Music Publishing LLC Administered by Sony/ATV Music Publishing LLC, 424 Church Street, Suite 1200, Nashville, TN 37219. All Rights on behalf of Galeneye Music Administered by Unichappell Music Inc. International Copyright Secured. All Rights Reserved. Reprinted by Permission of Hal Leonard LLC and Alfred Publishing, LLC.

"The Impossible Dream (The Quest)" by Mitch Leigh (melody) and Joe Darion (lyrics). © 1965. Andrew Scott Music and Helena Music Publishing Company. Used by Permission.

"Turn! Turn! Turn! (To Everything There Is a Season)" Words from the Book of Ecclesiastes. Adaptation and Music by Pete Seeger. TRO-© 1962 (Renewed) Melody Trails, Inc., New York, NY. International Copyright Secured. Made in U.S.A. All Rights Reserved Including Public Performance For Profit. Used by Permission.

"Walk Like An Egyptian" by Liam Sternberg. © 1986 by Peer International Corporation. Used by Permission. All Rights Reserved.

"Who Are You" Words and Music by Peter Townshend. © 1978 Spirit Catalog Holdings, S.à.r.l. All Rights Controlled and Administered by Spirit One Music. International Copyright Secured. All Rights Reserved. Used by Permission. Reprinted by Permission of Hal Leonard LLC.

"Wind-Up" Words and Music by Ian Anderson. © 1971 The Ian Anderson Group of Companies Ltd. Copyright Renewed. All Rights Administered by BMG Rights Management (US) LLC. All Rights Reserved. Used by Permission. Reprinted by Permission of Hal Leonard LLC.

"If I find in myself a desire which no experience in this world can satisfy, the most probable explanation is that I was made for another world."[1]

— C. S. LEWIS, *Mere Christianity*

Visit our website at
www.signalsoftranscendence.com
for links to purchase books online
and to iTunes and Spotify
to purchase songs so you can listen
and reminisce as you read!

Chapter One

I had been in these spots before. Life in upheaval, with both feet firmly planted in mid-air. I have intuitively learned how to handle these situations. They used to baffle me. Most times it is best not to do anything, just stand there. Floods, fires, deaths, just put one foot in front of the other. And that's what I was doing at my second oldest son's wedding with my mother lying in intensive care.

Was I restless? Maybe. Irritable? Possibly. Discontent? No. I was in no danger of drinking and hadn't been for many years. But there was a lot of ... "stuff" happening. I was sitting in a cramped folding chair, in a too crowded room, wearing a tuxedo. And being a life-long nicotine addict, I wanted to smoke. Other than that, I was cool.

Outside, fat raindrops splattered onto the surface of a small pond and in the flower gardens surrounding a beautiful white gazebo where the wedding should have been held. I could hear Mama saying, "You're not going to melt!" And at the front of the hastily arranged room was my second son standing among his groomsmen.

His lean body rocked in slow rhythm to an unheard song, and his brown eyes were bright and wide beneath his wire rimmed glasses. He bore a smile of great happiness and anticipation. In a few moments, his betrothed would march down the aisle to some beautiful song and take her place beside him.

Sons one and two, the groom, stood up front. Sons three, four, and five helped late comers find a seat. And the two youngest were in the back sporting dark shades and ear pieces like the Secret Service ready to take part in the processional. I sat next to my wife, a beautiful woman and proud mother. She gave me *that* look. You know, the one that says you ought to just confess even though you don't know to what.

My oldest sister's name is Lee. My other sister's name is Ann. Both of my sisters go by their middle names. I don't know why. My wife's name is Lee Ann. She dislikes using her full name, but Mama uses it so as to not get confused. I wonder what Sigmund Freud would say?

My mind—softened and made dopey by a drug to help me quit smoking— launched west to the ICU in Houston where my mother lay recuperating from surgery for an abdominal aortic aneurysm that happened only a few days before.

She was a tough old bird. Her flintiness and faith from her upbringing in North Louisiana shone bright. Two or three days before her surgery, I walked into her hospital room, a place of gadgets and blinking, whirring machines, to find her swinging her legs out of bed and heading to the closet. "Mama, what in the world are you doing?"

She looked up at me with that mischievous glint in her eyes. "I'm putting on my britches and walking out of here!" She'd have done it too if I had let her.

A day after the britches incident, Mama asked about the wedding. "It's this weekend, isn't it?"

"Yes ma'am, it is."

Her eyes wandered up from me and her lips stiffened then softened. She turned her eyes back to me. "I don't want to die on his wedding day. That should be a happy day for him." I almost fell over.

I wiped a tear away with the back of my hand. My mind wandered and a thought jumped in. Those can be dangerous. I wished I was sitting on the front porch at home with a cigar. The image was banished almost as soon as it appeared but it was too late. I was busted. The woman must have "ESPN" because she glanced at me like an errant child thinking bad thoughts. Mama always said mothers have two eyeballs in the back of their heads. And apparently, the ability to read minds.

I drove the five hours home to my small town north of New Orleans across Lake Pontchartrain that Thursday afternoon. I arrived just in time to dress and go to the rehearsal dinner. I was paying for it, I sure as hell wasn't going to miss it. The surgery had been Tuesday. It was supposed to take four hours, but after an hour and forty-five minutes the nurse called my oldest sister and me into a conference room to meet the thoracic surgeon. We braced for bad news. Why else would we be in here so early? He burst in with a big smile. The surgery had gone great and he drew me a nice picture.

No matter which way you sliced it (pardon the pun), it was a brutal procedure on an eighty-four-year-old woman. I didn't know if Mama would die the next day or what, so I stood there in cardiac ICU holding her hand all Tuesday night. She wouldn't let go and neither would I. I looked out the window and counted the lights on the building across the way. Over and over. The ICU nurse on the night shift was a big black guy. I told him flat out that we wouldn't have any problem as long as he wasn't an Alabama fan.

He smiled. "I went to Ohio State." OSU had recently beaten Alabama in the Sugar Bowl. I know, I was there with our high school football coach from the boys' school. The coach was from Youngstown and was a big OSU fan so I got him Sugar Bowl tickets for Christmas. He lets me coach.

Mom seemed to make it through under the circumstances and my sister shooed me to the rehearsal dinner. The goal was to get her well and home, but I had nagging doubts, like maybe we were just postponing the inevitable. I didn't dare say what I was thinking, least of all that I wasn't sure I could let go of her when the time came. I knew better. Like when Dad had died, I learned that no matter how ready you think you are, you are never really ready.

It was early evening when I pulled up the driveway to the house and rushed through the side door to get dressed for the rehearsal dinner. In what felt the blink of an eye, I was standing in a candlelit dining room, pausing before delivering a toast. I looked at the happy couple, both smiling, and then the expectant faces of our families. Time seemed to stop. I knew that in this moment we all shared the same sense of hope, joy, and promise. And my mother was there in spirit if not body.

I raised my glass of iced tea and began. "Things change and things evolve, and love has brought our families together into one. I am so proud to share this first meal, this first joyous occasion with our new family."

Glasses clinked, they all smiled, and all was as it should be in the world. I just wasn't really part of it.

# # #

There were several trips the next morning to the tuxedo rental shop to sort out the snafus. Then when Saturday evening came, we had a heavy rain. Wouldn't you just know? With everyone in the right tux, we rushed out into the rain to our cars.

During a break in the rain, we jogged into the reception hall and got organized, each guy off to their appointed duty. I said some hellos, moved to take my seat and tapped the breast pocket of my coat to be sure I'd remembered the scripture reading I was to give.

A few minutes earlier, I'd asked my son the groom, "I know you guys asked me to read part of Philippians, you know 'whatever is honorable … just … pure … lovely … commendable … worthy of praise, think about these things,' but I think I'd like to start earlier and read to the end. Is that okay with you?"

Number three's eyes perked up. I knew the verses. "Do not be anxious about anything, but in everything by prayer and supplication with thanksgiving let your requests be made known to God. And the peace of God, which surpasses all understanding, will guard your hearts and your minds in Christ Jesus." [2] I had been doing this for years. "Let go and let God." The theologians cringe at all that is left out and yet implied in this simple phrase.

He patted me on the back. "Start wherever you want Dad." He knew it was important to me even if he was agnostic in his beliefs.

Then son number three smiled. "Dad, just get up there and in your most officious Anglican impersonation of Martin Lloyd Jones say, *A reading from the book of Philippines.*'"

I wish he hadn't said that. I still have what some people might think are irrational or compulsive fears. Like the dream of standing up in court with my zipper down. I still check my zipper three times or more before leaving the bathroom. Now I had Manila on the brain.

I sat in the front row and repeated a few times, *Philippians, Philippians, Philippians* … until the sound of heads turning to the back of the room broke me from my mantra. Standing in the aisle were the bridesmaids. Each girl smiled nervously and was dressed in white with black, high-top sneakers. They looked at each other and then step, pause, step, pause … they made their way down the aisle.

Black high top sneakers? I racked my brain for statutes on motor vehicles. I mean is there a load limit? What if one of the bridesmaids had a blowout and careened off in to the crowd? There could be injuries. Would I have to call the State Police to investigate?

Then heads turned again and in the doorway, wearing white with black, high-top sneakers was the bride, beaming and blushing. She looked beautiful and the women tittered. Her eyes glanced toward the young man at the sound system and she took her first few furtive steps down the aisle as Darth Vader's theme from *Star Wars* poured from the speakers.

Wait, what was that? I had listened to loud rock and roll and shot a lot of ducks, so my hearing was not really up to snuff. Heads then turned to the young man at the soundboard as the room fell to silence. This was not good. The guy looked down as he worked to fix the error, then nodded like the issue was resolved.

The bride smiled and stepped back into the aisle, took three furtive steps and once again "The Imperial March" broke from the speakers. Bummer.

My addled brain thought to yell to my son to make a break for the exit. Inside I was screaming, *Run! Just run! It's Darth Vader!* But the bride looked up laughing, as if to say, *Nothing's going to stop me now.* Poor kid. And so, with the *Imperial March* as her accompaniment, down the aisle she came. He was smiling. Like they say, "Marriage is a great institution, if you like living in an institution!"

Looking at my son in his gray-blue tuxedo and long, wavy hair, the bridesmaids and bride in their high-tops, Darth Vader's accompaniment winding down, I remembered the weddings that had passed before.

My second oldest sister married a guy from New York who played trumpet in the LSU band. He may have been a genius, but Dad made him get his driver's license. You just can't have your wife drive all the time in Louisiana, even if you are from New York.

Then there was my younger brother whose two soon-to-be stepsons collapsed on a hot, humid day during the wedding ceremony. They were helped up and guided to pews where they sat with their heads between their knees with my sisters tending to them. Dad had looked up at the preacher. "Carry on," he said. Nothing flustered my dad.

Before my oldest sister got married, I'd finished my last law school exam. A course on contract law, (think *Paper Chase*) just before the rehearsal dinner. That night, I lost count at twenty martinis and they almost had to prop me up at the wedding the next day. After the ceremony, I stumbled out of the elevator into the reception. I snagged a bottle of champagne, which I nursed in a corner before bowing out early to my little apartment, where I slept until Monday. I was fried.

The family reverend had married my wife and me at our Presbyterian church when we were both two years sober. I don't think anyone would have advised us to get married so soon, but we never listened to anyone before. Why start now?

I have gotten used to expecting the unexpected. We have never done anything the way everybody else would. And it looks as if we aren't going to start now.

#

A few weeks before my son's wedding, the bride's grandmother had made it known that she wanted a Christian wedding. During premarital counseling, the minister set out belief in the Lord Jesus Christ as a prerequisite to him officiating. As it was reported to me, the bride said, "Not no, but hell no!" A friend of ours is a reformed Presbyterian pastor, and they agreed to let him perform the service just to keep the peace. I think he relished the task.

My son and I had engaged in several God discussions before. He told me once, "Dad, you know I argue with you over everything because you taught me to do that as a lawyer. But I must confess that whether you know it or not, I almost always end up doing what you say."

"Good," I said, "so you will agree with me that it makes no sense to paint yourself into a corner that you can't get out of. Keep an open mind, one of these days you may want to change it. I know I did. One day I just said, 'Hey, I was wrong about that. I've changed my mind.' After all, how can you be sure you even have a mind if you don't change it from time to time? It's not just a privilege reserved for women you know."

It was time for my part of the wedding. I rose, walked to the front of the room and began to speak, not in my most officious Anglican voice, just my regular lawyer's voice, "A reading from the book of Philippians." I read, looked over at number three, smiled and returned to my seat. Then it was my friend, the preacher's, turn. A good preacher knows how to use silence. My friend is a good preacher. He walked down the aisle, paused, and turned.

"When we come to faith, you do not choose God. God chooses you ..." From there he preached a message of love and solemnity for the couple with a note of fatherly warning. God works His will in our lives. It is not our place to disturb his sovereign choice.

I believe I heard most of it, but my mind wandered back to my front porch. Cigar smoke swirled past my nose as my number two son asked if he could speak with me Christmas before last. In his soft voice, he explained his plans for the future. He went on and on beating around the bush.

"Well, spit it out. Are you going to ask her to marry you or not?"

"Yeah, I am." He looked up at me. His eyes were shaded with apprehension looking for approval.

"Well, there is no perfect time. No guarantees. You have to make a decision and then make it work. Just be sure you have someone that you can go back to back with, lock arms, and fend off the world. Because that is what it will feel like sometimes, you two against the world. Sometimes you just have to take a deep breath and jump." I sounded like my dad and knew a little bit about the jumping thing.

For a while, my number two son had gone into his own subterranean world, but in the end, he found his way. Of course, I had to drive up to college and pull him out of school. Then the Saturday before Mother's Day we got a phone call that he was found virtually unconscious and taken to the local ER. I cajoled him into being admitted into a treatment center, and although it took a while, he got it. I am still working on him on the God part.

When to tell our boys that their parents met and married in recovery has been a subject of discussion in our marriage. We feared that if we told them that one parent was a recovered alcoholic and the other a recovered addict that they would feel doomed to repeat a failed scenario. Their fall into addiction would be a *fait accompli*. I came to faith in Christ through recovery, my wife at an altar call. Knowing that the remedy to addiction is a dependence on God, we purposed to raise them in church.

My wife would have liked our sons to come to salvation by raising them away from the temptations of the world, the flesh, and the devil. Me too. But I know that salvation rests on God's will, not ours. Whether my sons would have to travel the road through recovery was a choice not left to me. We have used public school, homeschool, and homeschool to seventh grade, followed by Christian schooling. The results have been mixed. I have sometimes felt like a man standing with his feet straddling a ditch. I would have preferred a foolproof answer.

Each of my sons is on his individual journey of faith. I know that. I have taught them the Bible. That God has made himself manifest in the birth, life, death, and resurrection of Jesus Christ. And I have tried to show them how there is more to life than what we can sense with our eyes and ears or what we experience in the day to day. After all I profess faith in a God that cannot be seen, heard, touched, or felt. Or can He?

As I look back both before and after sobriety, there were certain clues or signs, if you will, of God's presence and providence. These are to my mind the communicable attributes of God, or to borrow from Peter Berger, "signals of transcendence." [3]

I have shared my faith with my boys as they got to be of age, or so I thought. But I don't think I ever actually relived the journey with them. And without actually taking them on that journey, how can they really share my experience, strength, and, most importantly, the reason for the hope that is within me? When I hit my bottom, I was looking for meaning in booze, drugs, women, and other earthly things. I thought, *If this is all there is, then what's the point?* Then by the grace of God, I was saved, just as sure as if He plucked me from the path of a moving bus. I have to tell them who I was and where I came from so they will know who they are and where they come from. They need the whole picture.

#

I came to my senses as the happy couple read the vows they'd written for each other. It was clear that God did not put them together by accident. We had the reception right there in the hall with tons of good Italian food and a sound system that played more than "The Imperial March." I was happy and proud of my family. I do love them all to death. Then it was over. The newlyweds left for their first night as husband and wife, people sifted out into the evening, and we gathered our crew and drove home.

With the house a mess from the morning's rush but quiet in the wake of such a busy day, I stepped outside, alone for the first time since leaving Mama. The sky was clear, the air warm, and the stars shone bright. Reverberating around my mind was something written by Os Guinness, the English author and apologist:

> *Inevitably and inescapably, then, all who will not hear the signals of transcendence, and all who hear them but refuse to follow them, condemn themselves to be restless.*[4]

The trademark of the alcoholic, we are restless, irritable, and discontent.

I felt the absence of a lit cigar in my fingers. I worried about Mama. I thought of the pile of cummerbunds and other tuxedo paraphernalia I had to pick up around the house and return the next day, followed by depositions in north Louisiana, then driving back to the hospital in Houston. The BP oil spill case was ongoing with lives to be "made right." As always, there were the boys and endless school issues, football practices, and ceaseless appeals for more of me and from me. I was listening as loudly as I could.

This was not the first time I'd walked down my driveway wondering what was to come next. I looked up at the sky and asked the question I had asked God many times before, "Okay, what do you want me to do now?"

For thirty years I have lived through sobriety, marriage, childbirth, hurricanes, floods, fires, and death, knowing that no matter the circumstances, He would see us through. And yet, I still wanted some answers.

My wife called out into the night for me to come in and help her with the kids and the mess. I imagine that she worried that her husband, prone to flights of fancy, might have a lit cigar, and I wondered if she remembered that I'd already quit smoking for her once. I knew what to do. "Go slow and follow the signs."

I stepped into the house, shut the door, and flicked the outside lights off. Tomorrow was another day.

Non Posse Non Peccare

Chapter Two

I refer to myself today as a "two-by-four" Christian. God had to beat me in the head with a two-by-four until I finally surrendered. Off I would go down the broad path and bap! He would knock me back. Growing up, I didn't see God. I didn't see any signs. Hell, I didn't even look. I was only interested in what was in front of me to be taken at the time. But molding my life were the lessons and examples of my family. They taught me about God, justice, courage, kindness, and humor. They imputed to us goals and values which we knew were impossible to live up to, but we were to try anyway. Those expectations later weighed on me because I could see how far I'd wandered off the path. Then, in my darkest days, the seeds that had been planted helped me find my way back to who I was and where I came from.

#

Only in retrospect can I now see how the First Methodist Church in Winnfield, Louisiana had tied us all together through the generations like an immutable, omnipotent but unseen force. It was the center of my family and the community. With the persistent poverty and war that defined my grandparents' and parents' generations, the church was an anchor that folks hung on to.

If I close my eyes I can imagine a Sunday morning of my parents' youth in Winnfield. They are teenagers and passing acquaintances at best. It's summer and the air is warm and humid. Women flap fans to cool their faces, and the men have removed their coats rather than sweat themselves damp.

The Depression is a stubborn reality, and war will soon take many of the boys squirming with the desire to be outside from their homes.

Poppy, Ganny, Uncle John, Aunt Sarah, and Mama were probably sitting in a pew on the right. We always have sat on the right, toward the front as long as I can remember. It was from this roost that I remember Uncle John rising during a service past. I was a young boy, and my teenage cousins were cutting up as the pastor was in the meat of his sermon. "Excuse me, Pastor," Uncle John said in a serious voice. Every eye turned to him. "These two girls—" he pointed—"are misbehaving and they need to stand and apologize." Talk about being mortified. They did, and it was the last time they acted up in church.

My father's side of the family would have been there as well, though I had no idea where they would have sat. My grandparents had both died by the time I was born. I have to imagine that church was important to them as my dad's brother, Uncle Frank, and his wife attended during my childhood and in their later years as they were able.

What I do know is that Grandpa Shaw was born in Winn Parish after his father had come to Louisiana from Alabama as a young boy. (We call counties Parishes in Louisiana. It's a Catholic thing.) The City of Winnfield that greeted him was primarily a farming community with a modest downtown, composed of a handful of businesses surrounding the courthouse square.

Early in the twentieth century rather than trying his hand at farming, Grandpa Shaw opened a dry goods store to sell feed, tools, farm implements, clothing, and general merchandise. The store sat on the east side of the courthouse, which was one of those beautiful old buildings that would have ended up on the Historic Register had it not been torn down and replaced with a red brick pill box in the 1960s. (My Dad was not happy when the old courthouse was torn down.) Grandpa Shaw built his house atop a small hill a block up the street from the store. A block west is the First Methodist Church.

Grandpa Shaw's first wife died, and he subsequently remarried to Allie Mae Neal. They had three children, Uncle Frank, Elizabeth, who died in early childhood, and my dad. From all accounts, they were a happy family, the store prospered, and my grandfather was a well-respected member of the community—so much so that he was elected sheriff for several terms. This job entailed no small amount of risk.

In its earliest days, and especially after the Civil War, Winn Parish was a lawless, no-man's land. Things hadn't much changed when Grandpa Shaw served as sheriff. Winn Parish could be wild and violent, and the most dangerous places were the logging camps. Set up by northern logging companies they clear cut all the timber including the dogwood trees, which they used to make spools for thread.

As if the Civil War weren't enough, just to add insult to injury, they cut nearly every dogwood tree in the South. During the Depression, the Works Projects Administration (WPA) replanted many dogwoods, but not anywhere near what was lost. I remember Sunday drives through the Kisatchie National Forest west of Winnfield, usually around Easter, peering through the pines at the dogwoods in bloom with their white petals. Ganny would say, "Look at the dogwoods, but you can't see 'em." I've been told that the dogwood tree was used to fashion the cross of Jesus Christ. This is the legend:

> In Jesus' time, the dogwood grew
> To a stately size and a lovely hue.
>
> 'Twas strong and firm, its branches interwoven.
> For the cross of Christ its timbers were chosen.
>
> Seeing the distress at this use of their wood,
> Christ made a promise which still holds good:
>
> "Never again shall the dogwood grow
> Large enough to be used so.
>
> Slender and twisted, it shall be
> With blossoms like the cross for all to see.
>
> As blood stains the petals marked in brown,
> The blossom's center wears a thorny crown.
>
> All who see it will remember Me
> Crucified on a cross from the dogwood tree.
>
> Cherished and protected, this tree shall be
> A reminder to all of My agony." [6]

That was good enough for me. I was usually just ready to get home and eat. I guess it's apt that there is a contrast between the beauty of dogwoods in bloom and the ugliness of the timber camps where murders, stabbings, and fights were routine (and they weren't OSHA compliant, that's for sure).

Whenever there was trouble, Grandpa Shaw had to go out and investigate the murder or assault or some combination of the two. Confrontations were common, and one time he was chasing a suspect who got out ahead of him. As Uncle Frank told it, he was about to jump a fence when he thought better of it and stopped to listen. It turned out the suspect was waiting on the other side of the fence with a knife. The two remained there for some time in a standoff, but eventually the Sheriff got his man.

I'm not sure what happened to the fella, but I do know that justice had a sharper edge than it does now. Dad remembers public hangings in the courthouse square and one electrocution when the lights went dim, though I doubt they did that in the square.

There was also a more personal brand of justice. On Saturdays, particularly during the 1930s, farmers brought their produce into town to sell on the square and do their weekly shopping. On one busy Saturday, a local plumber by the name of Junior Barnes came face-to-face with the jealous husband of the woman he'd been bedding. The guy chased Junior across the courthouse square stabbing him in the back until he finally slit him in the throat, and Junior dropped right in front of the dry goods store.

Blood spurted out about six inches from Junior's neck as a local doctor tried to clip Junior's jugular vein. He couldn't and Junior bled out on the sidewalk. There was so much blood that fire hoses were used to wash it off the sidewalk.

Dad witnessed all of this at the ripe old age of seven. Feeling sick, he went to the back of the store and sat down. Grandpa came in. "You look a little green there son," he commented. It was just an observation. Dad made it clear to me just by telling the story that I would be exposed to life as it was. So, get ready.

#

When the Depression hit, life went from hard to desperate. This was true for everyone, but especially for the farms that surrounded Winnfield. These people were Grandpa Shaw's customers and most bought what they needed for the season on credit then paid when the crop came in. With the Depression, they found themselves in an impossible bind. Many, if not most, struggled to keep their accounts current at the store, but I don't believe my grandfather ever closed an account.

I suppose he had faith they would get current when they could. He also saw that no good would come of pushing these men and their families into destitution. You don't do that to a member of your community. The fact that you were in hard times because of something that wasn't of your own making wasn't held against you during the Depression. There were lots of people in hard times. Folks did for other folks as they could.

In several cases, farmers who'd reached their end, walked into the store and signed over the deeds to their land. Better to pay off their account than lose the land and buildings to foreclosure. Eventually, he came into several farms, which later served as timber parcels. I'm not sure who started that whole forty acres and a mule thing, but it seems like those parcels were about forty acres a pop.

I guess this is where the work ethic that was instilled in me came from. Of course, everybody pitched in and worked. But if you were a man it was required. My dad told me stories of unloading box cars full of sacks of oats, the 200-pound sacks that I heard about when his lumbago flared up. He taught me a few other things too, like a man is to work and support his family, don't judge a man by what he does for a living if he is earning an honest buck, and never ask how much money a man makes. It's just not to be done.

I wasn't born knowing these things; I was taught. This is why stories from the Depression days stick with me so much. They show that even as hard as life was, people did for one another. Grandpa Shaw didn't have to be sheriff, but he was. He didn't have to work with farmers on their accounts at the store, but he did. My Ganny's father was a doctor to his patients, whatever their need was. Her husband, my Poppy and grandfather, a pharmacist during the Depression, dispensed medical care to those who could not afford a doctor. What would have happened to Winnfield without these folks and the many others like them? They weren't forced or coerced into any of the roles they occupied. They did it because it was the right thing to do and they passed this ethic down to each generation.

I remember driving into Winnfield as a kid for vacation to see one of the buildings downtown on fire. Virtually every man in Winnfield was working to put that fire out. Uncle John waved hello as we passed. Not one of those men put a second thought to risking their own safety for the property of another. No matter the cost, they did for other folks before they did for themselves.

At the center of it all, was the churches. These people weren't do-gooders per se, but they understood that a community is more than a collection of buildings. They were in it together, and each person carried as much weight as they could, young and old, men and women. If there was a death, everyone attended the funeral, followed by a covered dish supper prepared by the ladies at the church.

I ended up becoming a fifteen-year-old selfish brat, but it wasn't because my family raised me that way. It would take some time for these lessons to sink in. One lesson, though, that I did pick up on early in life was that if you wanted a deviled egg at a picnic or covered dish supper, you had to get in the front of the line. All men of the South understand this. You don't want to come all the way down the line to find the deviled eggs are gone. Either you get to the front or you sweet talk one of the ladies into setting one aside.

#

I also learned that fishing is almost religion. After all, the disciples were fishermen. As part of Roosevelt's New Deal, the Works Progress Administration (WPA) dammed a handful of rivers north and west between Winnfield and Natchitoches to form a series of lakes—Saline, Black, and Clear. Within a short amount of time, these lakes filled with largemouth bass and the fishing was so good that folks from as far north as Chicago came down to fish them.

One of the best was Saline Lake, which is in Winn Parish and just a short drive west on US 84 from Winnfield. If the living was hard during the Depression, the fishing was easy. Every Thursday afternoon, the merchants of Winnfield—including Grandpa Shaw and Poppy—closed their stores to go fishing. It became such a routine for Poppy that he bought some land and built a small camp on the lake.

During the Depression, no one had outboard motors, so Uncle Frank or Dad had to row or paddle Grandpa Shaw, a rather large man, around the lake. They would cast for bass using plugs—a Lucky Thirteen or Green Darter, floating wood lures that resemble small fish with three treble hooks dangling from their belly. Make a cast, let it sit, give it a wiggle, then reel in whatever bass chose to make that his last meal.

I can imagine a lake dotted by these men, smiling, and enjoying the sacrament of a Thursday afternoon of fishing. I don't know how much time Grandpa Shaw and Poppy spent fishing together, if any, but the dry goods store and Poppy's pharmacy were on the same block. Everybody knew everybody.

Mama used to tell me that when she was a girl she'd run into my grandfather on the sidewalk in front of his store. She'd ask him how he was feeling that day and he'd reply, "Let's see…" Then he'd let fly a stream of tobacco spit. If he hit more than halfway across the street he'd say, "Looks like I'm doin' pretty good."

My maternal grandmother, Ganny (so named because my oldest first cousin could not pronounce *Granny)*, came from Atlanta, Louisiana, an even smaller town south of Winnfield. Her father was a physician called Daddy Doc. Through first my mother then my Uncle John, I heard tales of a gang called *The Nightriders*, the West-Kimbrell Clan located near Atlanta, south of Winnfield. Ganny never spoke of them.

During Reconstruction, quite a few people left the South and headed west following the El Camino Real from Natchez, Mississippi, to Natchitoches, Louisiana. The route ran south of Winnfield through Atlanta and on to Montgomery, Louisiana, where there was a crossing of the Red River. Travelers would often stop at the homes of these people. They didn't last long. There are stories of a clan mother getting mad at her daughter for not properly holding a woman over a bucket as she slit the woman's throat and blood got on the kitchen floor. They dumped the bodies in wells, and because they killed so many people, they had to dig a well every mile along a forty-mile stretch of road.

With the travelers dispatched, they sold their belongings, which made them rich and dangerous. The people of Atlanta became distraught and sent a rider to ask the occupying U.S. Cavalry for help. The Cavalry sent a colonel up to investigate. He was quickly murdered, his body thrown in the Red River. Rather than send troops, the Governor in New Orleans sent a whole slew of signed but blank "pardons" to the folks in Atlanta so they could act on their own behalf.

One of the leaders of the West-Kimbrell clan, John West, was a deacon of the church, and John Kimbrell was a church member. West taught Sunday school. To catch them off guard, the vigilantes waited to round up the members of the clan until Easter Sunday church services. Then they distributed shot guns—some only had rock salt so no one would know if they fired a fatal round—lined them up firing squad style and shot the whole lot. At least that was the tale.

No one spoke of it in Atlanta because there were still family members in the community and Daddy Doc had to make house calls. He didn't want to get shot while out on a dark, lonely road. I guess that's why Ganny always told us, "If you don't have anything nice to say, don't say anything at all." Good advice.

On my Mama's side, the first to set foot in Winnfield to my knowledge was my great-grandfather, Daddy Pole (for "Napoleon"). He bought some land at the top of what became known as Jackson Hill and started a dairy. When I was a kid, I could start at the top of that hill on a bike and gather enough momentum to carry me to Shaw house where Uncle Frank lived.

Daddy Pole married Mamaw and they had five kids including my grandfather known to us as Poppy. I don't know much about his childhood, but in the 1920s he rode a mule east to Clarence, Louisiana, where he caught a train to New Orleans to attend Tulane University. When he visited us in New Orleans, he still loved to get a café-au-lait and beignets, which we called French market donuts, at Café Du Monde. You can't breathe when eating a French Market donut or you'll get powdered sugar all over your clothes. And if you're wearing black you're really sunk.

Poppy was a Tulane football fan, even going so far as to travel to Pasadena in 1932 for the Rose Bowl, where undefeated Tulane lost to the University of Southern California 21 to 12. His love of football would later play an important role in my own life.

Poppy earned a pharmaceutical degree and returned to Winnfield where he worked in a drugstore just down the block from the dry goods store. I loved that drugstore. It had an old-style soda fountain with heavy Coke glasses and everything. We used to make cherry nectar sodas and root beer floats.

A few years later, he married Ganny. Before long, Aunt Sarah came along, followed by Uncle John and my mother. He eventually bought his own drugstore. And according to the children, it was a very straight-laced upbringing.

Church was a part of life and there was no tobacco or alcohol. Mom did not smoke until she went to Ruston to attend Louisiana Tech. Years later, I was mildly shocked to discover that Aunt Sarah also would sneak off and smoke a cigarette. I never had a clue. She was good, real good. No one smoked or drank in Poppy and Ganny's house or in front of them. That was just the way it was.

Uncle John would go on to play college football. He was a punter and tight end in Y. A. Tittle's day. He claimed Tittle could throw the football so hard he could knock you down. When he was recruited in high school, the LSU scouts came to a game to see him punt. He kicked the ball so hard, it went out of sight of the lights. Then it came down, twenty yards downfield. He kicked better after that.

Seems like Easter was one of Poppy's favorite holidays, selling all the Elmer's chocolate Easter eggs, baskets, and candy at the store and buying Easter corsages for all his granddaughters. That and the Fourth of July when the family gathered at his camp on Saline Lake for the family reunion picnic.

The camp has a boathouse, and fishing figured prominently at the reunion and through the year. Poppy was not only an ace with a bass plug, but he knew the lake so well that he knew the location of each cypress stump and the personal details of every fish lurking beneath those stumps too. As I said, fishing in Winnfield was almost religion.

At the picnic, we always ate fried chicken, casseroles with squash, green beans, and the like, roast and pork, salads and rolls. And the dessert table had every kind of cake and pie you could imagine. Blackberry and peach cobbler, pecan pie, chocolate pie with meringue, banana pudding. Need I continue? Sometimes I just hit the desserts first. I mean, why not? In the early years, we usually cut a Saline watermelon, which was good with a sprinkle of salt, and made homemade ice cream that you had to hand crank. Electric cranks came later. Seemed like cheating somehow. Of course, the homemade vanilla ice cream was topped with peaches from the orchard at Poppy's farm. And there were deviled eggs if you were lucky enough to get one or two.

When my dad was born, my grandpa was up in years. I don't think Dad spent much time bouncing on his knee. Not only was my grandfather busy in the community and with his work, but he seems to have been a bit of a hard man. When my nephew, Dad's first grandson, was born, we asked Dad what he wanted to be called? Grandpa? Gramps? What? Dad calmly replied, "He can call me Mr. Shaw." Some of my grandfather might have rubbed off on Dad.

Dad also looked up to his older brother, my Uncle Frank. Frank was several years older than Dad, and I can imagine Dad as a young boy following his older brother around. Dad's nickname for Uncle Frank was "Bud."

Growing up, I heard stories about "me and Bud." There was Dad getting clobbered with the brass nozzle of a firehose used in a tug-of-war between Bud and some older boys. Then there was the time Bud hooked Dad in the cheek while casting a Lucky 13. This story was usually told while we were fishing, along with the admonishment to look behind you before casting. Uncle Frank had to use his penknife to cut the hook out, and Dad used to show us the scar on his cheek. Even though it seemed like most of their stories involved Dad being hurt in some painful way, they laughed each of their tales off as good times.

I think the stories that meant the most to me, though, were of growing up in the Depression. When I was a kid and couldn't sleep, Dad would conjure up images of himself as a young boy sleeping out on the back screen porch, letting the chirping of crickets lull him to sleep. Above his head, a ceiling fan whirred and cooled the muggy, mid-summer air.

A couple times a week, an ice truck came by with a block of ice that they'd put in the icebox to keep their food cool, which included milk, butter, and eggs, probably from Daddy Pole's dairy. Dad remembers skimming the cream off the top of the milk, which was a real treat.

He told me, too, that people used to roll their own cigarettes from loose tobacco such as Bull Durham. Bits and pieces would fall to the floor of the dry goods store and Dad would sweep it up and roll whatever was on the floor for his cigarettes. Of course, that was the Depression and everybody smoked because they just didn't know any better. Everybody but Poppy and Ganny that is. Ganny always said that tobacco was a nasty and dirty habit.

Though everyone felt the Depression, none more so than the families farming the land just beyond the town limits. Dad remembers going to school with kids who had nothing more than a pair of coveralls and many times were barefoot. In the winter, they walked with a hot sweet potato to keep their hands warm then ate it for lunch. I don't know what they did for the walk home, but it puts a shine to the supposed misery of a yellow school bus.

My Grandmother felt privileged for the family to live in town close to the school. To her, education was a high calling, and she made sure that her kids made the best of what was offered to them. After high school Dad went off to college at LSU, transferring to Louisiana Tech in Ruston, Louisiana, after Pearl Harbor. It was closer to home but just far enough away to have to take the train and not be able to come home every weekend.

By this point, the war was raging and there was a premium placed on educated young men who were smart enough to fly a plane, but weren't smart enough to be scared. Recruiters made regular stops at Louisiana Tech, Georgia Tech, Texas A & M, and other southern schools because my dad said they liked country boys. "Despite our education, we were too dumb to know better," he said. They just wanted pictures in the cockpit with the flight jacket, helmet, goggles, and scarf.

Dad went to flight school on the west coast where he learned to fly Corsairs and Hellcats, as well as drop bombs and torpedoes with a degree of accuracy. Then they had to learn to fly off a carrier. Taking off wasn't so bad, but landing on a pitching carrier deck steaming across the ocean was a whole other matter. Three men in Dad's squadron lost their lives attempting their first solo landings. One hit the drink before reaching the deck, another spun off to the right, and the last hit the tower.

My exposure to all this was while tucked in Dad's lap as we looked through his flight school yearbook. He liked to tell me about the planes and some of the training. From where I sat, it was all wonderful and heroic. I dreamed of flying. Still do. Dreams where you stretch out your arms, catch some wind, and just float. It's awesome until you wake up. The Navy deployed him, but Dad never saw combat. I never asked him if he regretted that and he never said.

When the Navy discharged Dad, he came home and worked at the store, but dry goods didn't have the same level of excitement as flying planes. My take is there was some friction between brothers, but I never got the skinny on what happened between Dad and Uncle Frank, and there was no need to ask. So, I didn't. He did finish up his degree in Business at Louisiana Tech.

At some point "after the war," Uncle Dennis, Mom's first cousin, my Uncle Harold, a friend named John Peters, and Dad decided to take a camping trip and fish their way across northern Wisconsin and Minnesota. For several weeks, they caught walleye and pike and followed a labyrinth of dirt roads while exploring a vast, lake-filled area, living in tents. They loved it and years later I would look at the few pictures that Dad had of them camping. Their camping equipment and tents looked just like the stuff used by the Three Stooges and they looked so young and skinny.

Due to the friction between Dad and Uncle Frank, my grandfather suggested to my dad that he might be happier doing something else. So he enrolled at LSU Law School.

I know Uncle Frank and Dad had argued about the direction to take with the store. Uncle Frank wanted to ease off the farm supplies and sell upscale men's and women's clothes. Dad wanted to expand the dry goods aspect of the store and take it in the direction of a hardware store with a range of household items. He'd studied business at Louisiana Tech and thought adding to the current store and then opening a series of other stores, just like Sam Walton did, would work. Through the years, he talked somewhat wistfully about what it would be like to run a hardware store selling nuts and bolts and that sort of stuff. I guess being in business for yourself was in his blood.

My parents never told me much about their courtship. It just never came up. Funny, but my boys have never really asked about how my wife Lee and I met either. My theory is its part of that "Ewwww!" reaction that kids have when they see their parents smooching. A natural blank spot.

They knew of each other, of course, hard not to in such a small town, but Dad was several years older than Mom so they weren't classmates or anything like that. Their first "date" was my Aunt Sarah and Uncle Dennis's wedding. In other words, just coincidence.

What I do know is that Mom worked the soda fountain through World War II when Generals George Patton and Omar Bradley held war games in Louisiana before D-Day. As I heard it, Patton marched from Fort Polk to the southwest and Bradley from Monroe in the northeast with Winnfield right in the middle. The two generals met on the Winnfield Courthouse steps. If they could fight across the muck of Louisiana they could fight across Europe, and they did.

After graduating from college, Mom became a school teacher in the sprawling town of Calvin just north of Winnfield. Dad had graduated law school and they were married at the Methodist church in June, 1952. Mom taught school, Dad practiced law, and they struggled.

# # #

Winnfield may be small, but it gave birth to Huey and Earl Long, two of the biggest political personalities in Louisiana and the country. Huey is the better known of the brothers. He was a populist during the Depression who blamed the big banks for much of the country's woes and promoted a program he called Every Man a King. His rhetoric was big, inflammatory, and effective. As Huey rose up the political ranks to become Governor and then a U.S. Senator, Winn Parish was, as it had been before the Depression, trapped in a cycle of deep poverty. With rhetoric that spoke directly to the impoverished and those who believed the world gave them a raw deal—which was most people in the U.S.—Huey became one of the state's most powerful politicians.

There is one story about his successor as governor of Louisiana, whom Huey handpicked after he won his U.S. Senate seat. He too was from Winnfield, and his name was Oscar K. Allen, nicknamed "OK" Allen because one day the window to his office was open, a leaf blew onto his desk, and he signed it.

Huey was a Democrat and supported Roosevelt in 1932, but soon felt that he, the Kingfish, would do a better job. As he prepared for a presidential run and his notoriety reached its national peak, the son-in-law of a political rival shot and killed him at the State Capitol in Baton Rouge.

This left a vacuum, which Earl stepped into. Earl was a populist like his brother who also had a unique oratory flare that earned him the nickname, "Uncle Earl" and helped him win three non-consecutive terms as Governor. Judging by what he did, he was also crazy.

His wife Blanche committed him to the insane asylum in Mandeville after he compelled a state trooper to take him on a road trip through Texas, buying everything he saw, including a large number of cantaloupes. It probably didn't help his case with the wife that he was carrying on with a string of strippers, most famously with Blaze Starr.

Earl ran the state from the hospital by phone—there was no law in Louisiana that said he couldn't—and extricated himself from the asylum after firing the head of the state hospital system and replacing him with a friend. The friend ordered Earl released and life went on.

My Uncle Frank used to tell a story about a man who had a flat tire in front of an insane asylum. He took off the flat tire and put the lug nuts in the hubcap, which got blown into a ditch by a passing Greyhound bus. The man took off his shoes, rolled up his pants and his sleeves then started fishing around in the ditch, which was half-full of muddy water. The more he searched the muddier the water got. Frustrated, he stood up to see the bleary-eyed face of a mental patient at the chain link fence in a robe with bed hair.

"What the hell are you looking at!" the man shouted.

"Mister, if I was you, I'd take one lug nut off those other three tires, put my tire back on and drive on into town missing one off each."

Stunned, the man said, "That's a great idea. What are you doing in that insane asylum?"

"Hell mister, I might be crazy, but I ain't stupid."

Maybe Uncle Frank was talking about Earl.

With Huey and Earl, as well as other notable politicians, politics was an active pursuit in Winnfield, especially if you were a lawyer, as both Huey (who practiced in Winnfield) and Earl were. It probably also helped that Grandpa Shaw served as sheriff, but whatever the driving impulse, Dad decided to make a run for the state legislature.

Earl was governor at the time, and his representative passed through Winnfield and paid a visit to Dad in his law office. He told Dad that Earl would consider it a pleasure to support Mr. Frank's son, but that he expected Dad to vote the way Earl wanted him to. Dad refused, and failing to get Earl's endorsement, he lost the election. Years later after he retired, Dad would give tours at the Louisiana Political Museum in Winnfield. When it was opened, he and

Uncle Dennis, former Editor of The *Winn Parish Enterprise* newspaper, had bets on the chance that the entire museum, visiting politicians, dignitaries, and all would be incinerated by lighting during the opening ceremonies. Dad would start his tours by saying, "Welcome to Winnfield, Louisiana, home of three governors and not proud of any of them." The tours were very enlightening so I've heard.

After the election, Dad was a bit discouraged to go back to his sleepy law practice. He used to chuckle about a letter from a client who was a farmer in a particularly rural area of Winn Parish. The raging issue of the time was the open range law, which allowed farmers to let their livestock wander across roads and railroad tracks. An Illinois Central train struck this particular farmer's bull. The bull wasn't killed, but it lost a testicle resulting in the farmer's complaint that, "He ain't no good as a bull no more."

Bored and struggling, Dad looked for a way out, which came when Shell Oil Company offered him a job in New Orleans. He always said that a man has to go where the work is, so he took the job. It always struck me that Mom and Dad were the only two of their families to leave Winnfield. My other aunts and uncles stayed and didn't seem to have any inclination to leave. But as Mama told me when I asked, "I was kinda glad to be away because in Winnfield everybody knows your business all the time. It's hard to do what you want without the whole town knowing about it."

They moved into the Parkchester Apartments off Carrollton Avenue and my sister Lee was born soon after. My parents named her Elizabeth after my Dad's younger sister who had died as an infant. We always called her by her middle name, Lee.

My grandfather had been sick for some time. He lingered for a bit, and Dad administered morphine injections to make him comfortable before he died in Winnfield at his house just up the street from the store and the Methodist church. My sister Lee was just three months old. Then my other sister, Sarah Ann, was born and the family moved to a house in Airline Park. Grandma died not long after.

On March 9, 1957, at Baptist Hospital in New Orleans, I was born into the world, and as I was told by my Mom, given the name Sam. Apparently, Dad still had hard feelings over the dry goods store, which now sold men's and women's fashionable clothing.

Dad later consented to change my name to Frank, also his Dad's name. I have always wondered if my life would have been different with the name Sam.

Dad and I discussed my name. He made it clear that I was named after my grandfather and that you make a name what it is, the name doesn't make you. Made sense to me. Besides he always had some nickname for me. Knot-head, Bur-head (after shaving us with the clippers), Hot Shot, and Old Man were the most used. And he never wanted to name a child after himself. He said he figured that was the height of arrogance and would bind the child to a past, either good or maybe bad. My "little" brother John Robert was born two years later.

In 1958, it snowed while we lived on Airline Park. Snow is an unusual occurrence in New Orleans, Louisiana, and only happens once in a blue moon. I have no memory of that snowfall, but I know it happened. Through the years, we would pull out a shoebox full of pictures and among them was a Polaroid taken from outside the house in the front yard. It shows snowflakes angling across the screen in front of a picture window that frames a toddler standing in a playpen.

That toddler was me.

Chapter Three

I have no memory of the day that photo of the child staring out into the snow was taken, nor do I remember Airline Drive. That photograph symbolized to me the beginning of a feeling of fear. Fear of being alone.

It seems we all begin life as a blank slate. We then live our lives and write on our slates, choosing what we think is best for us at the moment. I sure did. And even though I was raised and taught different, inevitably my willpower could not resist the temptations of the world and the flesh, and I bought the plausible lie that therein lies true happiness. But I wasn't seduced. I ran to it. Try as I might, I simply had no ability to resist.

For the first thirty years of my life, I stuffed fears and feelings of aloneness with drugs and alcohol. As I caterwauled through life, there were signs from God I just missed. I ran from God. God didn't run from me. And when I turned, He was there.

Some have argued that it didn't have to be that way. That I could just have turned from my ways. Baloney. I was powerless over alcohol and life in general. I was a slave to sin. I was born that way. It took the disillusionment, bewilderment, humiliation, and humbling defeats to get me to a point where God changed my heart and entered my life. *Why me?* I have asked that question a thousand times, but it took what it took.

My slate was never really blank, and neither is yours. We just don't know what will be written. I might have been afraid of being left alone, but I could sense that I wasn't. I had a feeling that this world can't be it. It just can't.

#

I was born in the late 1950s to parents who survived the Depression as well as the inevitable pain and loss of World War II. Their world was a place capable of great evil and hardship, but they were somehow also able to see great joy in it as well. Or maybe it was their hope that the worst was finally over.

Like the rest of America, they sought to provide their kids with the security and comfort the Depression and war robbed from them. My memories begin on Melody Drive and like an aged reel in a projector, they come in flashes of what it was like to be a kid in the late 1950s and early 1960s. They overlap and twist around each other.

There were Christmas visits to Maison Blanche, a department store on Canal Street. In one of the large display windows, "Mr. Bingle" performed. He was a mechanical snowman that lived in a world of fake snow, candy canes, toys, Christmas lights, and a model train that looped around a track. He sang in a metallic voice and his gears stuttered as he moved, but he excited the imaginations of young children, including me.

As Christmas Eve approached, Mom and Dad loaded us into the car—none of us in a seatbelt and Mom and Dad smoking with the windows up—and drove to St. Charles Avenue. The houses were lit for the holidays with the best one being the home of the owner of a local dairy. There were the old-style lights with big glass bulbs, displays in the windows, a nativity scene, and a fat old Santa.

One New Year's Eve, it snowed. Outside was a rare delight while inside smoke and the voices of Mom and Dad gabbing over drinks with Uncle Frank and Aunt Martha filled the house. These were the post war years when doctors in advertisements said, "Light up!" and draining a bottle over the course of an evening was the norm. Years later someone said, "We used to talk about our problems over a cigarette and a drink. Now those are our problems." I had my heart set on shooting fireworks at midnight but fell asleep.

New Year's morning, there must have been six inches of snow, and I bounced on Mom and Dad's bed until bleary eyed and smelling of booze, Dad got up and went out with me. I shot a few firecrackers and he winced.

#

On Sunday mornings, Mother dressed us in our best clothes and then piled us into the station wagon for the trip to Metairie Methodist Church. When I was quite young, the whole thing seemed normal and natural, and I liked my Sunday school teacher.

Most of what we did was fun, but sometimes Miss Foil would go a little deep for a young, nervous boy. One day she talked about God and how big and powerful He is, and I couldn't help but wonder whether we are all just a small speck on a giant's toe. Mom thought that was somehow profound.

Another day, we sprouted an acorn and then planted it beside the church, a lone building surrounded by a white shell parking area and vacant lots. The area is now inundated with big box stores, strip malls, and restaurants. Right in the middle of it all is that small church and what is now a big oak tree.

Dad made it to church most Sundays, but there were plenty of times he stayed home. I think his excuse was to watch over my younger brother. As the story goes, the minute the car pulled out of the driveway, my brother filled his diaper. Mama always said, "That's what he gets for not going to church."

Though I liked Sunday school, church wasn't always my favorite thing. One Sunday before church, I climbed a china ball tree and refused to come down. We had just read the story of Zacchaeus in Sunday school taught in a children's song. Zacchaeus was a tax collector and an unpopular guy. Before Jesus came to town, Zacchaeus climbed high up a sycamore tree "for the Lord he wanted to see." Jesus stopped and said, "Zacchaeus, you come down, for I'm going to your house today." [8] The effect was to shock the crowd by His compassion for a man they loathed.

Dad came out to get me for church, and I refused to come down. He wasn't Jesus. "Fine," he said and walked into church. Well, it was a blazing hot July day, and it didn't take long for the heat to all but melt me and convince me that it wasn't fun sitting in a tree in the heat, alone. I got down and went inside. In my own good time. In my childish way, I had been looking for Jesus but missed Him because it never occurred to me that I really was Zacchaeus. I had a long, long way to go.

Bass fishing runs in my family and, in a kid's eyes, was the natural competitor to church. It made no sense. *We could be fishing right now*, I thought to myself as we walked into the First Methodist Church in Winnfield one Sunday. But I knew better than to say this to Poppy. Going to church was not an option. Poppy loved the church and made certain that I knew to give ten percent of everything I made. When church was over in June or July, it was as hot as all get out. The fishing wouldn't get good until things cooled in the evening.

Afternoon dinner followed Church and then everyone took a nap. Kids don't appreciate naps and neither did I. But I do now. Poppy and I would head to the lake around four in the afternoon and it was pure freedom. Like a breeze through a screen door. With daylight savings, we could fish until nine o'clock.

One Sunday, Mama tired of me whining about why I had to go to church and said, "For all God has done for you, you can't give up one hour for Him?" Earlier that week in Winnfield, she had made it a point to introduce me to a mailman whose name I am ashamed to say that I can't recall. When we were alone again in the car she said, "Let me tell you boys about that man. In high school, he could throw a ninety-five mile an hour fastball and was offered a contract by the New York Yankees. He asked if he would have to pitch on Sunday. When they said yes, he said 'no thank you,' turned down the contract, and has been a mailman in Winnfield ever since. So, I never want to hear you complain about going to church again." And that was that.

On the Sundays when we were out at the camp on Saline Lake, we would get up early before church and cast when the fish were active. As the sun rose and the heat took over, things calmed, but I still hated heading back to the camp. Down the road on US Highway 84 in the village of Cooley, Louisiana, is a little white-frame Methodist church that's probably been there forever. If you wanted to fish, you could go to church in Cooley. And the trip into town was just half an hour tops. There was no getting around going to church. I'd hate to think what Poppy would have done had I climbed a china ball tree in Cooley or Winnfield. Out of my own self-interest, I accepted that church was the more reasonable alternative. I only saw Poppy get really mad once when I almost slammed my brother's hand in the car door. I never wanted to see that again.

And in light of the threat of a spanking or a switch to your behind, I learned all the "rules." When spoken to I said, "yes sir" and "no sir," "yes ma'am" and "no ma'am." You stood when a woman entered or left a room, and you did what you were told. You only spoke when spoken to and always did for others before doing for yourself. If you didn't have anything nice to say, you didn't say anything at all.

Through the years, there were "important" occasions. For the kids it was Christmas. The adults seemed to prefer Easter. This was a special day for Poppy. We'd go to Winnfield for Easter. He would buy corsages and put them in the refrigerator at the drugstore to keep them fresh for all the granddaughters to wear on Easter Sunday.

One Easter, Mama made my brother and me white linen coats. Dad used his clippers to all but shave our heads as usual. We had black bow ties, black pants, and Mama bought us black dress shoes with white tops, which seemed like something Elvis would wear. We stood on the front walk of Ganny and Poppy's house and took a photo. I call it the Penguin Picture.

Dad drove an old red Dodge sedan, which was our only car until I was in kindergarten. We lived near Veterans Boulevard, which is one of the main arteries in Metairie, and Mom would take Dad to a bus stop on Canal Boulevard so he could get downtown to the office. Some days he took the car, and we had to make do without.

As the car aged, there got to be a rusted-out hole in the floorboard that he covered with cardboard. On rainy days, he had to roll his pants up or lift his legs so that his pants didn't get wet and dirty when he drove through a puddle. Behind the backseat, the dash to the trunk caved in so we could crawl right in. This was great for the drive to Winnfield. Dad laid a board down on the backseat so we could sleep in the backseat or crawl into the trunk. We never got pulled over and searched.

In those days, there wasn't a north-south interstate for us to speed up to Winnfield, so we took US Highway 190 which crosses the Atchafalaya Basin. Past Krotz Springs, we headed north on Louisiana Highway 71 into Lebeau where we'd hit a small truck-stop type of restaurant called Stelly's. They served seafood gumbo that was as dark as molasses with crab, shrimp, and oysters that we kids called "dead bodies" because they floated. Like dead bodies. It took us a while to realize these were good and stop letting Dad eat all our dead bodies. Then we would continue north to Alexandria through Bunkie and Cheneyville to Winnfield.

Though his job as a lawyer for a large corporation meant we lived comfortable, middle class lives, there was precious little of Dad to spread around. The trips to Winnfield each summer and holidays were wonderful. We would get up at Ganny's, eat breakfast, and head to town to visit. At the drugstore, we got ice cream and cherry nectar sodas. But back home in Metairie, time with Dad never felt like it was enough. So we had to make the most of what we had.

Some days Dad and I would pour through his Navy flight book from basic training and then try to spot and identify planes flying to and from Lakefront Airport, which juts out from the south shore of Lake Pontchartrain. My brother had an old metal fire truck that you could pedal around the driveway. We had just outgrown it when one Saturday Dad was hosing off the carport, and he hit upon the idea of building a ramp. He stacked up whatever he could find—a chair, a milk box, wooden planks, and I can't remember what else— and we perched at the top of the pile on the fire truck. It seemed like a mile high even though it couldn't have been more than six feet. With Dad's help, we launched ourselves down the ramp to the concrete below. I'm not sure how many times we fell off and hit our heads on the pavement, but it sure was fun.

One weekend, Dad trimmed the ligustrum bushes that lined the fence behind our house and helped us build a great fort. We took the branches he cut and hung them from a string we tied between the pear tree and the fence. We also had a tree house behind the carport. Actually, it was just a board in the base of a tallow tree, but it was a treehouse to us. And we would dive from the top of the clothes line into the ligustrum bushes. They would hold us up and we could just swim through the bushes. Except when they bloomed in the spring and the honey bees showed up.

One Sunday, Mom and Dad took us bream fishing up on the Lake Pontchartrain spillway. We were up in the treehouse and they started yelling for us to come on. My sister Ann got out onto the branch that we would hang from then let go and drop. She wouldn't drop for some reason. I bumped her to get her going and a length of kite string caught her front teeth and pulled them up so they poked straight out.

She yelped, and when I looked, there was blood running down her chin and tears flowing from her eyes. She ran to Mom and Dad who took her to the dentist to try and straighten her front teeth. They ended up putting caps on her teeth. For years, I felt terrible.

I do have to say that older sisters could make life difficult. Ann walked to the beat of a different drum, and had a mind of her own. Dad nicknamed her Pooh after Winnie the Pooh because she liked the story so much. And she knew how to use her special status by finding new and many ways to antagonize J.R. and me. On trips to Winnfield she'd just pick, pick, pick, pick until my brother and I would react. Then in a classic sister move she'd yell to the front seat, "They're hitting meeee!"

Despite having older sisters, I was a boy and I knew it. When I was a baby, Mama didn't want to cut my curls until one day my Dad was walking down the street pushing the stroller when a neighbor lady looked at me and said, "What a cute little girl you have!" He marched me back home and then off to the barber to have my head shaved. Next, he bought a pair of clippers, and my brother and I were from then on, the two, towheaded, crewcut, cotton top boys. In later years, we begged him to leave a quarter of an inch in the front that we could comb up with butch wax.

Mama and my sisters couldn't seem to get enough of dancing and sequins, and at times I felt victimized. Forget Guantanamo. We should make prisoners of war sit through dance recitals instead.

Then one hot summer day a line was drawn. My parents were on the carport barbecuing chicken while we played, when my sisters dressed me in a girl's bathing suit, stuffed tissues in the bra, put a swimming cap on my head, and pulled me to the wading pool calling me Francine. I was really little, but this I do remember. When Dad, the former Navy pilot, saw this he put a quick end to it. There was no gender neutrality in our house.

My room was in the front of the house with a Lionel electric trainset and a cherrywood dresser and bed. I loved that trainset and the time I spent playing with it. In the same room, there was a picture of two horses. One was white and the other black. In front of them a bolt of lightning arced from a dark cloud as the black stallion dug his hooves into the ground to protect the white mare. I loved this horse picture. In it you can see the danger in the world and the stallion's fight to protect both the mare and himself. You can also see the flared nostrils and the fear in their eyes.

With the Polaroid of me alone at the picture window looking out into the snow, these two pictures represent emotions of fear and loneliness—the two strongest emotions I would seek refuge from throughout my life.

When the aged film reel of memory plays, there I am, four or five years old, playing in our house. I look up to realize that I am alone. I call out to my mother—the single most constant protector in my life—but there is no answer. I call for my sisters and brother, but there is only silence. Frantic, I go to the front door and call out again, but there is no one to answer, only an empty street.

Gripped by an overpowering fear, I sit down in the middle of the living room. I am hysterical and cry and cry wondering where everyone went. They are just gone. Several minutes later Mama, my sisters, and little brother walk through the door. To me though it seemed like hours.

"What on earth is wrong with you?" Mama asks.

Still blubbering, I say, "I thought you all left me."

Mama laughs. "We were just next door visiting." But she looks concerned. I learn that if I am scared, I can't show it.

Of course, there was plenty to fear in the early 1960s. Surgery laid Mother up for a time after my younger brother was born. To help her out, Ganny and Poppy sent Nonnie, their black housekeeper and cook, to New Orleans. I have nothing but good memories of the time I spent with Nonnie, so I was happy that she was coming. Dad was glad too because she made banana pudding with meringue and a chocolate pie that was to die for.

As Mama got better, she and Ganny made plans for Nonnie to return to Winnfield and both felt it would be good for me to travel with her by train to pay a visit to my grandparents. Dad deposited us at the New Orleans train station with me dressed as if I were going to church and Nonnie in her white uniform. I vaguely remember walking down the platform to get on the train and a conductor stopping us.

"You can't sit in the white folks' car," he said to Nonnie.

She had my hand in hers like a vice and would not let go. "I am bringing this boy to visit his grandparents. Where he goes, I go."

A group of railroad officials conferred and concluded that despite the impropriety of it, Nonnie would be allowed to sit in the white people's car, but only because she was accompanying a white child.

On the train ride, I probably talked nonstop. This wasn't unusual for me. Nonnie and I talked frequently, though I have no earthly idea what about. After what happened at the station, I bet I turned it up a notch. I talked so much that Nonnie used to say, "That boy is going to be either a lawyer or a preacher." She was right.

I went to kindergarten at Mount Olive Lutheran Church. We brought mats for naps each afternoon. While "napping," I learned the mechanics of ladies' undergarments. I would sneak peeks up my teacher's skirt at her hose and garters as she walked amongst the prone class. Maybe that is why I still like naps so much.

Then in October of 1962, Mama sent me to school with canned goods, a toothbrush, a change of clothes, and a pillow in addition to my mat. We started having drills in which we ran into the church and hid under the pews. The nightly news talked of Russian ships steaming toward Cuba with nuclear weapons. I had no idea what a nuclear missile really was, and we went about our business as usual being told that everything would be all right. I just had to wonder though, "If everything was going to be all right, why was everyone in New Orleans so scared?" Little did I know that hiding under a church pew was totally useless in a nuclear attack.

#

That fall something great happened. I started playing football at Lakeshore playground. I was only five years old and don't remember anything about playing, though images of kids racing wildly around a field and crashing into each other comes to mind. What I do remember, and maybe this is because I was a bit anxious, was Mama saying the defensive coach would scoop me up before I got trampled by the onrushing herd of players.

About a year later I'd grown some, but was still feeling anxious about being hit. I told Mama and she said, "If you hit him harder than he hits you, it won't hurt." She was right.

Of course it was Dad who taught me about fighting. "Sometimes you have to stand up for yourself so if you absolutely have to fight, hit him really hard in the nose, most of the time that will do it."

Then he added, "But if it doesn't end the thing, you better be prepared to stand your ground."

I'm not sure how long it was after Dad gave me this advice, but while riding my sister Lee's bike, I passed a house where several older and bigger kids were playing. The bike was too big for me so I had to stand on the pedals to ride, which wasn't such a bad thing because it was a girl's bike. What I didn't realize—I was only six—was that I stood out like a sore thumb.

One of the kids stopped me and straddled the front tire with his legs. He was a sixth grader and big for his age, which made him look huge to me.

"What are you, a girl?" he sneered.

I looked to the other kids. That's when he started slapping and ridiculing me until tears streamed down my cheeks. He stopped and then yelled after me as I walked the bike back toward home, "You'd better never let me catch you on my street again!"

I had heard what Mom and Dad had said, but the question I had was what do you do if they are really big and you are scared? I would later learn that the definition of courage is being afraid and doing it anyway. Well I learned to do it anyway, but that did not tell me what to do with the fear. And as I got older, it got worse. I found an entire world of unhealthy ways to stuff fear. And they worked, for a while.

When my oldest sister saw me coming up the driveway crying with her bike she got angry. You just don't mess with family. And we couldn't just leave it alone and expect it to go away. It wouldn't. Every time I went around the block, I was afraid so it was worth standing up to the fear even if it did mean getting pounded. We had to do something.

"You go back around the block to where that kid is, but give me some time to walk around the street the other way. Okay?" my sister said.

I wasn't sure what would happen, but I said, "Okay."

She hustled around the block and I gave her a few minutes before standing up on the bike pedals and making my way to the house where the big kids were. When the big kid saw me, he launched out into the street and stopped me the same way he did before.

Before he had a chance to get a word out, my sister lit over from the opposite sidewalk with blood in her eyes. I thought she was going to beat the snot out of this kid—he was bigger than her, too—and in that moment, I believed she could. Instead, she lit into him like a banshee and the look of fear and shock in his face was priceless.

She told him that he didn't own the street, that he had no right to tell anyone what to do, and that if he ever touched me again or my bicycle that she would pound him into a small, greasy spot. Something to that effect.

Ever since then, I've done what I could to return the favor, but having my sister rescue me didn't exactly fit with the meaning of courage. I needed to start doing that on my own.

That was the street. By contrast, there was a sense of order on the football field. There were clear rules and they were enforced. I may have been a small kid, but no one could accuse me of lacking enthusiasm for football. I bought into Mom's advice one hundred percent. Just hit them harder than they hit me.

#

Anxiety is not a neat and tidy thing. It can be rational—fear of nuclear war. Or irrational—fear of Mom abandoning me.

I had both. Every day as Mom dropped me off for first grade, I repeatedly asked when she was picking me up at the end of the day. Going to school scared me to death, and walking from the car into the building gave me intense separation anxiety.

A bundle of nerves by the end of the day, I sat near the door and looked out the window across the yard to where the moms lined up their cars to be sure Mama was there. When I saw her car, I could hardly keep still, and the second the teacher said we could go, I uncoiled like a tightly wound spring, dashed across the yard and jumped into the car.

Then Mom made me ride the bus. This was like turning the heat up another notch, and my sisters became the object of my neurosis. Repeatedly, I asked when, where, and if one of them was meeting me at the bus after school. Getting on the wrong bus and ending up in some strange place without a hope of finding my way home terrified me.

The Bay of Pigs and Cuban Missile Crisis were recent memories and many of the survivors of the Bay of Pigs as well as escapees from Castro were in New Orleans. Cuba seemed so close and the fear of communism so acute among adults that to a kid like me it felt like the whole bloody thing was a few blocks away. The routine duck-and-cover drills reinforced that the communists had nuclear missiles pointed right at us and it was only a matter of time before it all blew up.

Adding to this unease was a tragedy close to home. My sisters had two friends, and the youngest sister was playing in a pile of sand near some road construction when the hole she was in caved and suffocated her. Both of my sisters had nightmares for God knows how long, and the thought of that happening to me or anyone in my family still gives me chills.

Then, on a quiet fall day as I sat in class, the loudspeakers crackled to life and the principal said, "It is my sad duty to report that a gunman assassinated President Kennedy in Dallas today ..." I didn't know what assassinated meant—obviously very bad—nor can I remember the rest of what she said. I do remember that it was enough to stop the world. Two days later, as TV news outlets broadcast police officers leading Lee Harvey Oswald to a waiting police car in the basement of the Dallas police station, Jack Ruby stepped from the crowd and shot him in the abdomen. I can still remember Oswald grimacing in pain.

The entire world drew a breath and wondered, *What in the world is happening?*

For three days, no one moved as images of the president's funeral played across black and white television screens. The City of New Orleans sat paralyzed, on edge, as if anything could happen at any moment. The adults reassured us that everything would be okay, but their voices were pensive, wishing it to be true more than knowing it to be true.

On Thanksgiving, our new president, Lyndon B. Johnson, came on the TV and said, "All of us have lived through seven days that none of us will ever forget … We are not given the divine wisdom to answer why this has been … From this midnight of tragedy, we shall move toward a new American greatness … We know tonight that our system is strong—strong and secure." Oh yeah? All I could think of was, *If God is so great and giant, as we learned in Sunday school and every adult said, then why are nuclear missiles pointed at us? Why did the president get assassinated? Why did my sister's best friend die?*

It had been Camelot, a time of calm and peace, but now it seemed that all hell was about to break loose. Racial tensions were high, and news shows were beginning to broadcast reports out of a place called Vietnam. Yet at home we felt loved. Things were safe and secure. Just don't venture out too far.

On top of it all, we didn't have a very good history with pets on Melody Drive either. Our dog Tippy died of distemper; one of Mama's friends started her car one morning with our cat huddled up near the radiator fan for warmth (what a bloody racket that was); our rabbit was devoured by a neighborhood cat which left just ears and a pile of fur; and Mom backed out of the driveway smashing our replacement cat which we had named Smut. And we witnessed it all, firsthand.

None of this meant I doubted my parents. Mom loved us and cared for our family. Dad was my hero and could do no wrong in my eyes. But at the same time, it must have felt like they were flying by the seat of their pants. They left Winnfield to live in New Orleans, which some considered a cesspool of sin. And despite the promise of post-World War II peace and prosperity, the world was apparently still a continually changing and dangerous place. Kennedy's assassination meant that evil could hit close to home, which further shifted the ground upon which they stood.

Then a curious thing happened. We were invaded by our allies the British. *Beatlemania* arose from a distant, friendly shore to swallow up teenage girls. Its attractant, like the sweet lure of honeysuckle, was a simple melody with simpler lyrics called, *I Want to Hold Your Hand*. My oldest sister was powerless in its grasp, and when word spread that the *Fab Four* were coming to New Orleans, she was apoplectic.

At ten years old, she was also out of luck. There was no way on God's green earth that Dad or Mom would even consider letting her go to such a thing. In fact, when Dad saw news reports of teen girls wailing, gnashing their teeth, and passing out from hyperventilating over *The Beatles*, he said, "What the hell, prisoners of war don't do this stuff."

Mom and Dad were of a different generation and of different musical tastes. Glenn Miller and the big bands were more their speed. One year they went to Biloxi where they saw the musical comedians *Homer & Jethro*, known as the thinking man's hillbillies, and bought their album on the spot.

I remember it well because I would sneak in and listen to it non-stop. The songs were heavy on drinking. And mental institutions. I thought they were so funny that at Saline Lake with Ganny, Poppy, and the rest of the relatives present I busted out with *After the Hangover's Over*:

"*Say pal, if you wanna stay single, this is my warning to you. When you're out drinking, don't mingle with gals who are lonesome and blue*—insert image of Mom drawing a finger across her neck to get me to knock it off—*If you don't wanna get married, don't mix your kisses with wine. It's twen'y to one that you'll end up with a female palooka like mine.*"[9] I had a good memory being so young.

Mother was mortified and Dad was in shock. The whole camp was just kind of quiet, like they were thinking, *Up here in Winnfield we're doing one thing, but down in New Orleans, they're having a bit of a different life*, which was true.

Dad had a saying: "Do as I say, not as I do." He said that about smoking cigarettes. But what I knew then and now is that you can't expect a kid to listen like that. I didn't listen, and I know that none of my sons ever has either. Then again, my wife and I never drank or smoked around our boys. So maybe the answer lies not so much in the credibility of the messenger as in the heart of the recipient.

While Dad could appreciate a thinking man's hillbilly, he also had a love for classical music. On Sunday afternoons, he would lay on the living room sofa listening to Bach or Beethoven to relax. But when my sister pleaded with him to go to the Beatles' concert, he shook his head firmly.

# # #

As time passed, it appeared our financial fortunes were improving. We had a second car, had moved up to sirloin steaks and not long after, Mom and Dad called a family meeting.

"We're moving," Dad said.

"What? Where?" the girls said almost at once.

"To a bigger house and a better location," Dad responded.

What he didn't mention was that there was a new school going up across the street.

The house they were building was on James Drive, which was a new neighborhood about fifteen minutes further out from New Orleans. When he said they were spending $45,000, I imagined some sort of palace. What it turned out to be was a nice, two-story brick house on a street where each home was about twenty feet apart. Our neighbor would complain that the light from the master bathroom at 5:30 am woke her up. Years later she complained that when we moved away she couldn't wake up on time because there was no light.

As we absorbed the news, my sisters protested that they would have to switch schools and lose their friends, among other worries. Somewhat exasperated by the inquisition and that the girls weren't as excited receiving the news as he was to give it, Dad fielded their questions with, "But it's a bigger house in a better neighborhood."

My main thing was don't leave me behind when we move and remember to pick me up after school.

Oh yeah, and sign me up for football.

Chapter Four

The house on James Drive was a two-story cape cod with two large upstairs bedrooms separated by a shared bathroom. Downstairs, there was a den with the ubiquitous TV, a kitchen, another bathroom, and a combination living and dining room where we had a piano and would set the tree up each Christmas. Both my sisters played piano, and they tried to teach me right up until sixth grade when during football practice, our center stepped on my two right fingers. I don't think he broke them, but it was enough to end my piano playing days.

I thought both of my sisters played the piano quite well. The pounding of the keys and sobs of anguish seemed over the top. They practiced before dinner, and it got to the point that we went about our evening routines with continual piano accompaniment. I remember when the oldest decided to step up her repertoire a notch by learning the March from Aida, and she filled the house with *dum, de dum, de dum, de dum, de dum, de dum, della, la, dah–dah* over and over again. It was a challenge for her to learn it, so in the midst of *dum, de dum* she'd hit a real clam of a note and we'd hear her scream, *Aaaah!* pause and then pick back up with *dum, de dum …*

Dad loved classical music so he thought it was great, and the rest of us learned to do our homework, set the dinner table, read, and so on to the never ending *dum, de dum …*

To break the tedium, J.R. and I often interrupted her to ask if she could, you know, play something a bit more contemporary. Since Mom and Dad liked it when we sang Christmas carols or hymns, Dad thought they may get us to do that more often if we had songs we liked better throughout the year. So, Dad used to stop by Werlein's music store in New Orleans and pick up some sheet music for them to play while we sang.

One of these was *The Impossible Dream*, which we saw Robert Goulet sing on TV. The sentiment of the lyrics had an effect on me, so it became something of a torch song that my brother and I—two towheaded, suburban kids—would sing in our best Robert Goulet voices. The nobility of the lyrics really touched me. *To right the unrightable wrong.*[11] I definitely put that one on my list.

The house was only two-and-a-half blocks from the elementary school and a block-and-a-half from the junior high. This eased my fears of being left on the bus or Mom abandoning me, and I managed to get used to walking or riding my bike to school.

It was also a tight-knit neighborhood, where people knew each other and generally got along well. Halloween, for instance, was a big neighborhood thing and Mom made popcorn balls, which was something no one else did. All the kids made sure to come by our house to get a popcorn ball, particularly the older kids who didn't feel right about trick-or-treating.

At Christmas, all the houses did their best to light up the neighborhood. On Christmas day, folks opened gifts at home then got dressed and walked to our house for visiting, which included some well-spiked eggnog or a cocktail, or two, or three.

The teachers at our schools cared about their students, and many of them lived within a few blocks of the school. Our sixth-grade teacher was a real prize. Her husband was a district court judge and would later be on the court of appeal. They lived just a block over from us. Everyone in my sixth-grade class had a nickname, which I wrote in my yearbook at the end of the school year.

As good as our new home and neighborhood was, it wasn't perfect. Shortly after we moved in, a kid down the street wearing a khaki uniform welcomed me by riding his bike up our driveway, into the carport, then back down again. He did this over and over so I went out to let him know we just moved into the house and lived there.

"No, ya don't," he yelled back at me as he turned in the street to do another loop in our carport.

"Yes, we do," I said pointing to the house.

He rode up the driveway and past me. "No, ya don't."

"We do, and you gotta stop riding up our driveway."

He stopped his bike and sneered. "I don't care who lives here. I'm gonna ride up and down this driveway and turn around in that carport as long as I want, whenever I want."

"No, you can't."

He stepped off the bike and let it drop onto the pavement. "You wanna fight about it?"

"It doesn't matter if we fight or not. I live here."

His dad must have given him the same advice as my Dad gave me because he punched me right in the nose. The pain shot up into my brain and my eyes watered. Then he punched me in the eye. We exchanged blows and a minute later he was pedaling down the street laughing at my bloody nose, swollen eye, and tears. I looked behind me to the side door of the house where there was a small laundry room. There was Mom. She watched the whole ordeal and let me deal with it on my own, which is something she tended to do. Her philosophy was to let us kids learn our lessons through experience and without her interference. Right then and there, I knew that I was on my own.

I entered second grade in the fall, and later that winter when it was about as cold as it gets in New Orleans, a kid took my hat. He was big and liked to pick on smaller kids. I'd worn a red stocking cap outside to keep my ears warm, and when I asked for it back he refused.

Eventually the teacher called the class back inside, leaving just us two outside. I demanded my hat back again. He refused. So, I stepped up to him, body stiff, hands at my sides and said, "If you don't give me my hat, I'm going to punch you in the nose."

He smiled and said, "No."

So, I punched him in the nose as hard as I could and suddenly he went from a big, bad bully to a crying, blubbering slob.

The teacher saw the whole thing, and in the next instant we were in the principal's office. The principal was surprised to see me there, and since the other boy was still crying, she asked me what happened.

"He took my hat and wouldn't give it back, so I told him if he didn't, I was going to punch him in the nose, and that's exactly what I did."

She seemed taken aback by how direct I was, and for a moment I thought she believed I was in the right. Then she asked, "Where in the world did you get the idea to punch someone in the nose?"

I proudly said, "My Dad." Funny, Mom asked me the same question when I got home that afternoon.

#

Second grade wasn't all about fighting. I found other ways to embarrass myself and get into trouble. My classroom was on the second floor, but the nearest bathroom was on the first. This wasn't usually much of a problem because our teacher told us that if we had a bathroom emergency, we should leave and explain later. Not all the teachers were as kind or smart, and the intercom often crackled to life asking Mr. Grunts—the janitor (I'm not kidding)—to clean up some spill of bodily fluids. Though his name seems like some sort of joke, it wasn't, and it didn't signify any particular sound he made. Instead, he was often silent with a dour expression.

One day we had navy beans and sausage for lunch, which on any other day would have been one of my favorites. This wasn't any other day. The beans made my stomach ache. I felt swollen as if I would burst. I was going to throw up. No doubt about it. Feeling this was an emergency as defined by our teacher's bathroom policy, I launched from my seat, ran out the door then down the metal and concrete stairs, praying for the relief of the bathroom below. I was almost home free having hit the bottom of the stairs, when I screeched to a halt in front of a pair of black janitor's boots. I let fly a Monty Python-esque volume of partially digested navy beans and sausage all over the boots and the floor and probably up the legs of the janitor's coveralls.

With the evacuation complete, my eyes wandered upward, tracing the portly frame of the janitor until I was eyeball to eyeball with the dour and disgusted face of Mr. Grunts. We stood there for a moment, silent, staring at each other, him disgusted and me wondering, What would a polite person do in this situation?

An answer didn't present itself, and since I felt much better, I turned and walked back up to my classroom.

#

As fishing was near to religion in Winnfield, football was my religion in Metairie.

I couldn't figure if Mom had a problem with me punching people in the nose if it was necessary, or what she considered necessary circumstances, but I did know that she didn't have a problem with hardnose football.

Our playground had so many boys that you had to try out and hope you didn't get cut.

I did my best to run through anyone who got in my way. During the many pickup games of two-hand touch almost-anywhere we played at a nearby vacant lot, I would instinctively lower my head and plow over people instead of trying to run around them. Dad made me quit playing because I came home with so many bruises on my head.

In second grade, I made the eighty-five-pound squad, and for as long as I played playground football—New Orleans' version of Pop Warner—I never did get cut. Ever.

Before each game, Mom gave me her flinty look and would say, "Go get 'em boy." During the game, I'd hear her yell, "Get 'em boy!" and I did.

Some folks nowadays think football is a violent, collision sport. Okay, it is. So, what. I was much more concerned with completing my assignment and blocking my man than any violent hits that may have come along. My teammates were counting on me. Collisions are just part of the game. I still don't like to fight. Never have. But when playing football, I never had to. It never felt violent or done out of anger or with the intention to harm the other guy, except to hit him hard. Violence and collisions were incidental to the goal of winning. That's life. Get used to it.

I remember, too, Dad showing me the scar on his shin when I started playing football. He said he got cleated while playing in basic training in the Navy. The wound got infected, so doctors treated it with streptomycin, which made the scar worse. The way he told the story, the scar was nothing compared to the thought of crashing a plane.

With duck-and-cover drills in school and adults tossing around talk of the Cold War, earning a small mark of manhood like Dad's didn't seem like such a bad thing.

#

Second grade passed and then came summer. There were daily trips to the swimming pool at the small club we belonged to—a novelty for my Winnfield born and bred parents—as well as weeks in Winnfield with family. By the end of summer, I'd fished and swam and did all the things any typical kid growing up in the early 1960s would do.

Then in early September, Mom and Dad started paying more attention to the TV and the radio. I don't ever remember not knowing what a hurricane is.

It's something that all kids along the Gulf Coast just seem to know about as if born with innate knowledge. It came from stories by parents of the big one they rode out and then grandparents remembering the devastation of the big storms that, from their telling, seemed to sneak in from the ocean.

So, when the news spoke of Hurricane Betsy, I knew this was something big and something scary. For a while it seemed as if it might miss us, but after it cut across southern Florida, then, strengthening as it passed the over hot, humid Gulf waters, it honed in on New Orleans. In the early evening of September 9, 1965, Dad turned off the radio. Worry lined his face as he walked out and backed the station wagon into the carport. Already, the wind blew so hard that it whistled and for the next couple of hours we sat in the living room listening to the radio.

Someone, not sure if it was Mom or one of my sisters, said we should watch the TV to distract ourselves. Dad nodded, but kept his ear to the radio. Being a Thursday night, it was doctor drama night. We made it through Ben Casey and were about halfway through Doctor Kildare when the pitch of the wind's moaning edged up, and the lights went out. There was only the sound of Dad's battery-powered radio and the announcer saying that Pilot Town at the mouth of the Mississippi river was gone. This could be a bad one.

I went upstairs to my room and looked out the window. The wind bent over every tree and bush, and the aluminum light on the street fluttered back and forth as if it were a pixie stick. The pitch of the wind was an unrelenting moan that I will never forget. If you ever hear it, you won't forget it either.

"Frank!" Dad yelled, "get down here!"

A beam of flashlight guided me down the stairs, and on the radio I heard the announcer say that Metairie would be under eighteen feet of water within a few hours. It was time to get out.

"Put your shoes on and let's go," Dad said. There was strength in his voice; as if it were time to get in the Hellcat and launch off the carrier. Don't second guess yourself or let fear be the pilot, just do what you must do. There was comfort in it, and there was comfort in Mom's resolute expression as we got in the car. She didn't need to tell us to be quiet.

Dad eased the car down James Drive through the neighborhood and turned on Airline Highway toward Baton Rouge. As we crossed over the Duncan Canal by Moisant Airport—now Louis Armstrong International Airport—there was a lone state trooper parked on the side of the road. As we passed, his headlights kicked on and he followed us. We must have been the last to get out.

Tree limbs and all manner of debris blew across Airline Highway, and at times it felt as if the wind was lifting the car onto two wheels. "Where are we going?" My sister asked from the back seat. J.R. and I were in the "way back" where, under normal circumstances, there would be luggage. There wasn't time to grab much more than the clothes we wore and Dad's radio.

"Uncle Nub's," Dad said, my Poppy's brother and my great uncle, which meant Baton Rouge.

The further we went, the better it got, but it was still windy and raining as we pulled into Baton Rouge. The storm followed us up along the Mississippi and seemed to slow when it hit land. My great aunt and uncle set us up in rooms, and I'm not sure where Mom slept, but Dad spent the entire night on the couch with the radio cradled in his arms. I'm sure he believed he was listening to the destruction of our home and everything in it.

Betsy was slow to dissipate and move on but we went back the next day. There was one photo I saw of New Orleans East that looked like a giant bayou dotted by roofs. Another showed the Lower Ninth Ward inundated by water. As we made our way back down Airline Highway, we drove by downed trees, light poles bent over like straw, signs floating in the water, fences busted up, and houses that burned down due to electrical shorts. Everything was down and everything was flat.

When we hit our neighborhood, it looked like it did when we first moved in. It didn't flood as predicted, but I could see from one end of the block to the other. There wasn't a tree, bush, or a fence left standing, and the 100-plus-mile-per-hour wind had stripped roofs of their shingles, which lay scattered on the ground with thousands of nails and shards of glass. I must have stepped on twenty roofing nails that year.

Several of our neighbors stayed through the storm and were picking through the debris when we pulled up. They looked stunned and shaken, but no one lost their life in our neighborhood.

One thing I learned about hurricanes is that there are many "worst parts." There's the storm itself, then the eye passes over and it is calm. Then all hell breaks loose again. Afterward, there's the tedium and discomfort of the cleanup. There was no water, so we had to go to the school where the Red Cross offered water and other necessities. There was no power. Hurricanes charge themselves by sucking the moisture out of the air. After they pass, the air is dry and hot, and boy was it hot after Betsy. For days, we lay in bed at night with the windows open. All we could do was sweat.

Dad helped the neighbors clean out soggy furniture and clothes from the houses that Betsy had stripped bare. We were lucky to be missing only about a twenty-foot circle of shingles, which I think was because of the slant of the Cape Cod roof. We had a few busted windows and the wood floors were buckled, but in comparison to other houses we were fortunate.

Mom emptied our freezer and cooked everything we had in a galvanized bucket filled with charcoal. Our grill was nowhere to be found. A few days in, she and I were standing on the back patio while she cooked butter beans. I looked down into the pot and pointed. "Mom, what's that?"

She tilted her eyes down to see a fat green worm floating in the boiling water. She scooped the worm up with a spoon and flung it into the yard. Then she looked at me with her not-to-be-misunderstood look. "Don't you dare breath a word to anyone, hear?"

"Yes, ma'am."

Every so often, she gave me the eye to see if I was going to break my promise, but I didn't. The food tasted fine to me. Besides, I hear worms are a good source of protein.

I'm not sure how long we lay in the heat without so much as a fan to cool ourselves, but around ten o'clock on what felt like the hottest night of all, a buzz passed through the neighborhood that the power trucks were near. Dad and I walked out into the yard and there they were at the end of the street. Both of us stood in a sort of awe as the juice shot through, and lights that were dead for weeks came to life.

You could hear the whooping and hollering through open windows from up and down the block. It wouldn't be long before folks shut their windows, turned on the AC and we wouldn't talk anymore. Life went back to as it was.

# # #

The summer between third and fourth grade was something like boy heaven. Mom and Dad let me spend time on my own in Winnfield with Ganny and Poppy, but even when Mom and Dad were there, they loosened the reins.

This is where I learned how to be a boy.

I caught bream and bass from one pond and catfish from another, but never more than Ganny said she needed for dinner. I shot turtles with a .22 and didn't shoot anywhere but toward the hill because bullets will skip off water and travel up to a mile, you know. I learned that a pocket knife could fold up on you and cut you if you weren't careful and that you need to toss a firecracker quickly because some fuses burn faster than others, and you don't want it to explode in your hand. Poppy taught me never to point a gun at anything I didn't intend to kill, and if I wasn't going to clean it and eat it, then throw it back.

I said "yes sir" and "no ma'am," "please" and "thank you" (most of the time anyway) and showed respect for my elders. I tried to ride calves, which didn't go so well, and helped Ganny and Poppy in the garden and in any way I could.

One morning, Poppy and Ganny loaded us up in the car to go pick the garden at the farm. Poppy and Ganny had company from out of town, so she came with us too. By now Poppy had sold the pharmacy—I did miss the soda fountain quite a bit—and we went to the farm to feed and work every day. On the farm was a peach orchard, hogs, cows, and horses. We walked behind the tractor in the July heat picking potatoes out of the red clay that had just been turned. I was told that was to build character.

The farm house remained unused, and over time reached a state where it wasn't much good for more than storing potatoes in lime beneath the porch. Out front there was a huge mulberry tree with berries that you could pick from the low branches without a ladder. J.R. and I loved mulberries, which are as good as black berries and easier to pick because there were no thorns or rattle snakes to avoid. Some days our hands were purple from the berries.

The ground beneath the tree was littered with berries that fell off the tree. We would gather up the good ones that the birds hadn't gotten. Poppy also had a bunch of goats up on the farm, which he allowed to roam. The oblong goat turds looked very "berry like" on the ground.

That morning, everyone went off to pick okra, tomatoes, squash, and beans in the garden while J.R. and I went to the farmhouse yard to look for a few good mulberries on the ground.

"What are y'all doin'?" asked the houseguest while standing in the lane in front of the house.

"Picking up berries," we said.

"Like these?"

My back was to her as I bent to pick up mulberries, and I didn't see what she had; neither did J.R. "Yeah!" we called without looking up.

About twenty minutes later we wandered over to the lane with purple mouths, and that lady had a five-gallon bucket about half full of the finest bunch of goat turds I'd ever seen. "Uh, you haven't eaten any of those, have you?" I asked.

She tilted her head up at me. "No. Actually, they don't smell too good.

What should I do with them?"

I looked at J.R. and he looked at me. It seemed proper to let nature take its course.

"Why don't you take those over to the others in the garden and show 'em what you got," I said, and off she went.

Throwing personal safety to the wind, we lit out through the barn and ran across the pasture that was home to the big turkey gobbler that attacked us if we wandered into its territory. Making it through the pasture we aimed ourselves down the hill to spend some time with the friendlier cows and calves. That is, until we heard Poppy's voice call across the farm, "Fraaaaank!!! J.R.!!!"

A spontaneous deafness overtook us, but it wasn't enough to save us. Ever since that incident, I didn't need to be reminded to be careful what you pick up. And for God's sake if you are not sure what it is don't put in your mouth.

Fourth grade passed without too many incidents. I did well enough in school, and my football team won the parish championship for the eighty-five-pound league. I still suffered from random anxieties, but for the most part, life was good. It seemed as if life would just sort of keep going as it was. Then I started to notice things.

One morning just before summer, I walked into the kitchen and announced, "Hey, did somebody cut themselves or something?"

"What are you talking about?" Mom asked.

"There's a bunch of blood in the trash can. What the heck's goin' on?"

Mom put her hands on her hips and looked at my sisters. "I don't know which one of you it is, but you got to take better care of your business."

Then she turned and saw that the whole blood-in-the-trash thing upset me. "No one is hurt. It's a female thing. Don't worry about it."

Don't worry about it? It looked like a slasher movie. I stood my ground. "There's blood in the garbage, and I want to know, did somebody hurt themselves or what?"

"Never mind, Frank, it's okay," my mom said, then she walked away.

I looked at my sisters, but I let it drop.

That summer we took a trip from Winnfield to Natchitoches with our cousins who were in high school. Out of nine grandchildren, my brother and I were the youngest and the only boys. I tended to revel in being the obnoxious little cousin.

On the way, we stopped for gas outside of Clarence, and I had to pee so I went into the gas station's bathroom. At that time, you didn't need to ask for the key, so I just walked in. As I did my business, I looked up and there were these machines with things that had exotic names and advertised ticklers and all sorts of stuff.

Well, I had a couple of quarters so I bought a few of them. When I got outside, the girls were standing by the back of the car looking as if they were melting from heat and boredom.

"Hey," I said, "have y'all ever seen one of these before?" And I held up the unwrapped thing that looked like a blue snakeskin with tentacles.

I thought seeing what a fella could buy in the men's room would interest them, but they acted as if I held a real snakeskin. With tentacles. "I can't believe you bought that!" they yelled. But they did laugh, a little. I threw the thing away as soon as the novelty wore off, which was pretty quick.

By now it seemed as if there was something going on that I wasn't privy to, and I didn't like it.

Later that year we went out to eat in New Orleans at a seafood restaurant called Fitzgerald's with Ganny and Poppy. The seafood platters were awesome, and the shrimp remoulades had so much horse radish they would make Barq's root beer bubble out your nose.

I went to the bathroom, and when I got back to the table I asked, "What does f**k mean?" The table went silent. Dad's fork stopped in front of his mouth with his head leaning out over his plate. "Where did you hear that?"

"It's written on the wall in the bathroom."

Poppy leaned back in his seat and looked at Dad. Dad glanced up at him then back to me. "I'll tell you later. It's not something we should talk about now." I looked down at my plate. Message received.

The morning after we got home, I walked into the kitchen and Dad said he had to speak with me.

"What is it?" I asked, worried I may have done something wrong.

"Well, you know, we need to have 'the talk.' So here goes. To make babies, a man and a woman, when they are in love and married, well, the man takes his penis and puts it inside the woman's vagina and, you know, he produces sperm and it fertilizes the egg and then she gets pregnant and has a baby." I was kind of shocked. I just wanted breakfast.

"Is that what you and mom did?"

"Yes."

I started laughing. I couldn't help it. That was the most ridiculous thing I had ever heard in my life. "You have got to be kidding me. Why would anybody in their right mind do that?"

"I don't know. That's what it is."

"Well, I don't have to worry about that then," and I was laughing my behind off as I walked into the den to watch TV.

Behind me I heard him say to Mom, "Well, I told him."

"Yeah, I heard."

With my introduction to the mechanics of conception complete and my questions answered, I turned to important business. Football. To be sure there weren't oversized kids playing against undersized kids, they separated everybody by weight. The first was eighty-five pounds and below followed by one-hundred pounds and below. This year my friends and I were to move into the second weight class, but that caused some stress because you had to make the weight.

Too much and you were at risk of getting creamed by bigger and older kids or not playing at all. Too little and you got cut. I never had the too little problem. The big moment of truth was the weigh-in. I went into the locker room to get weighed with my buddy the center and after we stripped down to our drawers he said, "Hey, ya got hair on your weenie yet?"

Coach was standing right there and rolled his eyes. "Man, you know not to even ask that question." I can imagine him thinking, *Here I am in a locker room with these two boys in their drawers and one of 'em's gotta start talking like that.*

We laughed. I was too embarrassed to say anything, but it did get my mind to thinking that we were going to change. My sisters were going through something, and it wasn't just the blood in the trash can that tipped me off, and so would I. I would start to not be a boy anymore, and there was something unsettling about it. I wanted to grow up and be a man like Dad and Poppy, but at the same time there were parts of it I just wasn't sure about.

Gary Puckett and Union Gap, a band that modeled their outfits after uniforms worn by the Union Army, had a song called, "This Girl is a Woman Now" that became popular. I wasn't sure, but I believe it had something to do with a guy who talked this girl into doing something she ought not to have done. That bothered me—a lot. I was starting to put two and two together.

Mom and Dad and the other adults in my orbit taught me that a man and a woman fall in love and they marry. Then because of their love they have a child.

Implicit in it all was that they would care for the child and remain loyal to each other. This was all assumed. Love and sex are inseparable. The notion of recreational sex didn't exist in my mind, or at least my parents and other adults weren't putting it there.

Meanwhile, sex was everywhere. TV shows hinted at it in rather obvious ways like the painted women on "Laugh In." Music lamented it ("I Can't Get No Satisfaction") or celebrated it ("[Come on Baby] Light My Fire"). Magazines splashed it across their covers (from a 1967 Cosmo cover with a voluptuous woman: *The new pill that promises to make women more responsive*). Movies embraced it with gusto ("Barbarella" and on and on …), and it was in ads for everything from suntan lotion to men's ties. The culture made it all look so easy and harmless. Yep, it was a regular revolution. And all you needed was *Good Lovin'*.

For a fifth-grade kid, sex was unfathomable and a changing and complicated culture undermined the lessons my parents wanted me to hear and believe. I started looking down and checking for hair on a regular basis.

#

Though church was important to Mom, Dad was something of a lapsed Methodist. Work took him from New Orleans to Houston frequently, and when he was home the thought of sitting in a pew couldn't compete with playing golf and doing whatever he could to forget he was a lawyer for a couple days. I was in fifth grade, 1967 to 1968. The world was changing, uncertain, and I think Dad just wanted to focus on what he knew. Work and family.

Then Reverend Bob Malsbary came by to have a scotch with Dad one Saturday night. He was the pastor of a new Presbyterian church, which at the time was in a temporary building until they could build a proper church. So, we became Presbyterians. From my view, it seemed like the only difference between Methodists and Presbyterians was that Presbyterians drank scotch. I figured that since they could talk and have a drink together that Dad thought Reverend Malsbary was an okay guy.

But as I thought about it, it felt like there was something going on just beyond my vision, again. And it wasn't the scotch. Dad had a come to Jesus moment. There was a definite change, and when it was time for prayer during the service, he'd be at the end of the pew with his hands folded and his eyes closed like he really meant it. Turns out he did.

#

Fall and fifth grade meant football, sweet salvation. I was the starting center for the one-hundred-pound team. Most, if not all, of the other starters were sixth graders and they were good. Especially one kid who was the toughest and most mental football player I've ever been around. He just refused to let himself be beat.

That year we were undefeated and earned a spot in the Parish championship game, which we played in a high school stadium. That was a big deal. Near the end of the game, the other team had the ball and the running back ran a sweep. Our linebacker, the star, had him in his sights, but instead of lowering his shoulder and taking the guy out of bounds, he gave him a shove. The runner managed to tiptoe down the sideline and score. We lost by one touchdown.

The loss devastated me, and I cried the whole way home. Nothing and no one could console me, and for the next year that game haunted me. There wasn't a day that I didn't spend time mentally picturing what it would take to get back to that game. I was obsessed. I thought about it non-stop. I talked to my teammates and classmates about it like a little Ahab. Strategizing about how to win was my default mode, and in some ways, it's where I began to learn what it takes to win. You think about it—all the time.

That spring and early summer, assassins murdered Martin Luther King Jr. and Robert Kennedy. Lyndon Johnson refused to run for his party's nomination. The Soviets invaded Czechoslovakia and more, and the war in Vietnam claimed an ever-growing number of American lives. In the summer, the Democratic National Convention descended into chaos, and the Republicans nominated Richard Nixon to be their presidential candidate.

These events filtered through the fever of football and did their work to create unease and anxiety, but my desire to return to that game overwhelmed my fears. By the fall of 1968 when I entered sixth grade, nothing else mattered. All that existed was football and winning. And my teammates were with me. We put cage facemasks on our helmets because the offensive linemen for the Green Bay Packers wore them. Green Bay was the most dominant team in football—little did we know they were embarking on their first losing season since 1958 that year—and in our minds, we *were* the Green Bay Packers.

We set out to dominate the one-hundred-pound league and we did. We went undefeated and then won the parish championship. I still have the photo of us holding the trophy at the West Jefferson High School stadium as well as my championship jacket.

In later years, I tried to cast my mind back to a time when things worked right, and despite my fears and anxiety, everything seemed put together just as intended. Inevitably, I dreamed of sixth grade and that undefeated season. For many years, it was my high mark and a measure of how far I'd fallen and how lost I was.

Summer was its usual boyhood escapes of swimming and riding horses. There were trips to Winnfield and time spent there without Mom and Dad, when they left me on my own like some sort of suburban Huck Finn. Life, for the most part, felt normal, but then came seventh grade. And football was the first thing to turn on me.

I made the team in seventh grade, but for the first time ever, I didn't start. Football was no longer limited by weight or age, and rather than being among kids relatively my size, I was one of the smaller kids on the team. I hated that the coach relegated me to the bench, but at the same time, I was afraid that my size was a deep liability. A 250-pound lineman confirmed this when he fell on our quarterback, crushed his femur and dislocated his hip.

As I watched paramedics work for almost an hour to pick up the mess that was our quarterback, a certain uneasiness crept over me that I hadn't felt in years. At 120 pounds, I knew I was out of my league. I didn't play much that year, but when I did I was afraid of being hit by any one of a field full of kids that were easily twice my size. The next year was the same.

It was about this time that I would take refuge in my sisters' room and listen to albums on their Zenith turntable. My sister had this poster, and I couldn't figure out who Norman was—"Norman is an island …" But Simon and Garfunkel's song, "The Boxer," was one of my favorites. There was something to the sad, dissonant melody that caught me. That was me. I was a fighter, yet without football, there was a huge hole. Football was my life, and it had moored me to the ground. Without it, I had to figure out who I was, and in a hurry because seventh grade was when the culture came crashing in.

The things that defined me and enabled me to fit in before seventh grade—good grades, sports, making my parents proud—were now things that made me the outsider, the boxer. I was a blank slate with short hair and bad clothes. I oozed conformity when the intention of everyone else was to give the finger to authority, whether it was the school, the ill-defined establishment, or our parents. And the markers of being accepted or an outcast were having the right attitude, hair, and clothes. And my boys say I know nothing about peer pressure?

Like the kid I was, I turned to Dad for help, but clothes for him were a nonstarter. He grew up watching kids walk to school in threadbare overalls with a hot sweet potato tucked in their pocket to keep them warm. As an adult, clothes were a suit for the office and khakis and a shirt for home.

Hair was no different. Most of his generation put Brylcreem or Vitalis in their hair to give them the wet look. The only change occurred when some famous person or company announced, "The wet head is dead." Hair was a whole other matter in seventh grade. With the Beatles, Jimi Hendrix, the Rolling Stones, Janis Joplin, and everything else that kids happily digested, the test of coolness and acceptance was how you wore your hair, which Dad and Poppy found hysterical. Kids with crewcuts were social outcasts while Dad and Poppy laughed at anyone with hair over their ears. You know the comments. "Is that a boy, or a girl?" For a kid like me, who only recently managed to convince his dad to not shave the front so close so I could sweep it up with a little Brylcreem, it was enough to make me neurotic.

And I was just as lost with trying to figure out the right clothes to wear. With older sisters, there wasn't anyone to blaze a trail for me in terms of what was cool and how to fit in. My oldest sister stepped out with her fashion and attitudes a bit, but I was still only twelve or thirteen and relied on Mom and Dad to help me figure out what to do.

It didn't help that nature and genes conspired to give me a healthy body. That means chunky. It's still hard to find clothes for a kid shaped like that, and back then it meant shopping in the *husky* department, a laughable place to teenagers when the cool look was being tall, ridiculously thin, and wearing tight clothes. The ideal was Mick Jagger and John Lennon, but I looked more like Spanky from the Little Rascals.

Mom and my sisters did what they could to help—Mom was even starting to try to keep current with some of her clothes—but I was too twisted by anxiety to follow any advice they gave me.

The result was that I settled into a standard outfit of blue jeans and a shirt. In eighth grade, I added a pair of leather harness boots. This was about the time the movie "Easy Rider" came out and the band, James Gang, put out their first hits. "Easy Rider" was without any doubt cool (even if I hadn't seen the movie), and James Gang were from Cleveland so they had a tougher, blue-collar look that I could pull off at school and without my parents minding too much.

Beginning in eighth grade, certain cliques started to establish themselves— most were refractions of what older kids were doing—with clothes, hair, and music the defining characteristics. There were two that stood out among the rest—the Pitts and the Frats. The Pitts were the guys with pointed-toe Beatle boots—good for kicking a guy in a fight—leather jackets, and tight pants. The Frats were the button-down shirt, penny loafer, surfer haircut, preppie guys who were also good at sports so they were kind of tough.

Tension periodically flared between the two groups with word spreading through the school that so and so was going to fight so and so. I think the Frats got the worst of it because the two toughest guys in school were Pitts. This gave the Pitts a certain aura, which, from where I sat, meant if they let you hang out with them, you were cool. I wanted to be cool.

I got my chance when there was a sock hop kind of thing at the gym. A few of the Pitts guys got hold of some wine, and somehow, I managed to be standing in the right place at the right time wearing my jeans, shirt, and tough guy harness boots. They passed the bottles around, and I didn't have more than a sip or three, but afterward I put on a good show. So good that I walked up our driveway singing:

Bottle of wine
Fruit of the vine
When you gonna let me get sober?
Leave me alone
Let me go home
Let me go home and start over [12]

Sure enough, Mom was sitting up on the front porch in the dark where I couldn't see her. "Did we have a good time?"

"Oops."

"Let's get in the house there Mr. Fruit of the Loom," she said as she stood and pointed to the door.

It was also around this time that tobacco entered my life. My friend came to the house one day and asked if I wanted to go up to Lake Pontchartrain and fish. Then he added, "I have two big 'gars," and proceeded to show me two long, green cigars that he stole from his father.

Off we went to the lake where we fished and smoked the cigars down to their nubs. On the way home I turned my bike down our street, and as I did so, a feeling came over me that I will never forget. I got cold, clammy, and began to sweat. My stomach twisted, my mouth became watery, and I barely made it to the front porch before I barfed in the bushes.

That's when Mom came out. Her timing was good.

Mom gave me her look, "You sick?"

I said nothing. What was I supposed to say?

"You been smoking?"

I looked up at her. "Yes, ma'am."

"What have you been smoking?"

"A cigar," I croaked.

"Well, that should be a lesson to you. Those things will make you sick as a dog." Then she shut the door and went inside.

That should have been enough to keep me away from tobacco, but it wasn't.

A little while later a neighborhood girl and I sat in her backyard thinking how cool we were smoking Marlboro menthol cigarettes. We smoked the whole pack, and from then on, I pilfered cigarettes whenever I could. To my mind, I liked smoking—smoking was cool, and I was hooked.

#

Girls and my notions of love were the next things to crap out on me.

Sex, commitment, and love were inextricably tied in my mind, but what was love? Theologians, mystics, and philosophers have for centuries cogitated on this very question with sometimes profound results. However, the philosophers I consulted wrote songs such as "I Want You," sung by an aching John Lennon declaring, "I want you so bad it's driving me mad."[13]

It wasn't that I didn't have plenty of examples of what a committed relationship looked like. There were Ganny and Poppy as well as Mom and Dad, but these began before I did. There wasn't any romance, any deep desire that drew them together, that I was around to witness.

Instead, music, television, and the movies made the case that love was life altering. People didn't merely like each other, their love was all consuming, life or death, and its fulfillment led the angst-ridden couple into a state of enduring bliss. Anything less wasn't true, authentic love. I know, I know. What a bunch of malarkey! It was and is a myth, but it's one that teenagers have bought into since Shakespeare penned "Romeo and Juliet." And what if it was true?

I bought into it full-bore and believed that if I could fall in love with the right girl it would somehow change who I was and define me in some unknown and indescribable way. The flip side of this was that I would have some similar effect on the girl. I would save her and give her life meaning as well.

In seventh grade, we put on the play, "Butch Cassidy & the Sundance Kid." I played a guy drinking whiskey in a bar who gets shot and killed by Sundance.

Then at the end, I played one of the Mexican soldiers that shoots them down. There was a red-haired girl in the play who lived near me, and after one performance, she walked home with me as I pushed my bike with a banana seat and angel wing handlebars. We stopped in the middle of the street, and she tilted her head toward mine and we kissed.

Wow! It was the sweetest thing, and I was super high. If anything could confirm the myth of love, it was that kiss.

And if anything could confirm that we were being sold a myth, it's that I don't remember her name. I also don't remember what happened to her other than that she went to a different school. But like any good drug, I wanted that high again.

In eighth grade, the girls started to wear miniskirts and too much makeup. Everybody went steady with someone and exchanged ID bracelets, except me. I don't know what it was, but all the girls went for the blond-haired guys with bangs and killer eyes, named Bobby. It was never the stocky guys with short, wavy hair, named Frank.

I soured on love and became disillusioned with the whole relationship thing. It all seemed so phony and I got angry, but really, I was jealous and still wanted that transformational love. Mom always said, "Don't worry about it. God will give you somebody when you're ready," and that type of thing. I wanted to believe her and chose to believe her, but at the same time the heart wants what it wants.

My next big moment was a dance down at the swim club. My latest crush was on a girl who was two years older than me, but despite the clear difference in our ages, I held out hope. It was the time for hippies so I wore a tie-dye t-shirt and sandals to look cool. I think she felt sorry for me and perhaps thought my attention was cute, and whoever she was truly interested in wasn't there. We danced for a while and that felt good, but it didn't go anywhere at all.

She ended up becoming a urologist, and after I got sober a friend of mine, who is a lawyer, developed a urinary tract infection after some sexual indiscretions. It turns out, he was going to see her so I told him to say *hello*. Bet that went over well.

The next crush was a big one, but followed the same script as the others. The right guy for her didn't buy his clothes in the husky department and he wasn't named Frank. The whole thing was emotional turmoil followed by heartbreak, which generated frustration and more anger.

As eighth grade faded into summer, it was clear the girls had the equipment, but it never seemed they were willing to consider me. That summer, my buddy and I went to the swim club almost every day. We looked at all the girls in bikinis, and the loudspeakers played song after song about love and sex and desire, and it felt like we were staring at a buffet from which we were not allowed to eat. Girls with whom I could find transformational love, the love that gives life meaning surrounded me, but I was alone.

I went through heartache and heartbreak without any kind of a relationship, and I finally said *screw this*. I wanted my life to have meaning, but girls weren't going to oblige. This didn't stop the crushes, but it did open me up to finding some other ways to fill the hole left by football and the lack of a girlfriend. What I didn't realize was that the hole I needed to fill was more about the fears and anxieties that would lead me down some dark paths.

Meanwhile, politics, race, and war intruded on life.

This was nothing new. The Vietnam War was churning just as hard as ever and political upheaval was routine. In seventh grade, race and the country's response to racism came to my school when it became one of many across the South to enact a court-ordered desegregation plan. This meant that the district bussed kids in from Bunche Village, a predominantly black area in Metairie a few miles south of where I lived. Most of the parents of my friends and many of my friends did not react kindly to this change.

To say the least, navigating race for a twelve-year-old kid like me was complicated. Notions of race and racism were deeply embedded in the South and my family was no exception. For Poppy and his generation, as well as many in my parents' generation, that's just the way it was. But it didn't make it right.

When the bussing of students from Bunche Village started, I can't say it surprised me or that I worried about violence. One of the new students in seventh grade was a tall, surly kid named Charles. My biology teacher sat him next to me. I imagine that Charles, a kid who was as much of an outsider in our mostly white school as one could find, saw me as a tempting target. He started picking on me almost right away, and as the taunts of the other kids toward him increased, he got meaner with me. It felt unfair and just cruel. Why me? Wouldn't he want to lash out at the kids who were being mean to him? I was stuck.

"Maybe he just needs a friend," Mom said in her usual Methodist way. "You know, you have to be a friend to have a friend."

With J.R. and me old enough to take care of ourselves, Mom worked in the school as a substitute teacher to bring in a little extra cash. Unbeknownst to me, she kept better track of us than I ever knew. I listened to what she said, then weighed my options. I could stand up to Charles, and he would beat the snot out of me. Or I could try to make friends with him. Friends it was.

I talked with Charles and tried to find a way to calm his anger and be a friend. Before long it became clear that he was just a kid in a strange place struggling with his schoolwork, especially biology. I made a deal with him. He could pretend to pick on me, which might help with getting the other kids to lay off him, and I'd help him with his biology. In return, he promised to be more of a friend to me, and if I needed protection he would help me out. In the end, Charles passed biology, we became friends, and I didn't get beat up. Clearly a win-win.

I also managed to live a lesson Mom was trying to teach. "Don't judge a book by its cover. Men look at the exterior of a person while God looks at the heart." For her, this principle was inextricably linked to her perception of what it meant to be a Christian and was summed in her belief that there is good in all people. Her Christian ideals and sense of justice wouldn't have it any other way. And she lived those ideals.

As I was wrestling with how to manage my way with Charles, Mom hired a middle-aged black woman named Mae to come clean our home once a week. She was a nice woman. Each week, Mom would pick her up, then in the afternoon take her home. We gave clothes we outgrew to Mae's son, Jerry. They weren't really hand-me-downs as we grew so fast that some of the stuff was brand new. Then Mom helped Mae get her driver's license, and we sold the family station wagon to her rather than trade it in. When Mom realized Mae couldn't read, she helped her get started in a reading course. This led to more courses, and eventually Mae earned her GED. We recognized that change was coming one way or another so Mom welcomed it and did what she could to bring it on, one person at a time.

As a kid, I knew right from wrong and seeing the injustice and hypocrisy of racism ticked me off then just as much as it does today. I would like to say we've totally moved on, but we haven't. As a lawyer, I represented a black woman from Mississippi who was injured due to a faulty car seat. She was a paraplegic, lived in a trailer home, and had to get around either in a wheelchair or by crawling on the floor.

We lost the case in the trial court, and I had to go to this woman's trailer and tell her we lost. That was almost as bad as calling my partners and telling them I had lost with over six figures of expenses into the case.

The lawyer who was responsible for getting me the client in the first place was older than Methuselah. We had lunch one day as this was going on and sort of out of nowhere he says, "You just love 'em, don'tcha?"

"What?"

"You just love 'em, don'tcha?"

This was in the late 1990s, and I just looked at him totally shocked. "What age are you living in? I can't believe this." Sometimes time just doesn't go by fast enough. The adverse verdict was reversed by the Mississippi Supreme Court and the case later settled.

There was another case of a woman who was hurt after slipping on yogurt left on a grocery store floor. When I went to ask the store manager for the security video of the injury he said, "Do you know who you're representing?"

I did. I also knew she was in Section 8 housing, received welfare, was among the poorest of the poor, and black. Just asking that question did it. He might as well have spit in my face because I was going to the mat. I played dumb. "What do you mean?"

After no reply, I said, "You know, I'm going to do what it takes to find out what really happened." I gave him a wink.

When I got the security video, I saw that someone had cut several minutes out of it, but because they were so stupid, they put the missing minutes at the back of the tape. And what they cut was the assistant manager passing by the spilled yogurt before the accident without doing a thing about it. Then my client comes down the aisle looking up at the top shelf for a liter of Coke and, zwoop, down she goes and busts her butt. Just like she said.

The most misquoted verse in the bible is, "The truth will set you free." That's not really what it says. John 8:32 says, "And you shall know the truth, and the truth shall set you free" (emphasis added). My life's job is to be sure the truth is known. Sometimes it has not made me very popular.

Over twenty years ago, my law partner and I started representing children living in New Orleans housing projects in lead paint cases. It's bad enough to grow up in poverty in a housing project in the middle of crime and drugs. It is even worse to live in a housing project filled with chipping lead paint that can cause permanent neurological damage. We worked that case with many other concerned caring lawyers to a successful conclusion. You do what you can.

# # #

Then, there was Vietnam.

There was no other issue in which the stakes to individuals, often people I knew, were higher. In about fourth and fifth grade, I would come home to Walter Cronkite reading off the body count and news of the war. Often, the reports included scenes of fighting in cities and parks, with people running through streets that reminded me of New Orleans. This wasn't the war Dad fought in. This felt uglier, more real, and did not have the distance of time and the assured outcome of Dad's war.

By the time I reached eighth grade, my sister was well into high school and was increasingly strident in her political views. Being the lawyer that he was, Dad would invoke the Socratic Method in his conversations, which usually took place at the dinner table.

This was nothing new and something he often did when confronted with an indignant kid who'd made the mistake of stating an opinion in front of him, which led to a lot of stupid arguments between us. One of the more memorable ones was a fight we started at the dinner table and carried into the den. I was in fifth grade and arguing that good football players make their own breaks. Dad took the opposite side even though he had said to me many times that good football players create their own luck. He argued that the bounce of the ball ruled the day. He characteristically took the side opposite me, whatever it may be.

"How in the world can you say that a player can't make his own breaks?" I asked.

"You never know which way the ball is going to bounce."

"No. Players make their own breaks."

"No. It just happens randomly."

We had chosen sides and now would fight to the death.

But with my sister and the war in Vietnam, he was more thoughtful. Vietnam was the biggest thing I can remember discussing as a group at the dinner table. In these conversations, his stock phrase to almost any statement was, "Why do you think that is?"

My sister would respond, "Well, people don't want to go off and fight and die in a war that doesn't mean anything."

"How do you know it doesn't mean anything? Are you for communism?"

"No, but this is an unwinnable war and one we shouldn't be fighting."

"We stopped them in Korea. What makes you think we can't stop them in Vietnam?"

"We're not committing the resources to actually do it, and we don't have the support of the people."

"But if we don't stop the flow of communism, and we have Cuba right to our south, that would be dangerous, so don't you think we need to do that?"

"We're just spinning our wheels getting people killed just trying to hold the status quo on something that's about to give out anyway."

Depending on how entrenched you were in your opinion, it could get irritating, but later he would say, "I'm just trying to get you to think and work through your thoughts." As frustrating as he could be, I was thankful for two things. The first was the respect and patience he showed us at a time when the social, political, and cultural changes of the 1960s was tearing other families apart. If nothing else, we could talk and disagree.

The second is that he did force us to think. Both Mom and Dad did what they could to get us to think through our own problems and the issues of the day, whether it was Vietnam or a kid from Bunche Village being mean to me. They wanted us to be independent people capable of using our own intellect and morals to reason through things as opposed to knee-jerk reactions or deciding upon a conclusion without thinking through the complexities of the issue. Answers to difficult problems are rarely easy.

Despite Dad often taking the opposite side, I'm not sure he was totally decided that the war was worthwhile. His experience in World War II and then seeing how Korea played out gave him a political, moral, and personal perspective, and I'm not sure he believed Vietnam was the kind of war we could win or that we should fight.

But when it got down to whether a person would leave the country rather than allow the military to draft them to fight, he was consistent. "If your country says it needs you, you should do your duty." He wouldn't cotton to draft dodgers.

At about this same time, my sister's friends began serious discussions and thoughts on what they would do. For them, the question of fighting or seeking a way out wasn't theoretical. The draft was starting to find some of them. She hung out with a group of friends who had a band that often practiced in our living room. I remember because there was the constant need to keep the little brothers out of the way, and Dad watched what was going on like a hawk.

There was a kid with blond hair who lived a few streets down from us who we knew from the horse stables. Having a horse at the horse stables was nothing hoity-toity. If we gave trail rides on the levee, we got a stall to keep a horse. It was my oldest sister's horse, but I did whatever she asked so I could ride.

His number came up in the draft and off he went. He completed basic training, came home for one last visit, and then left for a one year tour in Vietnam. Within a few weeks, he came home in a coffin. Boy, did we have some discussions at the kitchen table after that. The tension ticked up a notch too because the draft loomed large for those in the band.

I was in seventh and eighth grades as these discussions played out. With the thought that my time could come to think through this same issue I decided I couldn't leave my family and everything I knew to go to Canada and become part of some subculture. Dad's service also had an influence on my thinking, and after seeing the John Wayne movie "The Green Berets"—now recognized as a sales pitch for Vietnam by the Department of Defense—I decided that if it came to it I would join the Marines.

I may have mentioned it to Dad and the others at the time, but at age twelve or thirteen, the draft seemed far enough off that it was more than likely Vietnam would be settled by then. Thankfully, the war ended, and after going through a rough time in my junior year of high school, I told Dad I might just enlist in the Marines anyway. He looked concerned. "No, don't do that unless you want to make a career of it. If they want you, they'll draft you. Otherwise you should go to college and get on with your life." Good advice that I took.

In January of 1969—I was still in sixth grade—my first cousin married a guy named Mike at the First Methodist Church in Winnfield. It was a Saturday and it sleeted three inches, then snowed one more. We had to put the chains on Poppy's truck to go feed the cows at the farm. We tied a rope from the bumper to a sheet of old plywood and Poppy drug us around. It was fun. Only problem was eating the exhaust pipe on the truck when he stopped and we didn't.

Mike was a local boy from Winn Parish with dark hair and jet black eyes. He had played tight end on the high school football team, but could not avoid the draft like so many others who received college deferments or who got into the National Guard. Mike enlisted in the Army Rangers, and after he and my cousin married and the rice was thrown, they headed to Fort Benning in Georgia for basic training.

That summer, I spent time in Winnfield with Poppy and Ganny, and I remember my cousin getting excited each time she received a package from Mike. These were audiotapes that she listened to privately, but she shared snippets of stories such as the officer who spit polished his boots every morning only to step out of his quarters into ankle deep mud. And on the radio, like a soundtrack to life, Credence Clearwater Revival's songs about those unfortunate ones who had to run through the jungle and not look back[14] played over and over.

In the summer of 1971, I was fourteen years old and on the verge of entering high school. I was still just as lost and neurotic with how to fit in, and I was in a deep depression by the fact that love hadn't found me yet. Maybe my parents felt I needed a change, or maybe they thought it was time for me to get out of the house, but whatever the reason, my Uncle John in Winnfield offered me a job.

He owned a car dealership that also offered mechanic service and sold Conoco gasoline. I lived with Ganny and Poppy and worked nine and a half hours a day Monday through Friday and then a half day on Saturdays for $35 per week. I had a job and was making money at it. From what I could figure, I was making 67 cents an hour! Pretty good, huh?

As a kid, I sold mail-order Christmas cards door-to-door because I wanted to buy a dog. After explaining this to the neighborhood ladies, I sold a lot of cards. When the cards came in the mail, I went back to each one of these ladies to deliver their purchase, and each one asked me the name of my new dog. Well, I'd forgotten about the whole dog business after selling the cards. But it was a good year while it lasted.

There were a couple other kinda, sort-of jobs, washing cars and cutting grass, but working for Uncle John was my first real job, and I liked the sense of responsibility it gave me. Each morning I started the used cars to warm them up, followed by washing and detailing the new cars that arrived at the dealership. Through the day, I also took out the trash, manned the gas pumps, and did anything else anybody asked me to do.

There were also a couple guys I came to respect. One was a mechanic named Willie, who used to pour a pack of salted peanuts from the vending machine into the bottle of Coke he drank for lunch every day. One day he gave me one of the best pieces of advice about work I've ever received. "Listen up," he said, "you know what the best insurance is you can get to keep from getting fired?"

"No, sir."

"A broom." He smiled, then added, "Don't ever stand around and do nothing. Grab a broom and sweep if nothing else."

His advice saved my butt a few times.

I pumped gas along with a black man named John Henry. I followed him like a shadow, and before long I would come running when the loudspeaker called me to some new chore with my new nickname, Frank Henry. If there was such a thing, I was John Henry's apprentice and enjoyed his company.

The dealership sold Barracudas, Super Bees, Chargers, and Challengers, all with 440-cubic-inch engines and Holley carburetors. In the early mornings when I started the used cars, especially the muscle cars, I loved their throaty rumbling and the vibration of the engine that traveled up through the steering column into the wheel and then through my hands.

I'd turn on the radio as the cars warmed up, and more often than not, "Alone Again (Naturally)"—the most depressing song in the history of mankind and a big hit—came on. I wonder now why I tortured myself so at age fourteen, but when that song came on I felt an incredible sadness.

Here was a guy jilted at the altar, his dad was dead, his mother died of heartbreak, and he is left a sobbing mess. No wonder he asked about God, *"If He really does exist, why did he desert me?"*[15] Meanwhile, I was hooked on cigarettes, would never be an athlete, no girl would give me five minutes, had no idea what the future held, and had no real idea of who I was or who I was supposed to be. I was asking the same question.

When I was in Winnfield that summer, there was no doubt about it, I was in a funk. Dad called it the blues and it was my impression that everyone got the blues every now and again, but why was I so depressed? I wasn't alone, far from it, but boy was I lonely.

Adding to my own teen angst was Dad's angina attack earlier that year. He was in his mid-forties and the onset of his angina was so bad we had to call an ambulance to transport him to the emergency room because he thought he was having a heart attack. Seeing Dad so vulnerable and scared panicked me.

He was a heavy smoker who drank and ate a high fat diet with lots of meat, butter, salt, and everything else that most people did at the time. After leaving the hospital, he went to a cardiologist and got the edict: "You have to quit smoking, change your diet, and lower the fat." I don't know if he was kosher, but the doctor wouldn't even let pork in his house. With Mom's help, Dad quit smoking and changed his diet. He had already started down the Presbyterian path with Reverend Malsbary, and this event triggered a renewed vigor to his faith.

In the middle of that summer, my cousin's husband Mike came home from Vietnam after a second tour where he and other Army Ranger paratroopers made a jump into Cambodia. He seemed a little edgy. Gone were the soft eyes and demeanor of a young man. He was tall and lean, tattooed to his right forearm was a black panther, and he smoked Kool cigarettes almost constantly. In my eyes, he was the most badass dude that ever walked the face of the earth.

I tried to go everywhere Mike did to the point that I'm sure I was a pest. I also used to bum cigarettes off him, then sneak to the bathroom to smoke. One day while changing a tire on an outside tire machine, he walked behind me as I dropped a tire iron to the ground, which clanged loudly near him. He whipped around so fast that I thought I was a dead man. There was something in his eyes, something he brought home from Vietnam that I would never understand.

"Don't do that again," he said. It wasn't menacing. It was like he was asking me to do him a favor.

If he was around, I never did anything like that again.

And then, in the blink of an eye, the summer was over. The next thing I knew, I was back in East Jefferson High School looking out a window in the dark of a morning. Through the window, I stared at the shell road that led up to the back of the school, trying to figure out what was happening. A line of guys, organized and orderly, stood with platform shoes and long hair. One guy had plastic baggies of some sort of vegetable material that he was handing out while another guy collected ten dollars from each person in line.

"What is that?" I asked a dude near me.

"Pot, they're selling pot, you know, four finger bags of Acapulco gold."

I looked at him. "That's illegal."

He just smiled and walked away.

What I didn't know was that my world was about to open up into rebellion. But we just called it high school.

Chapter Five

I started high school in 1971 with short hair, the son of a teacher and oil company lawyer, living in a good neighborhood, with an upbringing steeped in the outdoors, football, church, and family.

And yet, with all this—the signs and evidence of a classic, middleclass upbringing—my profound restlessness grew steadily worse. The lessons taught to me by my parents did not square with life as I saw and experienced it. Rather than a place where there is good in everything and everyone, at least a little, there was plenty to fear and reasons to question everything. In response, I channeled anger to overcome fear and anxiety. And if you wanted me to do something, all you had to do was tell me not to do it. My feet were preprogrammed to run straight to the wayward path, the broad road, or whatever you want to call it.

What could go wrong?

# # #

The first day of school, I walked to the bus stop anxious and wondering what this new school held for me. There was no football to obsess over, though I'd decided to try out for the wrestling team, and unlike elementary and junior high, there would be no girls at school. You couldn't segregate based on race anymore, but by gender, absolutely.

Maybe the lack of females would calm my overburdened desire for some soul defining relationship. Or at the very least, limit the time I spent mooning over some girl who decided I was a nice boy and therefore not at all a romantic possibility. I milled about the bus stop with other kids for whom this was the first day of some new adventure or the boring continuation of something they must endure. The bus came, and silently we stepped up, consigned to our fate.

When we arrived, we got off the bus, tired and sullen, anxious and unsure, to coaches and teachers pulling random students out and sending them home for violating the school's hair regulations.

"If your hair is more than halfway down your ear or touches the collar of your shirt in the back," boomed a male voice, "tell your parents to take you to the barber, because until you get a haircut, we don't want you here." This rule—the grooming code—in my estimation was responsible for the t-shirt being the overwhelming shirt of choice at school.

I didn't have to worry about anyone yanking me out and sending me home. My hair was barely to the tops of my ears because Dad, Poppy, and the other old geezers claimed that you couldn't tell the girls from the boys if it was long enough to fall over of its own weight. I thought that was a crock. The girls were the ones with nice butts and boobs. Any fool could see that.

A few weeks later a group of students organized a sit-in at the school's quadrangle to protest the hair code. My neighborhood friend and I watched from the second story hallway until the wrestling coach—a squat but muscular man—came by and fussed at us to get back to class. We stood looking at him, then back out to the burgeoning chaos in the quadrangle.

His face reddened. "If you agree with them—" his tone escalated—"then get out there with them! Otherwise, get back to class!"

I looked at my friend. This was 1971, and protests on campuses, even high schools, were in full swing for everything from the Vietnam War to feminism to civil rights, and on and on. Most of them I agreed with, so why not hair? As far as I was concerned, we had the right to wear our hair down to our asses or shave it all off.

So, we went outside and joined the protesters, many of whom were making stronger statements with their appearance—clothes and hair—than my t-shirt, jeans, and short blonde hair. Nonetheless, it felt good to be part of something, especially for a freshman.

Teachers and coaches yelled, threatened, and tried to cajole us into returning to class, but we shouted over them. Then the sheriff's office arrived and began arresting and loading us "protesters" into paddy wagons. A couple officers grabbed my friend and me, but before they could cuff-and-stuff us, the school disciplinarian spotted us two shorthaired freshmen and pulled us aside. "I'll deal with these two idiots," he said.

The disciplinarian knew Mom because his daughter was in her Girl Scout troop. As a kid, I'd gone camping with them, made slingshots and that sort of thing, so he knew me, too. I guess he thought he was doing Mom a favor, but I wanted to find out what jail was like. The whole thing felt like a big adventure, and here I was missing out on the best part.

"I'll be speaking with your parents," he said as he hustled us back to class.

When I got home, Mom asked why I'd joined the "civil disobedience."

"Well, my wrestling coach told us we should join 'em if we agreed with them, so I did." She crossed her arms on her chest. "After all, you taught us to stand up for what we believe in, right?"

Caught in her own words, she shook her head. "I guess I did."

Wrestling turned out to be the hardest but best sport there ever was. We ran three miles to warm up, exercised out on the field, and then came inside and wrestled in the gym where we engaged in one of the most brutal workouts I've ever done called *posting*. The post man would wrestle a three-minute round with each of the guys in his weight class, usually six or seven, without any kind of break. Then the post man would switch out and it was your turn to be the post man. Then there were bridges. You start on your back, and then using only the soles of your feet and top of your head, you arch your back as far up as you can go to form a bridge. For good measure, a guy sat on your chest as you did these. After that we lifted weights for about an hour and then hit the showers. Mixed in with all this was the constant need to make weight and stay in the right weight class. By the end of practice, my body ached and my legs shook as I walked to Mom's parked car, where she sat reading a book as she waited.

"Another good time abusing yourself?" she'd say with a smile.

I'd look at her and nod.

"Good. Don't forget your homework when you get home." The engine would rev to life and off we went.

I liked wrestling, especially the physical challenge of it. But as a freshman, I was at the bottom of the totem pole. I didn't have the excuse of the other guys being twice my size because we wrestled in our own weight class. The other guys were just older and better.

The point of it for me was the challenge, but before too long I would lose that point.

# # #

At Thanksgiving dinner that year, Dad let me drink a glass of wine, which he'd been allowing my older sisters do for a few years. It was dark red and tasted strong, but I liked the way it bit at the tip of my tongue.

I sat at the table feeling a bit more grown up with my glass of wine and waited with Dad and John Robert for Mom and the girls to bring the food out.

"Hey, check this out," Dad said as he placed a pea on the end of his fork then smacked the tines with his hand so that the pea flew up and stuck to the popcorn stucco ceiling.

"Cool," said J.R.

By the time Mom came into the dining room weighed down by the turkey in her arms, the girls had joined in too, and there were green peas everywhere. She wasn't happy.

Dad sliced the turkey, and we passed the remaining peas and other dishes. With plates full and eyes wide, we fell into the silence of the laying on of dinner.

"Have I told you about a Greek friend of mine who owns a restaurant?" Dad asked as he put his knife and fork down on his plate. We groaned.

"Well, he has this fella from China working for him, and when my Greek friend has had enough to drink he'll ask this employee to say *fried rice*."

"Uh huh."

"So, the Chinese guy says, 'Flied Lice' and my Greek friend laughs it up."

"One day, the Greek is walking with his girlfriend when he sees his Chinese employee coming the other way down the sidewalk. 'Watch this,' he says and says to his employee, 'Hey, say fried rice!'"

"The Chinese fella puts his hands on his hips and stares right at his Greek boss and says, 'Fried Rice, you Gleek plick!'"

We'd heard Dad tell this joke many times over the years, but it always made us break down laughing. In later years, he'd just say the punch line and that was enough to get the same effect.

At Christmas, Dad made homemade eggnog using his mother's recipe. This entailed separating the egg whites from the yolks on Christmas Eve then beating the whites while spooning in sugar until they were shiny and nice and fluffy. He saved this in a big bowl in the refrigerator for the next morning. Then he beat the yolks gently while spooning in bourbon, followed by a spoonful of bourbon for the cook, then a spoonful for the yolks and a spoonful for the cook … you get the picture. On Christmas morning, they were folded together in a big crystal punch bowl.

With the eggnog mixed and the spirit of its maker shored up, the neighbors began to arrive on Christmas morning. The adults helped themselves to glasses of eggnog and other cocktails, while the kids played with their new gifts. Everybody was smiling, laughing, and happy, which made it one of the most wonderful days ever.

That is until I realized that I could sneak bourbon and cokes (we rarely ran low on either). I managed to hold the liquor well enough that nobody noticed, all's normal on the outside, but on the inside the feeling of my growing intoxication was tremendous. I'd never felt anything like it, so as I finished one, I followed it up with another.

Meanwhile, the younger kids played with their toys, we all put on our new Christmas clothes, the adults indulged in eggnog or harder drinks, and one of our neighbors, an engineer, decided to experiment with the self-cleaning feature on our oven. Maybe he wasn't a very good engineer or it was the alcohol, but he didn't bother to look to see if there was anything in the oven. He should've. Even though Mom caught the error before a fire broke out, the jacked-up oven cooked our turkey in about half-an-hour. It was a little dry.

Later that afternoon things began to spin, and I raced to the bathroom where I threw up my dinner and the bourbon and cokes.

Shortly after Christmas, my closest friend in the neighborhood told me that his of-the-age-of-majority brother might be able to help us out. He and his girlfriend were "hippies" as it were.

"He can go up to Time Saver and buy us some booze."

The idea had some merit.

"But we gotta be careful, really careful so we don't get caught."

"I'm in."

We paid for some Dixie Beer, Boone's Farm wine, and cigarettes from the Time Saver store. Like spies picking up a drop, we made our way to his car, then took our supplies to a vacant lot where we used to play touch football and had a little party. We didn't get caught, but like the idiots we were, we didn't think about the fact that the house on one side of the lot was the home of a district judge and across the street was the home of the district attorney. We could have been apprehended, charged, and convicted all within a block of my house.

I quickly realized that it didn't make sense to pay for a six pack of beer just to vomit it up. Forget the fact that evacuation is the body's way of saying, "Stop poisoning me!" Real men held their liquor so that's what I did.

#

With the holidays past, it was time for the wrestling season to get into full swing. I was miserable. The season ran from just after Thanksgiving through Mardi Gras, and I was trying to drop a weight class which meant I had to starve to death. I could eat any vegetable I wanted if it was green (no potatoes or starches) or any meat if it wasn't breaded and fried. My body screamed for carbs. And beer.

During practices and workouts, I wore a plastic garbage bag sweat suit to lose weight. You just pulled open the elastic sleeve to let the sweat pour out. I wasn't the only guy so outfitted. Trying to wrestle a guy slipping around in a garbage bag was a challenge made worse by the fact that the only exposed part had breath that could drop a horse from halitosis. By the time Fat Tuesday came around, all I could do was walk the parade route and try not to pass out.

I didn't wrestle in any of the meets. The only exception was when the starter in my weight class got sick, and I got bumped up from the number four spot to number three. Only the top two spots wrestled, but number three got to dress out and ride the pine. But this still didn't mean I'd wrestle.

I sat down, pulled my uniform from my bag, and laid it out on the locker room bench. I was just going to put it on and run out there to warm up with the team, but as I sat on the bench looking at the uniform—the socks, skin-tight singlet, and wrestling shoes—an overwhelming anxiety came over me. *No, I don't want to do it,* I thought.

"Go ahead man, just put the thing on and dress out," one of our Captains said.

I looked up at him and anxiety got the better of me. "No." Put the thing on and go out is all I had to do, but I didn't want to do it. And I didn't. "I'm not really the number three guy, so no."

#

My relief at the end of wrestling season was short lived. My homeroom teacher was the running backs' coach for the football team, and one day I made the mistake of wearing my parish championship jacket to class.

"You play football?" he asked.

"I did."

"You won a parish championship?"

My eyes glanced at the clock. "My team did."

"Spring football starts in a week. I expect to see you out on the field."

I wasn't so hot on playing football, especially after seeing our quarterback in eighth grade get crushed, but football is a big deal where I come from. East Jefferson had a good team and had recently graduated a young phenom of a quarterback by the name of Mike Miley. He went on to start at LSU, where he earned the nickname *Miracle Mike* and became an outstanding professional baseball player for the California Angels until he died in a car crash in 1977.

My sisters were also on the dance teams at East Jefferson's "sister schools," so I grew up going to all the games with my family, which was a big deal. The stands were always packed, and people stood two and three deep around the fence that surrounded the field. At the end of the north end-zone were two large, steel letters—an E and J—soaked in diesel. The school's mascot—the E. J. Warrior—would run out, do a war dance with a lit torch, and set the initials on fire, which always got the crowd going.

During the game, Mom would revert to her, "Go boy, go," style of cheering, but who could blame her. Throughout my family's time at East Jefferson, players such as Terry Bradshaw, Joe Ferguson, Bert Jones, and Norris Weis were out on the high school football fields of Louisiana. It was an incredibly exciting time to be a high school football fan. So, when that coach told me in homeroom he expected to see me out that spring, I had to play.

Spring football was nothing more than practice for the next season, but it was still full pads and a chance for kids to prove themselves to the coach. They hit hard and it was serious business. I should have died. After starving myself all winter I looked like a midget compared to the upper classmen who towered over me like hulking giants.

They moved me to wingback, which took getting used to as I had always played guard, then fullback, followed by linebacker. In each position I felt like I was one blindside hit away from leaving this earth. This isn't to say I didn't love football. I did and still do.

The one bright spot was my locker assignment. The coach, or whoever does these things, put me between two juniors, a tight end and a linebacker. The linebacker was big, mean, and ugly. For some reason they liked me and gave me a ride home after practice. When the neighborhood kids saw me emerge from that car, I had some cred and it gave me a bit of a boost.

Somehow, I managed to survive spring football as well as the remainder of ninth grade but popped out the other end without a job. I didn't want to go back to Winnfield so I went down to Jim's Clearview Shell and told Jim I'd always wanted to work there. It actually wasn't that much of an exaggeration. When I was a kid, we would drop our car off at the neighborhood Shell station for service, and one of the guys would drive us the few blocks home. There was something about them I thought was cool.

"Really?" Jim said.

"Yeah, and my Dad's a lawyer for Shell, too, so this seems like a good place for me to work."

Jim folded his arms and sort of frowned.

"Look, let me work here for a week, and if I don't do a good job, no problem, I'm done. I'll even work for free, no sweat." This was actually Mom's idea.

A week later Jim called and said he'd give me a try on the 6 p.m. to 10 p.m. shift helping the night man tend the pumps and clean the place up. My friends thought I was nuts to work nights, but I wanted the job so I took it. My biggest worry was making sure Jim wanted to keep me and getting enough shifts to make it worth my while.

About a week later the heat and humidity crept ever higher and I went waterskiing with friends. I hit a tugboat wake and launched at least ten feet into the air. It was so cool. Predictably, I lost control, the skis flew off, and I flipped upside down before hitting the water. No problem, except one of the skis splashed down before I did and hit me dead square in the forehead. That was a bit of a problem.

I bobbed up to the surface and tasted blood running into my mouth from a deep, inch-long cut in my forehead just above my hairline. A doctor in the emergency room stitched it up and joked that I'd appreciate his work when my hairline receded, as of course it has. Good work, doc.

I showed up to work that night with stitches in my head that throbbed as the xylocaine wore off. Despite the pain and it being an exceptionally hot and humid night, I kept at it. After that night, Jim knew I meant what I said about wanting the job and that he could rely on me, no matter what. I never had to worry about my hours or keeping that job again.

As I showed my willingness to work that summer, even when in considerable pain, it became clear to me that one of the main recreational pursuits in our neighborhood was getting loaded. The adults were the children of The Great Depression and the soldiers and caretakers of the home front during World War II. They appreciated having a few drinks with their downtime. Where we lived, everyone had good jobs, worked hard during the week, and on Saturdays, after they manicured their lawns and swept the sidewalks, they broke out the glasses, bottles, and ice. This was the era of the cocktail party. My friends and I watched and absorbed it all as we listened to Creedence's "Down on the Corner." The joy of drinking wasn't lost on us. Earlier that spring, we'd had our own kid versions of the adult cocktail party in the vacant lot. By summer, we were sneaking booze from our parents and meeting up with friends to drink beers and smoke cigarettes, to which I was now thoroughly addicted.

Then in June, on a dead summer's day, my friend said, "I got some weed, man."

Hmm, I thought, *interesting.*

"My parents aren't home so let's go."

I was all in. He got the stuff from his brother, and as I watched him roll a loose joint with a reasonable level of skill, I realized he was doing a lot more adventuring than me. He lit it then passed it to me, and I took a big drag.

"Hold it," he said, but I coughed up the harsh smoke.

He took another hit, held it with his chest out and eyes closed, then let a steady, slow stream of smoke escape. I pinched the joint between my pointer finger and thumb and pulled on it, but a seed exploded in a shower of sparks and half the joint went with it. We smoked it down to a little brown roach, and I looked around the room.

Nothing. Didn't feel a thing.

"What do you think?" he asked.

"I don't know, maybe we didn't do it right."

"Yeah, we didn't smoke enough."

He rolled another, we smoked it, and then I felt it. It's hard to describe, but it felt like that initial euphoric sensation you get right when you start to drink that just goes on and on. And instead of getting mellow, clumsy, and slurring your words like drinking, you just break out in great bouts of hilarity at incredibly foolish things. Then it started to wear off and I was ravenously hungry, just like I used to get after swim practice. We ate two boxes of Captain Crunch and then went to the convenience store for more.

At work, I advanced to working a day shift on Sundays, which Mom didn't like because I missed church, but a job is a job. The Sunday manager was a young guy who had medium-length blond hair and worked during the week for the railroad.

I also got to meet a couple of the other day crew guys. One was a fella named Cotton who wore the old-style gas station uniform with the hat and everything. I worked the night shift with him. When the phone rang he always answered very nasally, "Jim's Clearview Shell." He drove a 1949 Ford with a Flathead V-8 engine that was pretty sweet. God only knows what that car is worth today.

Cotton was from Alabama, called me Pardnah all the time and said an-tic instead of antique. When I first saw his car, he looked at me and said, "Pardnah, one day that car is going to be an an-tic." He also used to call traffic lights *single lights*, not *signal lights*. Being that we were near Interstate 10, we were the GPS and Google Maps of the time. When someone pulled into the gas station and asked Cotton for directions, he would say in his thick drawl, "Y'all go down to the first single light, and you take a right to the next single light, then ..." By the time he got to the third "single" light, the person was so confused they didn't know where the hell they were going. They just floored it to get away and go ask someone else for directions. And he claimed great intuition in discerning which female customers were interested in the Bo Hawg grind.

The other guy I liked working with was a big, black guy with a beard, who drove a dark blue two-door Chevy Impala. One sunny, Sunday afternoon as we were working the pumps, I noticed him and the Sunday manager disappearing into the washroom at the back of the bays. They'd peak out every so often if they heard a customer pull in and the bell ring. Despite them telling me to watch the front, I went back to the washroom.

"What's up?" I asked as I opened the door and walked into a cloud of pot smoke. The Sunday manager didn't know me very well, so he got upset and worried that the fifteen-year-old kid would rat them out.

"No, he's cool," the big black dude said. Since I'd all but been his shadow at the station, I'd told him all about the joints with my buddy and the cereal binge.

"You sure?"

"Yeah, I'm sure, I'm sure." Then he passed me the joint, and from then on, I liked working Sundays a whole lot more.

#

Working in a gas station with cars and hearing the rumble of muscle cars as they came and went made getting my driver's license an obsession. As soon as I could, I signed up for driver's education and then chomped at the bit to get behind the wheel of a car, any car. The written portion of the class was first, which was simple enough. After that, they tried to scare us with a movie that showed all sorts of horrible crashes with bodies—mostly of teenagers— hanging from telephone poles, lying on the ground, and so on. The one I remember the most was the sliced-up bodies of a couple drunken teenagers after they flew through the windshield. It seemed simple enough to me: If you don't crash you won't die. Duh.

To further educate and prepare us to be safe drivers, they put us in a car with a P.E. coach who barely looked at us before telling us to drive across the Huey P. Long bridge over the Mississippi River to get his laundry.

"Pull in here," he said pointing to a laundromat and dry cleaners. I wheeled the car in and parked, and then he went in and picked up his laundry.

"You," he said pointing to my friend in the back seat, "your turn."

The state built the bridge in the 1930s with two lanes running in either direction and railroad tracks between the lanes. With the size of cars in the 1970s and the famously narrow bridge, there was about a two-inch clearance on each side of the car. The Parish dump was also on the other side of the river, which meant garbage trucks frequently crossed. God help you if one passed while you were on the bridge on a windy day.

If you survived crossing the Huey P. Long bridge, you passed driver's education.

With my driver's license in hand, I borrowed Mom's car and drove out to a small suburban neighborhood where the Sunday manager and his wife lived. Both worked, they had a child, he had a boat and loved to bass fish, and they were, to the teenage me anyway, super cool. I was there for dinner, but I also, for the first time, scored some pot of my own.

Afterward, as I sat parked in the car, I took the baggy from my pocket and looked at it in my hands. The adrenaline rush was unbelievable! I was happy to have it, sort of proud to have the resources and connection to buy such a thing, but at the same time it scared me. I knew if I got caught I would be dead.

It would kill my parents, too.

But none of that was enough to get me to stop. Looking back on that summer and that moment, I know now that something within me changed. I loved and respected Mom and Dad, which was maybe unique among my generation. I loved Poppy and Ganny and all my family, too, but I was no longer the wide-eyed recipient of their wisdom. Everything was to be tried and tested.

By the time summer wound down and I entered my sophomore year, I'd begun surrendering. I questioned the established order of everything. I turned to pot and drinking and began down a road of moral decay that years later would bring me sobbing to my knees.

To a kid relying on inductive reasoning—making decisions about the world and my place in it based on what I saw and experienced—the deductive reasoning of my parents and church was no match to what I was seeing with my eyes. They could tell me what to think or believe and how to behave, but my experiencing the world was opening new paths as old ones closed.

#

There was no way out of playing football. Part of me relished the new season—putting the pads on, the smell of rotting grass and tepid water puddles, red ants, mosquitoes, jock itch, and bruises—but the same fears were there. I also knew I'd never be a starter. We did have junior varsity games scheduled, but only a few, and they felt like a booby prize rather than a chance to work my way up the ladder.

The coaches also didn't seem to care about anyone other than the bigger and better varsity starters. The only bright spot was that the J.V. coach slotted me at middle linebacker, often referred to as the quarterback for the defense. I appreciated him giving me that responsibility.

But the thing that really did me in as a football player was smoking cigarettes. People who say that tobacco is not an entry drug are fooling themselves. Smoking and being addicted to nicotine set the stage for other drugs.

One day at practice, I had a running back squared up and was about to make a photo op tackle in the open field. My shoulder was just above his belt, my head was on his side, and I was wrapping him up to take him down when my defensive teammate flew in from the side. His head was down and he speared the crap out of me instead of the ball carrier. Instantly, the hit sent a burning, electric-like fire down my now paralyzed arm. I would later learn players call this a *stinger.*

I lay on the ground for a second or two then rose to my knees with my left arm drooped down to the ground as the coach yelled, "Get up! Get up!"

My arm felt like it was on fire. To this day my neck still burns, but only when I type.

During one of our few J.V. games on a cold November day, I was out in my middle linebacker position. It was first down, and for some reason, the transition between the offensive and defensive teams taking the field was a confusing mess with guys running in and then back out and all over the place.

We'd finally lined up and the other team's quarterback was calling out the count when I looked up.

"TIME OUT!" I yelled.

I looked to the sideline and the coach was apoplectic. His face was fire-engine-red, and his eyes were bugging out of their sockets. Mom was in the stands watching this.

When he could finally manage to form words, he shouted so all could hear, "What in the hell are you doing?!"

"Coach, we only have ten men on the field."

Eyes wide, face red, he used his finger to help him count the number of players on the field. "Oh, right."

Mom got a kick out of that.

That year in spring practice I made a fatal mistake. I don't like to criticize coaches—I'm one now for my kids—but the coaches were cold and distant at East Jefferson. There were the players and then there were the coaches who walked through the locker room to their offices and closed the door without a word; the overt implication being, leave us alone.

We were practicing, and I was alternating in a fullback spot, which is a position I wanted to play much more than middle linebacker. We had three offensive huddles going when a wingback ran past and asked me to give him a breather because he was running in two groups. I didn't want to blow playing fullback by running wingback in another huddle too. I guess it could be done, but I was staying where I was until told to double up.

I didn't say it loud, and it was just as he ran past. "F**k you, man." Even I was a little shocked at what I'd said. But it wasn't really the language. This was an all-boys public high school. Not a monastery. The coaches said worse. No, I was to be the example.

"What!"

I turned in the direction of the deep, male, and angry voice to see the head coach standing behind me. He blew his whistle, which stopped everything, and it seemed that for the first time ever he knew I existed.

"Your teammate is asking for help and that is all you have to say? Start running."

So, I started running around the field. Practice started up again, ended, and I was still running. Everyone left the field. I kept running. The sun set, and it got dark as I ran, and then I was the only person left.

Then I stopped. Something in me died. They didn't care about me, I didn't care about them, and I knew right then that it was over for good. I didn't quit the team until spring practice ended, but I couldn't care less about football. I was only a body on the sidelines—I don't think they noticed one way or the other.

In two years, J.R. would come along at six-foot-two-inches and two-hundred-ten-pounds. They noticed him. I was jealous and proud of him when he became something of a football star and was named All District Guard.

I talked to Dad about some of the challenges and my frustrations with the team. He listened, offered advice and was sympathetic, but he didn't really want me playing. He stressed academics and knew I was small compared to the other players. I think he worried I'd get hurt. But I don't think he realized that as I pulled away from sports the pull toward drugs, alcohol, and questionable friendships was all the stronger.

We weren't bad kids nor, to our way of thinking, were we delinquents. We smoked as much pot as we could get our hands on and rode around listening to music. When we were younger and got bored, there were a whole range of activities we could engage in. There was ring-and-run—ring a doorbell and run—and pull-the-string—car comes down the street, we kneel on either side, car gets close, we act like we pull a string up, car slams brakes on, and we run away laughing. And we could improvise. Like setting fire to a bag of dog crap before ringing and running. Or roll or egg a house. As '72 became '73 and then spring led into summer, I worked as much as I could at Jim's Clearview Shell, and our antics crossed the line from devious to deviant and just plain stupid. Like mailbox baseball. One house used brick and put the mailbox inside of it. *Kapow!* the bat ricocheted off the mailbox, flew back, and smashed a window on the car. We left the brick ones alone after that.

In the early mornings before school, Mom would stand at the kitchen sink facing east watching the sunrise. Above the sink was a needlepoint.

"This is the day the Lord has made. Let us rejoice and be glad in it" from Psalm 118:24. My cousin says this was my Poppy's favorite verse.

I'm sure glad Mom was praying for me. I sure needed it. And I know I tested her patience.

I had one friend who was kind of a funny guy. He was held back in the grades and was one of those kids who could grow a full beard from the time he was ten. Seems he was easily influenced into mischief. His dad was an airline pilot, and we could swipe about as much booze as we wanted in those little airline bottles. We got loaded at our bus stop before school pretty regularly.

My friend would come by to get me before school, but he wouldn't knock, just stand by the back door on the carport and wait. Mom would be cooking breakfast and the dog would start to growl so she'd go to the back door.

"Can I help you?"

He started every conversation with, "Did you know ..." and some strange fact he'd picked up. "Did you know that if you put a tennis ball into a PVC pipe with a can of Coca Cola that you can explode the ball out and maybe even kill a bird with it?" Stuff like that.

That Christmas, he bought a huge peppermint stick. It was about a foot long and four inches around and he decided to lick the thing until it was gone. You'd see him walking down the street licking his peppermint stick.

"What are you doing?" I'd ask.

"I'm still licking on this peppermint thing." It took him three weeks before it was finally gone.

Then he broke his foot, not sure how. We used to play around with fiberglass, which I learned how to use while building a boat. He used it where he worked so he mixed some up, took a shoebox and cut holes in it, put his foot inside and spread fiberglass on it like a cast. He came walking down the street with this fiberglass shoe box on his foot.

"Hey Frank."

"What?"

"Guess what?"

"What?"

"You got a box on your foot."

"Yeah, guess what's around it?"

"I got no idea."

"Fiberglass."

"Why do you have a fiberglass box on your foot?"

"Because I broke my foot. Jump on it. You can't break it."

I said no, but that is what he was like. I didn't like getting him into trouble or anything because I liked the guy and we were friends. At the same time, he either found trouble or it found him. One night we had drunk a bunch of Singapore slings with dates from some uptown New Orleans finishing school. We had dropped off his date first. Drunk luck was with me and my date let me in her house, but before anything could get going we heard this loud hhh-*hhoooonnnnkkkkk!* out in front of her house.

I ran out front to see my friend passed out with his face planted on the horn. The car was in gear so it had pushed up against the back of the car parked in front. Pretty funny sight actually. Before I could get to him, a neighbor came running across the street yelling, "Hey, hey, hey!"

"Hey, hang on just a minute," I yelled.

He woke up, saw this guy yelling, and for some unknown reason reached across to his glovebox like he's going to hand the guy his license and registration or something. The guy thought he was reaching for a gun so he jumped into the car, grabbed him as if he were in a fight for his life, pulled him out of the car, and dumped him on the pavement.

I ran up yelling, "Hey, we're leaving. He didn't do any damage to that car."

The guy let go, and I picked him up then pushed him into his car as I yammered at the guy about how we meant no harm, there's no gun, all a big mistake, no need to worry, and so on. Then, after he left, we laughed our butts off.

Beyond this and quite a few other adventures, we spent our time sneaking around the neighborhood smoking cigarettes, filching beers from garage refrigerators, making illicit booze buys, and smoking pot whenever we could get our hands on any.

But we weren't bad kids. Right?

I think the counterbalance or the thing that kept me from completely falling off the edge was my parents. Dad was as engaged in our lives as he could be and set a good, strong example of hard work and honesty. I did my best to live up to the work ethic he set even if I wasn't living up to my parents'—and my own—expectations for honesty.

Mom worked hard in and out of the home as well and didn't ever give up on or compromise her desire to see me accept her Methodist values. She encouraged me to join the church youth group, and despite my strong objections—basically, *it isn't cool*—she didn't give up. She also continued to talk with me about God and describe the reasoning behind her faith. She lived it. You could tell by the way she just did for others.

I was watching all right, but to me the signals were mixed. Justice, equality, and freedom all seemed to fall on the side of rebellion. And I had to clearly see it and experience it to know if it was true. I had lots of questions.

How could I have any faith in the presence and goodness of God if I'd failed at the things I truly wanted for my life, things that are inarguably good? I wanted to be an athlete, especially with football, but I not only failed, I was made to feel horrible. I wanted to find love but this was, in my own mind, denied to me. What girls came my way, and there were precious few, did not lead to transformational love, only heartbreak.

If God was so good and faith so redeeming, why was I so miserable when I tried to be good? At least, that's what I thought.

At the same time, experience was teaching me that drinking, smoking pot, and the rest of it gave me at least something. It gave me that feeling of ease and comfort. I was cool.

I remember hanging out in my room, which now was my lair, listening to Jethro Tull's "Wind Up." I have to give Mom credit. When every other parent was freaking out over the direction of the music we listened to, she was genuinely interested in how and why it spoke to me. We talked about music, not just as a source of noise and rebellion, but to its meaning and how it questioned justice and the purpose of man. It led me to ask, *What does it all mean? Is this all there is?*

I kicked back on my bed and could hear the gurgling of some homemade wine I was trying to ferment. I had a gallon milk jug in my closet filled with raisins, grape juice, and yeast. The top was a rubber cork with a tube in another gallon jug of water that let fermentation gasses out, but no air in. It went b*lurp, blurp, blurp* every few seconds. This was my second batch. The first had been pretty good.

Mom poked her head into the room to the lyric, "He's not the kind you have to wind up on Sunday." [17]

"Well, what do you think about that?"

She paused, gave me that amused look, then said, "That's what I have been trying to tell you."

I completely missed her point. I was looking for hypocrisy in her and everywhere to justify my own failings, not any kind of redemption.

It would be wrong to say that nothing my parents did affected me. While I pushed the limits and did the inverse of what adults said I should, I wasn't stupid. Mom and Dad set some limits on my behavior and the choices I made, like hard work and education. That was non-negotiable. I had a sense of right and wrong, smart and stupid. I also had what I thought was a sixth sense for knowing when to back off and out of the group just before trouble hit.

For example, I knew to leave one of our "parties" just before things got out of hand and they busted up a sofa and got in trouble for it. Another time they wanted me to go on a homemade zip line that my parents—all our parents— said was too dangerous after one kid fell and split his hand open on a sapling stump. I said no, I had to work. They went and one kid fell and broke his arm. Then I passed on loading into a convertible to drive up a lawn and throw a brick with lit firecrackers through an erstwhile friend's front window. The police tracked them down and jailed them for a night. Or the Sunday afternoon when I had to work and my friend ended up speeding in a twenty-mile-per-hour zone with pot on him. The cops nailed him, and I went with his father and my Dad, the lawyer, to bail him out.

There are more—many more—stories like these when friends fell off the edge, some of them drowning in their mistakes. For some reason, one that I can only explain as my *Spidey Senses*, I crept to that edge, sometimes with my toes and most of my body leaning over but somehow knew when to pull back.

Maybe I just got lucky? Or as Mom said, maybe Someone was trying to tell me something.

#

I am a hopeless romantic, and there are times when I wonder what would have happened if a girl, any girl, had taken an interest in me. For a long time, I finished second or third or fourth to guys who fit the narrow box of what girls were looking for, or I got shot down and humiliated. It was the girl next door, across the street, or some wistful daydream at the pool. And with each hard crush, the pain of it sent me further toward things that eased the angst and sustained that little ember of ego I'd managed to protect.

The fall of 1973, my junior year, I had quit football and wrestling. With my grades—believe it or not they were good—I had one foot lingering in what my parents expected, the established order of things, but the other foot and my body leaning hard toward drugs, smoking, drinking, and trouble. Then for the first time, I actually fell in love. Or so I thought. The truth is she was the first girl to show any interest in me.

I had a cousin who was a year older and we'd become friends. He was dating a girl from across the street, and over the Christmas holiday her parents had friends visiting from Alabama and they had brought their daughter. The perfect double date. I was pumping gas at Jim's Clearview Shell about six hours each day and ripe for someone to fall in love with.

I'm not sure if it helped that she didn't know me, except maybe by my cousin, but it didn't take long for us to become sweet on each other. She met my basic standards—female with a pulse—and it didn't hurt that she was an attractive and sweet girl.

Other than when I had to work, we spent as much time with each other as we could, either going out or burrowing into a sofa where we could be alone listening to Elton John and Bread. When we weren't together, we talked on the phone, or I walked around work and our house like a moon-eyed puppy.

The only hiccup was she didn't like my smoking. She said it was gross, like kissing an ash tray. Little did she know that she was denigrating my beloved first drug of choice. Cigarettes gave me something to do when bored or waiting. They created a look, an aesthetic, and an identity that I embraced. And I was addicted to nicotine.

She asked me to quit, and I wanted to oblige. I tried cutting back one day. By the next day I was back to where I started. I tried stopping cold. It was more than I could take. I wanted nothing more than to be the person she desired and deserved, but she was going to have to accept me as a smoker, at least for now.

I think Mom, Dad, and my siblings appreciated the relative calm that came with my first supposed girlfriend. I imagine, too, that Mom and Dad hoped this meant a change in direction for me. For the first time in a long while, probably since sixth grade, I was happy and the knot in my gut softened. Finally I was living out what I'd dreamed of for years and that I'd jealously seen happen to other guys often with girls I had crushes on.

A few days before New Year's my uncle pulled some strings and got tickets to the national championship Sugar Bowl game between Notre Dame and the University of Alabama at Tulane Stadium. When I looked at the schedule at work, I was horrified to see I was on the night shift New Year's Eve.

"Jim," I said, "I need New Year's off. I really do. I need it off."

"Maybe. Let me see."

"Come on Jim, you gotta give me New Year's off. I'll work double shifts, whatever you want."

"I dunno."

"Please, Jim, I really need this."

"If I say no and you go I'll have to fire you. You know that?"

"Jim, come on, when have I ever asked for time off?"

"You're gonna go no matter what I say?"

"Jim, please, I have to have New Year's off."

He wiped his mouth and thought for a moment. "A football game?"

"And a girl."

The wheels turned and he finally said, "Fine, whatever. I don't want to have to train a new guy after firing you."

Notre Dame eked out a win 24 to 23 over University of Alabama. Although we lost, it was an awesome game. I looked at my girlfriend as we left the stadium, and she was crying over the loss even though she was an Auburn fan, not a 'Bama fan.

"Hey, let's go out? It's New Year's after all," I said.

She looked at me as if someone had died. "No. Take me home."

"What?"

"Take me home."

"You gotta be kidding? It's New Year's Eve! And it was 'Bama that lost, not Auburn." I had seen Bert Jones and LSU beat Ole Miss in 1972 on the last play of the game with one second on the clock, so I was used to tight exciting ball games. It was at that point I had subconsciously decided I would be an LSU Tiger.

She stopped walking and gave me a hard look. "I know. But it's still my state. I'm upset about it. I want to go home."

I was so head-over-heels in love that I let it slide and took her home.

The whole whirlwind romance lasted less than two weeks. It seemed forever.

She went home with her family, and later that same day I started writing the first of what would be many love letters. She dabbed hers with perfume, and since she was a senior in high school that year we talked of me graduating early so I could go to—and I can't believe I ever considered this—college at Auburn.

She said that I had the hands of a surgeon. I'm not sure how a high school senior would have such insight, but I believed her and became as soft as putty.

"You'd be great in medical school," she said on the phone one night.

"Well, maybe," I said, not so sure.

"Wouldn't you like to be a doctor?"

They made bank, that's for sure. "Maybe."

"Then how about it?"

"I am taking the ACT in a few weeks."

I'd signed up for the February ACT date, and with the female urging, I did what I could to prepare. The night before the test, after working at the service station until 10 p.m., I bought a six pack of beer and smoked a joint or two. It was Friday night, and I really did reel it in some. I was in bed by midnight, but the next morning, I was a little hung over.

By the time I got to the natural sciences section of the test, the fourth and final section, the hangover hit, and a light headache kicked in. Screw it. I raced through science, skimming the questions and selecting whatever answer seemed right so I could finish the thing and head home. I answered the last question as they called time.

I did well on the rest of the test, but on the science portion I got a thirty something which put me in the ninety-eighth percentile. It was just dumb luck attributed to reading comprehension, and since then I've considered standardized tests as somewhat of a joke. Unless you are testing for time management and reading comprehension.

When I called my girl and told her my score, it was a done deal. She decided I was going to medical school. I had my doubts. The next step was to go tell Dad what was shaping up.

"Dad, we need to talk."

He was in his bedroom at the dresser after a game of golf with a cold beer. He gave me a swig.

"Look, I think I'm in love—and I don't know if this is it or not but I've got to find out. I want to go to Auburn."

He looked up. "For college?"

"No, for the weekend, but maybe."

He snickered, but to his credit he didn't burst out laughing. "Okay."

I bought a Greyhound bus ticket and left that Friday. We love birded it up that night, then the next day she took me to a state park with a lake and a slimy dam.

She pulled her coat around her shoulders. "During the summer, you can slide down the dam because the water at the bottom of it is deep."

"I'll give it a try." This wasn't the first dumb thing that I had ever done.

"Oh no, it's too cold."

I took my shirt off. "Nah, sun's out. Can't be that cold." It was February.

There's just being stupid and then there's being stupid for love. This was both. I pulled a picture perfect shallow racing dive into the lake. The water was so cold that it sucked my breath from my body and I convulsed into a ball. It was such a quick and involuntary reflex that the ring I got for Christmas slid right off my finger and is still at the bottom of that lake. Damn, that lake was cold!

I surfaced and managed to breath, then forced a smile.

"You're going to die of hypothermia."

"Maybe."

We did have fun getting me warm again.

That night there was a fraternity party on the Auburn campus and we went. They had jungle juice, which was a mixture of Hawaiian Punch and crystal clear liquor. Powerful stuff that tasted akin to antifreeze. I drank three, four, five cups of it and thought, Hey, I'm doin' good. She drank one cup of the jungle juice and loosened up a bit. Then she had another and maybe one more before she pulled me to the side and said we had to leave.

"I don't want to leave."

She looked at me and her eyes rolled back and her cheeks poofed out. We made it out to the sidewalk and she bent over and ralphed in the grass. I held her and made sure she got to the car safely and then home.

The next morning it was time for me to go. I'd brought the Bread album with me, which we did put to good use, and I left it on her sofa so that she'd see it when she got back from the bus station. We walked into the bus station together and when the speakers called my bus I kissed her.

"Frank?"

"Yeah?"

"You really need to quit smoking cigarettes."

"Okay, I'll see you later."

I got on the bus and waved to her as we pulled out, then lit a smoke and settled in for what would be the longest bus ride in history. We stopped in every Podunk town in Alabama and Mississippi. Not long after we left Auburn, a fifteen-year-old badass girl with a carton of Marlboros got on the bus and sat right next to me. I'd already filled the tiny, metal ashtray in the arm rest, but she just flicked a few of the butts out and stubbed her cigarette out.

"How ya doin?" she asked, and I knew I was in trouble. She lit one cigarette after another and described how much she hated her divorced parents, that sadistic nuns filled her Catholic school (a cliché, I know), and generally how much she loved rock music and getting high and all the rest. I lit one cigarette after another, nodded my head as she spoke, and told her about getting high with my friends. She laughed, I laughed, and by the time the bus pulled out from the first meal stop, we were making out. She got out somewhere in Mississippi, and I knew I would never see her again. I also knew I was no longer in love.

Some thirteen hours after we set out from Auburn with the seam in the back of my Levis permanently imbedded into my sacrum, the bus pulled into New Orleans. The next day I wrote a letter, "I want to go to college, but I think I need to stay closer to home than Auburn. I'm thinking about LSU and you're at Auburn and I'm here and it's not fair for us to tie each other down, so maybe we should see other people. I will always be here for you. Frank."

What I didn't tell her was that I couldn't quit smoking to save my life, and I didn't want to anyhow. And I wanted to go to LSU.

I received a nice letter in response, "If that's the way you want it, I'll always be here."

I read her letter and thought about that girl on the bus. Whatever restraint I'd felt was gone. My course was set, and it was going to go how it went. A girl wasn't enough to get me to change the path I was on. When I think of her now, I don't wonder if love could have saved me. It couldn't and didn't.

#

In October of 1973, the Arab Petroleum Exporting Countries (OPEC) proclaimed an oil embargo to punish the United States and other countries for supporting Israel during the Yom Kippur War that same year. The most immediate effect was a sharp rise in the price of gas from about thirty-five cents to fifty-five cents, a price that was unheard of back then.

Over the next couple of months, as supplies dwindled, states started all sorts of rationing schemes such as odd/even license plate days or green (all welcome), yellow (only commercial vehicles), and red (no gas) flags. With the holidays, states asked people not to put up holiday lights and use other strategies to lower power consumption.

For those who didn't live through it, it was a mess.

At Jim's Clearview Shell, there were long periods of boredom followed by being busier than a one-legged man in a butt-kicking contest. We'd get a truck load of gas and there would be a line of cars winding out of the pumps and down the street. Like word had gotten out. We pumped gas so fast it was dizzying. We didn't check hoods, put air in tires or clean anything. We stuffed money and credit card slips in our pockets and moved on to the next car. Within a few hours the pumps were empty and the line disappeared until the next load came in.

Even though Louisiana is a gulf state, we had rationing, which meant the station was only able to be open two hours in the morning and two hours in the evening. Jim hated to do it, but there were other guys who needed the work more, and a bit after Christmas he laid me off.

Not working wasn't something I could do. Having a job helped define me. It gave me something I was proud of and helped mediate the anxiety that was my constant companion. I needed a job to keep me sane. And I needed the money. Fortunately, I didn't have to go too long without work. My friend worked at a cafeteria at a local shopping mall and got me a job. I worked the 2 p.m. to 8 p.m. shift after school and full-time on weekends.

There was a well-established hierarchy in the cafeteria based on the food you served. Simple foods such as drinks and bread meant you were on the low end of the totem pole. Entrees put you among the elite. New employees started at the beverage station, which was a counter filled with glasses of iced tea, red drink, purple drink, lemonade, water, and some sodas. If you excelled at beverage, you quickly moved up the ladder to bread. People slid their trays along the rail, often distracted by conversations and choosing what they were going to have at the next stations. They never asked for bread, but just pointed to what they wanted and gave a little grunt after I asked, "Bread?" The next question, "Butter?" got the same response. After working at a busy gas station, where the boss and other workers respected me, this job drove me nuts. "Bread?" "Butter?" "Bread?" "Butter?" *Aaggghhhh!*

Excelling at "bread" meant you moved up one more station to "vegetables," and if you were really good you'd get to move to "entrees." The top position was line runner, which was the guy who passed the pans to and from the kitchen through a little, slotted window. The next stop after this station was probably insanity, quitting, getting fired, or all the above.

One of the perks of this job was getting to eat as much as you wanted each shift. The wonder and thrill of this lasted about five days, at which point I lost my appetite for food altogether. Familiarity breeds contempt, after all.

This was true even though I went to work as stoned as I could get. School too. Creative writing was my first class in the morning so getting stoned at the bus stop seemed like good mental preparation. I had to keep a sharp eye out because Dad would leave the house for work about ten or twenty minutes after I left for the bus stop. Most days the bus had stopped and left by the time he pulled past in his car, but on a few occasions, he pulled out of the driveway, drove down our street and turned at the corner where our bus stop was.

"Wait, wait," I'd say holding a lit joint behind my back, "here comes my Dad." I smiled and waved to him as he passed.

Our closest Cheech & Chong impression happened after we scored a large bag of weed. We rolled three huge joints in Esmerelda strawberry papers, lit up, and passed them around while giving each other shotguns, which is a way of blowing more smoke from a joint so more smoke forces its way into the other guy's lungs. The normal students just looked on.

As we stood in a cloud of smoke, backs turned to the street and bug-eyed stoned, a horn blew behind us, which nearly gave me a heart attack. We turned to see the school bus idling, the door open, the other dudes looking out the window at us and the bus driver giving us a bored stare.

(Our bus driver was cool. When I was in ninth grade we smoked cigarettes the whole ride—he let us, we didn't have to hide it or anything—and when we turned the corner close to school he'd yell, "Throw 'em out boys.")

"Are you all going to get on or what?"

Oh, crap.

That Easter, I had to work, so Mom and Dad left me at home when they went to Winnfield. On Saturday morning, I made plans to hook up with a friend that night and go to the French Quarter. He and his parents lived in Fat City, the section of Metairie with the majority of bars and nightclubs.

His parents were already out when I stopped by their apartment. I noticed a bowl of pills on the kitchen table. His parents filled it like a Halloween candy bowl with red pills, green ones, blue ones, you name it.

"What are these?" I asked.

"Take what you want," he replied.

I didn't want to mix them so I picked out a small handful of something, I can't remember what, and took them. After a few drinks and joints, things in the Quarter deteriorated so much that I didn't remember anything. I woke up laying in an alley with my erstwhile friend trying to force milk down my throat.

"Man, what are you doing?" I asked.

"I've been trying to get you to drink milk so you'll throw up."

"What?"

"You're OD-ing on me, man."

That's how it happens. Overdosing isn't like the movies. There's no background music or dramatic buildup. You start taking drugs. You slide down the slippery slope. And then you screw up, or you get something that is beyond what your body can handle. If you're lucky, someone's there. If not, things run their course.

I pushed the milk away and told him I was okay, but then my memory cut out again. The next thing I remember is a phone ringing and ringing. I opened my eyes to see that I was lying naked on the bathroom floor of our house. *Ring, Ring, Ring* ... the phone wouldn't stop, so I got up, put pants on, and went to the phone.

"Hello?"

"I've been calling and calling you," my friend said. "The manager is mad as hell at you, and he's going to fire you if you don't get down here."

I looked at a clock. Easter Sunday is a huge day at the cafeteria, and my shift went from 10 a.m. to 2 p.m. It was 12:30.

"Well, let him fire me. I'm done." There was no way I was in any kind of condition to go to work, no way, and especially not around food. And I was scared, really scared.

I cleaned up, and when Mom and Dad came home, I don't think they noticed a thing. I did get fired, but it didn't last long. Somehow, they took me back. By then I'd worked my way up to entrees, and there was still another station to go before the job drove me insane.

If my parents didn't suspect anything about my near overdose in the French Quarter, it wasn't because they weren't concerned. I no longer asked if I could go out at night. I just did it and ignored the pain in their faces. They knew what I was up to.

Then one night I stayed out all night, and Dad had had enough.

He was standing at his dresser. "There are rules in this house and you need to stick to them like everybody else."

"What rules?"

"Like not staying out all night for starters, and cleaning up your act."

"If you don't like the way I'm living, 'just leave this long-haired country boy alone.'[18] I'll move out." It was a laughable threat. I was making minimum wage. He should have smacked me and thrown me out of his room.

For some reason, he was silent. I must have hurt him. His oldest son threw all the years of his love, sweat, and toil in his face like it was nothing.

He didn't say a word as I walked out of his room. He was afraid, not of me, but of what I could do to myself. That morning I was too tired, drunk, and stoned from the night before to act on my threat. When I woke up there was a tense peace, and I didn't move out, but Dad and I knew I'd crossed a line.

#

In the spring of 1974, the oil embargo lifted and with it, gas stations started hiring again. I couldn't wait to free myself of the cafeteria, and soon found a job at West Esplanade Shell. It was a much finer establishment and boasted a sign at its full-service island that read, "The World's Best Service." Then it read, "As a customer you should expect: To have your front and rear windows cleaned without having to ask, your litter bag and ashtray emptied, and your hood checked."

A man named Virgil, who served on a submarine during World War II in the Pacific, owned the station with Ray, his gambling and bass-fishing younger brother. The night man's name was V (yeah, just V), a squat Puerto Rican with a heavy brush mustache from New York who told gang stories that would curl your hair. There was also an ex-Marine, a black guy named "Get-Right" Robert, another fella called Railroad Bill, and a Jehovah's Witness, who picked up the conversation when it lagged. In the back, the main mechanic had a long beard that made him look like the spitting image of the Zig-Zag man. *Man,* I loved that place.

With my career as a gas station attendant restored, the next big thing was the junior prom. We held it at a hotel in downtown New Orleans and like any teenage boy, I was monumentally curious about sex. With as much necking and snuggling as I had done, I'd managed thus far to keep my virginity intact. Reflecting back, with the drinking and smoking crowd I hung with, I shouldn't have been that surprised that my date, an overweight blond, wanted to be with her friends more than me. I am pretty sure I was the only guy who asked her to the prom. I managed to get drunk and stoned and remember driving home in a light rain just barely able to see the painted lines marking the lanes on Interstate 10 in the glare of the headlights. Overall a disappointment.

I think the only good thing I can say about that spring is I finished the school year with good grades and that I got on well at the new job. In fact, I got along so well with Virgil that he spotted me $400 cash—he was the only guy I knew that carried a large roll of hundred dollar bills in his pocket—to buy a black, 1968 Chevrolet Camaro.

I paid him back the next day and started to figure out how to turn what was a nice Camaro body with a six-cylinder engine into a slick piece of work. I went to the junkyards off Chef Menteur Highway and found a 396-cubic inch V-8 engine from a Chevrolet Suburban. Then bit by bit, I ordered factory motor mounts, coil springs, wiring harness, radiator, alternator, dual factory exhaust, all from GM. At a buddy's who owned an engine dolly, we dropped the V-8 into the Camaro and bolted up the motor mounts and transmission. I ended up with a flat-black Chevrolet Camaro SS-396. When the engine turned over for the first time, I heard the sweetest, deepest *vvvrrrrroooommmm*.

I loved it and spent as much time driving my Camaro as I could or just sitting in it trying to look cool, which wasn't hard in that car. Sometimes we'd ride out to Laplace and back, smoking pot and listening to eight-tracks of the Doobie Brothers and what not.

As cool as the car was and as good as I looked in it, the Camaro wasn't exactly a babe magnet. I tried dating a girl from church, but when we parked down at the boat launch—a known make-out spot—and I made my move, she froze. I mean like ice. The fear of being touched was palpable, so I quit and took her home.

The girls from the local Catholic girls' school were a tad different. They were cute with their wool skirts with two-tone buck shoes and sweaters tied around their waists. And they all wanted to date bad boys from the public school, or so they thought. When they found out we really did play loud rock 'n' roll, drove fast, drank, smoked, wanted sex, and did drugs, they bailed.

I worked on the Camaro and found other ways to occupy my time. That summer Virgil made things a little easier by switching me to the 6 a.m. to 2 p.m. shift and then Sundays off after Mom said I needed the time to go to church. During the week and on Saturdays, I burned the candle at both ends, and on Sundays, church was the last place anyone would find me.

My friends and I would hit the road on Saturday after work and head to my buddy's parents' camp on a river north of Lake Pontchartrain. After heavy rains, we'd stop to pick through pastures looking for cow patties with distinctive mushrooms growing from them and turn them into a tea that got us bugged out. At the camp, there was a Cypress tree higher than a telephone pole hanging out over the water. You could jump off, but you had to be sure you didn't look down before hitting the water because you'd get water deep behind your eyeballs. Other times, we tied an inner tube behind the boat and took turns skimming along the top of Lake Maurepas, which is what the river by the camp fed into. When the lake was smooth as glass you could cut the boat in circles so the tube was like a slingshot hissing across the water until it hit the boat's wake and shot up in the air. The guy who bounced across the water the most times won a six pack.

One of these weekends we brought two girls, valium, beer, vodka, and pot. The only one of these that wasn't a sure thing was the girls. Beginning Saturday afternoon, we drank, I popped a couple valium, and then things went dark. I came to that evening as my friends described how I'd slalom skied—one ski instead of two—through lily pads while grabbing low overhanging moss. Buck naked.

"You're full of it," I said.

"Nope, you were naked and doing great."

"Nope, don't believe it."

"I got a movie of it."

Sure enough, he had a camera. I must say, I skied pretty well.

The next day, I decided we needed to make a run to the store. Before we left, I had visited the vodka bottle a few times and polished off a couple beers. One of the girls foolishly let me drive her car, and after a few miles, I drove off the road into a ditch and tore up the front end.

While she worked through every possible way to call me an idiot, a sheriff's deputy pulled up, promptly arrested me for driving drunk, and took me off to jail. My friend and the girls got the car out of the ditch and called a lawyer—Dad. He headed to the jail, but before he got there the police released me on my own recognizance. They did that back then. I went back to the camp. Meanwhile Dad arrived at the jail loaded for bear.

"He ain't here," the deputy said, no doubt smiling. I'm sure he could tell that Dad was well into his launch sequence for kicking my ass.

Back at the camp, it was more waterskiing, beer, pot, and fun. By the time I got home Dad, was really ticked. I was sunburned and wasted. He tore into me, but by now I was just coming and going as I pleased. Anything he had to say about it was water off a duck's back. There wasn't anyone, as far as I was concerned, who had any say over what I did. A few days after school started, a football coach saw me in the hall. "So, you're hanging out with the drug heads now, huh?"

I looked at him. "Whatever. I'm not playing football."

#

The fall of my senior year was my last semester of high school. I had enough credits to graduate and wanted to be free of school. I told my folks that I wanted to earn more money rather than spend six hours each day in school earning credits I didn't need. They said okay since I'd done well on the ACT and been accepted to LSU for the following fall semester.

I settled into a relatively comfortable routine of school, work until 10 p.m., driving around smoking a joint, and then picking up some beers for home or finding where the party was. On Fridays, I got off in the evening and would pick up two six packs of Budweiser tallboys and head home. I'd come in with dirty hands, fingernails, jeans, and khaki Shell shirt unbuttoned down the front.

Dad would be home cooking cheeseburgers. We drank beer and talked. As rough as I got, Dad never stopped wanting to spend time with me and talk. He was always Socrates and a football fan, especially LSU, and I respected and loved him. We never said it. Didn't have to.

I could not wait to graduate at midterm and turn eighteen that March. Living in Louisiana and Dad working for Shell, we knew all about the offshore rigs. There was good money to be made out there; many men earned better than decent livings and these guys were the tough of the tough.

If you were a *roustabout* or *roughneck*, well, that meant something to me. I'd sometimes daydream about the Gulf and think, that's me. I wanted to be on one of those rigs; I wanted to be one of those guys.

On Friday nights with Dad, I was happy. He usually went to the Friday night high school games to see my brother play. He would feign shock at the cheer emanating from the student body of an all-boys school after a fumble or a messed-up play. "OOhhhhh … sh*t!" There's education, and then there's real education.

My home was principled. We were honest and hard working. We believed in what was right. Status didn't matter. Like the guys at the station used to say, "You know the difference between a porcupine and a Mercedes Benz? With a porcupine, the pricks are on the outside." We loved each other and believed in God. But it was better to live it than just say it. Everything I needed to know I could find at home, but I had to do it my own way.

#

My last day of high school was the day before Christmas break. We got loaded, as usual, and then it was over. No fanfare, just done.

On Christmas Day, there was the usual eggnog and cocktails. The biggest thing was when a neighbor caught her daughter having sex with a friend of mine in their garage. She came to our house stunned, and the father raced to the scene yelling, "What is the meaning of this ..." over and over. Good question that I had asked myself many times.

After the break, a friend and I took our version of a senior trip to the Great Smoky Mountains. Our plan was to drive up through Gatlinburg to Newfound Gap during the day, hike the Appalachian Trail in the snow, and party each night. We began our first drive up the mountains in a light snow with the morning sun a dull glow behind us in the east.

He looked at me as he drove. "How cool would it be to drop acid with the snow falling?"

"I'm not so sure that's a great idea." I was against LSD. Taking something that created another world while you walked off a building or in front of a truck just seemed stupid to me. So, I either never did it or faked doing it by taking just a little hit. Two times. That's it. This was number two.

"But look at this snow and the trees and everything."

It was beautiful. "I don't know, man."

"Come on, let's do it."

We were out of our minds.

The wind howled, snow piled up, and the cold, snowy air formed frost feathers on icy tree branches. The hiking was hard and left us breathless, but it and our modest winter gear wasn't enough to prevent us from becoming numb from cold. We didn't last long and soon enough turned back.

"We've got to put the chains on the tires," he said when we reached the car. I looked at the road, which wasn't yet iced or piled with snow. I was fine. A little stimulated, but otherwise fine. His eyes were the size of Frisbees. Like I said, LSD was never my thing, so I only took about half a hit. He ate I don't know how many hits and was tripping his ass off.

I looked back down the road, which wound down the mountain to our motel about twenty-five miles. "There's not any snow on the road."

"We gotta do it."

No we didn't, but why waste breath arguing with a lunatic.

The first chain didn't go on easy, and he became frantic. "Screw this. We gotta get out of here." He jumped in the driver seat and put the car in gear. I barely got in the car before he hit the gas.

The car, with only one chain on a rear tire, went *baboom, baboom, baboom* as he drove. Meanwhile, the acid was hitting him harder and he was beginning to hallucinate and have an epic panic attack.

Then he looked at me, totally freaked out, and screamed, "You're the devil!"

I was more worried about him driving off the mountain, so I pulled down my hood. "I'm Frank, just Frank! You know me!"

The car swerved from one lane to the next and back again. "No, you're the devil!"

"No, my cheeks are just red from the cold, and this is the green jacket I always wear, I swear it!"

He tried to drive and pull his body away from me. "The devil, you're the devil!"

"No, I'm Frank! Let me drive!"

"No way, man, I'm driving."

Somehow, we made it the rest of the way down the mountain in one piece. Our motel was coming up on the left of a four-lane road. He looked at me, slowed the car and did what any normal person would do. He jumped out.

"Oh, you son of a bitch!" I yelled as I slid across to take the wheel. Then I heard the brakes of a semi screech as he ran across the median, to the other side of the highway in front of the truck, up the hill, and into our room. I whipped a U, headed up the hill, parked, and tried to open the motel room door, but he pushed back from the other side. I used my foot and then my body to force the door open. He finally let go, and I fell into the room as he ran cackling into the bathroom. I sat on the edge of the bed wondering what to do next, but the nut was one step ahead of me. He leapt out the bathroom door laughing.

"Would you sit down," I said. "Do you have any idea where you are?"

He kept bouncing around, so I turned on the TV and found a station playing cartoons. Like a little child, Bugs Bunny calmed him, and drew him close to the screen. For about four hours he zeroed in on the TV until all of a sudden he said, "Where am I?"

"You're in the motel room, you idiot. You took a ton of acid and almost killed us up on the mountain."

"Oh, that was cool." Cool? Really? Not from my vantage point it wasn't.

We returned home after a week, and I don't think I spoke to him for months.

I was pissed, but I also had a new distraction. She was sweet, attractive, and lived in my neighborhood. From the moment we first met, we connected; she was an addict of the first order and would do anything to get loaded every day. She'd come over to my house in the afternoon when I'd get home from work, then ask Mom, "Is Frank home?" Then to Mom's chagrin she just bounded upstairs to my room. I liked it. Most days we'd head out and spend time smoking pot and doing whatever else we could find.

Like every other crush, I lived with a hope that somehow, someway I'd be able to get her to like me and be more than a buddy to get loaded with, but it wasn't ever going to happen. She wasn't interested in me emotionally or physically. It was just, "Let's be friends and use," and that's pretty much the way she was with everybody.

Even though I had graduated at midterm, I did walk across the stage at the East Jefferson Senior High School graduation that May. I know there were at least 300 of us, all boys. The disciplinarian gave a stern warning. Any monkey business, no diploma. With a last name starting with the letter "S," I never had to wait long. Sure enough we didn't even make it to "L" before a kid slipped his inside arm into his graduation robe and crossed the stage sporting the largest erection in the history of mankind. And a big smile as he shook the disciplinarian's hand who just looked disgusted and gave him the diploma to our cheers. Not something Ganny usually saw teaching third grade in Winnfield.

I carried a torch for my "girlfriend" well past turning eighteen and taking a job working offshore as a roustabout. The company operated out of Morgan City, about one hundred miles southwest of New Orleans. Our job was to finish painting and preparing an offshore platform, then help install it on the Outer Continental Shelf.

We lived in the yard, where we worked twelve-hour shifts, 6 a.m. to 6 p.m., which meant we had to find something to do with the down time. At night, we would sneak off to a seedy little joint beneath the bridge at Amelia called The Neighborhood Bar. It made the bar in Star Wars look tame. I stuck close to the guys from my drilling company. If you got into a fight in this bar, you'd more than likely end up dead. We were far from what I knew, and we hadn't even left shore yet.

While we worked in the yard prepping the rig, there were some engineering students down from Louisiana Tech who may have been book smart, but they didn't seem to know what they were doing. One day they ventured out amongst the various scrap equipment and poked around. I guess they were bored.

"Hey, what the hell are you idiots doing?" a supervisor yelled across the yard.

They were throwing some white, fluffy stuff they'd found in the air and watching it disintegrate. I guess they thought it was mysterious or something.

"Put that crap down, you morons! That's asbestos!" Oops.

Then there was the yardman named Smooth. He'd suffered a range of injuries, the most noticeable were numerous missing fingers. Smooth loved giving life advice to the college boys, like describing the relative merits of placing rubber fishing worms in a hot water bottle.

"Then what?" I cringed.

"Why, you stick your pecker in, what else! It feels just like a real woman."

I don't think any of those boys took Smooth up on his advice. I know I didn't. I can't help thinking of ole Smooth though every time I'm bass fishing and rig up a purple worm.

With the rig prepped, we rode out on a derrick barge to the drilling location. There were thirty roustabouts, no power, no potable water, and no bunks. We spent twenty-one days working almost around the clock, sleeping on life preservers or whatever we could find that wasn't made of metal. We were so tired that the two tool pushers—the guys responsible for the safe, efficient operations of the rig—walked around passing out Black Mollies, prescription speed.

When I got back home for my few days off, I went straight to Fat City where I sat in Dirty Pierre's until 3 a.m., eating cheeseburgers and drinking cold beer. I had the biggest paycheck I'd ever received, and the burgers and beers never tasted so good. In that moment going to college seemed very far off.

The next morning, I went to my female friend's house. She wasn't around, and her mother had no idea where she was. Over the next couple mornings, I expected to hear her bounding up the stairs after a brief salutation to Mom, but she never did.

A few days later, her mom called. "Frank, have you seen my daughter?"

I always had good relationships with girls' mothers, which was the kiss of death.

"No ma'am." This was no lie. I had been looking for her since I got home and hadn't seen her. I did hear she might be in a house in the neighborhood though. I didn't mention that. The people who owned the house, a boy's parents, were away for a while, and their son and his friends took it over. These guys were into pills and needles, not just pot, and had turned the house into something akin to a suburban shooting gallery.

The second thing that I wouldn't cotton was needles. I didn't want to get hooked and turn into a junkie. Or worse, overdose and die. Fresh from high school, I had enough experience to ease into whiskey, beer, and pot. That's it. I just couldn't see the need for anything else and had to take frequent breaks even then. Getting burned out was no fun, no fun at all.

"Do you know where she is?"

"Well, I think I might, but she'd get mad if I told you."

There was silence from the other end, then a mix of sadness and anger. "This is no time for whatever code you may have. I haven't seen her for days," she took a breath. "I'm scared. You've got to tell me."

"I'll go get her and bring her home." I had always been taught to say what you mean and mean what you say, but I didn't know if I could deliver on this one. But I guess I'd die trying.

I thought of getting my Tennessee friend, but I was still pissed at him and wanted someone who could handle himself when we got to that house. The first name that came to mind was a dude I'd played football with. He was a year ahead of me and halfway through his senior year, his mother kicked him out of their house. For a week or so he was living out of his car until my aunt felt sorry for him, so he stayed at my cousin's house most of the time.

He too worked offshore and drove a two-door, dark blue, Chevy Impala with a 283-cubic-inch engine. A few nights earlier, we smoked a few joints while riding around in his car, listening to a new band, Aerosmith. He had set the idle so high that the car did twenty miles per hour without touching the gas pedal. When "Sweet Emotion" kicked in, he eased the car up past the sidewalk, and we lazily putt-putted through front yards, around bushes, trees, trash cans. The further we went the funnier it got and the more we laughed. The song ended when the block did, thank goodness.

I figured he'd be good in a pinch.

We made some calls and figured out where the house was and drove there in the Impala. We didn't knock. We just went in. It made me sick. Skinny, longhaired dudes laying around. Trash and filth filled the place.

"What the hell are you guys doin' here?" some freak said as he walked up to us in the foyer. Like the others, he was rail thin with track marks running along the veins in his arms.

"Give me any crap and we're gonna to beat the snot out of you," I said. "Where is she?"

He pointed down the hall to the den. And there she was, lying on a couch with a guy who had what looked like the worst case of acne in the history of the world and hadn't washed in weeks. She didn't look much better and was totally wasted.

"You shouldn't be here," she said.

"I'm here to take you home."

"What the f**k for?"

"Your mother's looking for you. You need to go home."

A smile wandered across her lips. "Well, I don't wanna go."

"Yeah, she's good here," said the putrid kid.

I looked at him hard and cocked a fist.

"This isn't a good place for you," I said.

"This is a fine place for me," she said and smiled at the kid.

We spent some time trying to get her to leave, but she refused. She was sick, lost, and hopeless. I figured they were using her for sex, and she was using them for drugs. I was pissed.

Rather than bust the place up, which both of us wanted to do, we left. When I got home I called her mom.

"Where is she? Is she okay?"

"No, she isn't okay," I said and told her what I saw. "I tried to get her to leave, but she wouldn't, so here's the address of the house."

I never talked to her again. Looking back on it, I should have beat the crap out of those guys, but if I'd physically removed her, she'd only have gone back. Some people just get sucked up into things they can't control and have no business doing, but they can't help themselves.

#

Sometime in July, the company assigned me to a rig out of Venice, Louisiana, at the mouth of the Mississippi River in East Bay. Our crane operator was a dude from Stuttgart, Arkansas, and when he wasn't working the crane he was an auctioneer back home.

To offload cargo that came by crew boat to the rig, a few roustabouts would climb onto the personnel basket suspended from the crane and be lowered to the boat. Our crane operator took great pleasure bouncing us off the rig's steel-framed legs then dunking us into the water. We'd probably have complained, but at other times he would pull out his pig sticker knife and wave it in our faces to let us know what a bad-ass he was.

The most frustrating thing he did was talk to us nonstop on the squawk box rigged to his crane while we toiled in the unrelenting July heat. One day, the heat coming off the water must have been around 110 degrees and so humid you could see the air. It felt as if it grabbed you and weighed you down with an extra hundred pounds.

"Come on, get with it you worms!" came from the squawk box.

I was on the rig's deck with another guy stacking muddy tubing pulled from the well on the pipe rack as fast as we could as the roughnecks slid the pipe down the V-door. We were on the fifteenth day of a twenty-one-day hitch.

Suddenly, I had a revelation.

A few days before we came out, I spoke to Mom and Dad.

"Listen, I'm making good money, more than anyone I know, so it seems like a good idea for me to delay college."

"What?" they said at the same time.

"The money's really good and I like the work a lot. I'll go to college later."

Mom was flexible on a lot of things, but on this she was a rock. "You are going to college."

Dad worked for Shell and had spent time for one reason or another with rig workers. He knew how hard the work was and how hot it got out in the Gulf. "Frank, you know I'm with your mother on this." He had been firm, but less insistent than Mom. I think he knew me better than I knew myself.

"Move yo ass boy!"

Suddenly an air-conditioned classroom at LSU seemed like a great idea.

Chapter Six

I asked this God a question
and by way of firm reply
He said, "I'm not the kind you have to wind-up on Sundays." [19]

    —"WIND UP," JETHRO TULL

I did my last offshore hitch and walked onto terra firma with mixed emotions—joy and happiness. Being a roustabout gave me an identity. When asked what I did, it was a not-so-nonchalant, "I work offshore." College would check another box. I wanted to go, but telling folks I was a college student didn't do much for me. I was already blue collar. I welcomed the mental and physical challenge. Offshore, the work pushed my body to its limits. Living in a dorm and sitting in a classroom seemed a pale comparison, on first glance.

I walked through the gate to my car, the '68 Camaro with the bumper sticker that said, "Pray for me, I drive Hwy 90!" and as I did so I passed from roustabout to college freshman. The next thought was food, followed by what do I want to drink? Cheeseburgers answered the former and a bottle of Jack Daniels took care of the latter.

Later that night my high school gang and I took turns on a minibike out of boredom. The thing had welded foot pegs so they wouldn't retract like they did on most bikes and a governor on the engine that kept it from going fast. The engine was a Briggs & Stratton; it was basically a two-wheeled lawnmower. But if you steered it with one hand and used the other to override the governor, it could do about thirty-five miles per hour. Not bad.

"My turn on that thing!" Primed and ready I throttled up the bike then overrode the governor so that in a few moments I was tearing down a suburban street drunk, tilted to one side, and going fast. Before I knew it, I'd reached the end of the street and needed to negotiate a more than sharp left turn. I leaned the bike over to cut the turn tight to the curb when the welded foot peg hit the concrete and threw the bike to the right. Instinctively I planted my right foot, and the speed and momentum of the bike pulled my leg down against the pavement with enough force to tear the meniscus and anterior cruciate ligament in my right knee.

I kept drinking that night, but the next morning my knee was so swollen that I had to cut my jeans off. If I put any weight on it, the pain was overwhelming, and the knee just gave out. Mom took me to the emergency room. The doctor looked at my knee and then the x-rays like the mechanic at West Esplanade Shell surveying a seized-up engine and shrugged. "There's nothing I can do here. You need a specialist." He wrapped it up, prescribed some pain meds, and sent us on our way to the Saints' orthopedic at Tulane who confirmed that I tore the meniscus and ACL. He believed in letting nature do the healing first before considering surgery.

At the time, knee surgery was no small thing. Laparoscopic surgery was unheard of as were many other modern techniques, which meant the scar would run from below the hip to just above the ankle like a zipper and the recovery time would be long. My knee was still swollen, so he inserted a large needle and pulled big syringes of blood and fluid until it was close to normal size. He had to do this a few more times over the next two weeks as I was on ice and crutches. Then he fitted me for a stiff, straight-leg brace.

"You'll need to wear this for six months and then we'll see what it looks like," he said.

I'd thought of trying out for the wrestling team at LSU, but the injury did in whatever hopes I had to play a sport. The thought of surgery wasn't appetizing either, so I just accepted that my career in team sports was now and forever done. In fact, I didn't get the surgery for my knee until well into my fifties and it still bothers me.

A few days later, Dad helped load my belongings into his red Dodge Demon—a midlife crisis car if there ever was one—and he drove me up to LSU in Baton Rouge. My dorm was Johnston Hall, which is one of three dorms on the east side of Tiger Stadium, and my room was on the fourth floor at the far back left corner of the building. From my window I could see Tiger Stadium, a golf course beyond that, and some of the Mississippi River.

Nice view, but no elevator. And no air conditioning. The stairwell had handrails so that on the way down I could sling my crutches over my shoulder and swing on the handrail. Going up was a bitch. On that first day, Dad parked in front of the dorm and helped me with the few things I'd packed. It was late August and, of course, being Louisiana, it was hot and humid. By the time we finished, our clothes were wet with sweat.

I followed Dad to the car, and for the first time since deciding to go to college, I felt the moment in my heart and gut. The second he pulled away I would be on my own, again. Sink or swim, it was up to me to survive college and my own worst instincts. I also knew that despite being a royal turd with the partying, attitude, and the rest, I was going to miss Dad, his Socratic wisdom, and sage advice, as well as his steady presence.

I walked with him to the sidewalk in front of Johnston Hall, and when we neared his car I paused and leaned on my crutches. He shook my hand, then walked toward the car. Halfway between me and the car, he hesitated, turned, and walked back to me.

"I want to offer you one final piece of advice."

"Yes, sir."

His eyes glanced down at the hot sidewalk then back to me with a slight smile. I waited for something profound.

"Don't screw this up."

Then, without waiting he turned, started the car, and left.

#

College accepted me in the fall of my senior year, but I didn't accept college until a little after my offshore awakening. This meant I hadn't registered for classes, and so my first stop was the registrar's office, where they handed me a paper catalogue of courses. I had no clue what to do.

My sister, Ann, was a junior, a member of a sorority, a Golden Girl on the LSU dance team, part of the Tiger Marching Band, and had arrived on campus days before me. I finally got her on the phone.

"Ann, I need your help."

"Already?"

"No, come on, seriously. Can you help me figure out what classes I have to take?"

I begged her some more and she relented but said she'd have to meet me later at a McDonald's near the band practice field.

My roommate and I were friends back in Metairie. For some reason, I never got around to telling him I might not go to college, which turned out to be a good move. In the meanwhile, though, he and his girlfriend managed to have a wee little accident. Rather than try to hide her pregnancy or run off, they told their parents they were expecting and wanted to get married.

Both parents said, "No way." They would put the baby up for adoption and their relationship was over. He and his girlfriend were seventeen, and though I'm sure they could have run away or snuck around together, both accepted their parents' verdict. But my friend was mad. He loved her, but he was also adopted and understood exactly what his child would go through. None of it seemed fair to me, and it triggered a fleeting fantasy to be noble, marry his girlfriend, and somehow keep their nascent family together.

When I staggered up the stairs to our dorm room one day, there he was smoking pot with some guys. His parents worried that if he had the baby, it would make college impossible and ruin his life. Well, now all he wanted was to be out of his parents' house and on his own so that he could smoke as much pot as he could get his hands on. I don't know if it was luck-of-the-draw or that every dorm had its own collection of pot heads, but he was in good company.

I didn't want any trouble at LSU as my Dad's cousin of some degree was the Dean of Men, and word would get home quickly. Besides I had graduated from a public high school. Drugs were old hat to me. I had my business face on and there was plenty of beer to drink anyway. So, when it became apparent that they weren't leaving, I split in time to limp down the stairs and go to McDonald's to fill out my registration form. I sat across from Ann with a burger, fries, milkshake, and no real clue. I had a real healthy fear though. It was do or die time.

"Let me see that," she said as she grabbed the catalogue from me and pulled out the course registration form. "Okay, your ACT scores placed you into this English and that Math," and she wrote the courses down in the form. "Oh, and you like science, so I guess you should take Chemistry, that would be good. You like politics so here's *Intro to Political Science*. Hmm, do you like business?"

"I guess so."

"Then you should take this Economics class, and I know you like History so here's *American History*." She pulled her head back and scanned the form, then looked at me. "There ya go. It's eighteen credits, which is kind of a lot, but this is what you should do."

I nodded and shoved a small mass of French fries in my mouth. What I didn't know was that Ann had signed me up for Honors Chemistry, sophomore year Economics for business majors and sophomore American History.

"Thanks," I said.

Ann smiled. "No problem."

My first day of classes was an eye opener. The guys in Honors Chemistry wore Texas Instruments calculators strapped to their hip like six shooters. I dropped chemistry in a heartbeat. So much for medical school. By the end of my second day, I was completely intimidated. For a few days, I wondered if I'd made a mistake and that I'd be better off going back offshore. For the rest of the week and into the next, I felt insecure and overwhelmed. In each class, it seemed as if the professors and students had some insider knowledge on how things worked that no one shared with me. There was an expectation of a base level of competency that I doubted I possessed or could ever possess.

Then one day I limped into class. The weight of my books made the crutches even more awkward and a few students turned to look at me. Their eyes were impassive, not frustrated by the disturbance I caused, but uncaring as to my plight and unsure of how I fit into what they must have felt was their school. I stood near the back of the room to look for a seat on the end of a row so that my braced leg could stick out into an aisle. As my eyes wandered from seat to seat, one back of the head to the next, I realized that I was different from these people.

I couldn't imagine that any of them stood in one-hundred-degree heat with air so thick you could taste it on a platform out in the middle of the Gulf while a guy yelled abuse at them through a squawk box. I doubted any of them had ever washed their hands with gasoline and pumice then scraped them against a cement block wall to wear away embedded oil and grease. I was also damn sure none of them had the experience of flying in a helicopter as huge thunder storms whipped it around and the pilot, who learned to fly in Vietnam, desperately searched for the landing pad on an oil rig in the middle of the ocean.

I stood in a room filled with people I figured did not know or understand the value and dignity of hard work in the way I did, and with that I reached the conclusion I would not fail out of college. From then on, it was the grease monkey versus the world.

After class, I carried myself across campus to my dorm and climbed the four flights of stairs, dragging my crutches but lifted by a sense of purpose. All I wanted to do was study to gain the upper hand in my classes, but when I walked into my dorm room there was my roommate, stoned and lying in bed with his new girlfriend.

I turned around and lugged my books and body to the library. The next day I walked into the room after classes ready to get to work, but this time there was a bunch of guys smoking dope. Again, I turned and walked to the library. The next day, it was the stoned roommate and his girlfriend. Back to the library. The next it was a party in the room followed by the girlfriend.

"Enough," I said.

"What's up, Frank?"

"I need to study."

"So, study."

"I can't with you in here. If you want to smoke pot and just hangout, do it somewhere else." That's what he did. A lot. I don't think he was bothered at all about studying nor did it particularly worry him, but it bothered me.

And so with my room as a sanctuary and my knee keeping me hobbled, I began to evolve into a college student. In the first few weeks of that semester, I found an ability to focus that I didn't know I had. I studied for hours at a pace and competency that no one who knew me thought possible, especially the grease monkey himself.

By the middle of the semester I was doing well in all my classes and acing my midterms. The last of these was my Economics midterm. I studied until three in the morning and then set my alarm to be awake in time for the 7:30 a.m. class, but it didn't go off. My eyes popped open with the sun, and I grabbed the clock.

"Oh crap," it was ten minutes to eight. I leapt out of bed, wrapped my brace around my leg, grabbed my books, hobbled across the quadrangle and boom, I burst through the classroom door. Everyone's heads turned as I limped into the room. The professor was a graduate assistant monitoring the test, which was in a pile on the desk at the head of the room. I grabbed one and sat down to start the exam.

Except for the scratching of pencils, the room was quiet. I looked at the first question but had to take a deep breath to settle my mind enough to read the words.

"Hey, wait a minute," the professor said. He'd walked to my seat and bent over to whisper. "Come out in the hall for a second."

We went out and closed the door.

"Aren't you a freshman?"

"Yeah."

"What happened?"

"I overslept after studying for this thing until three, and now I only have half an hour to take it."

He looked at my crumpled hair and the shorts and t-shirt I'd slept in. "Don't worry about it. I know you're a freshman so just take a seat out here in the hall and look at your notes. I've got another class taking the same test next period. If you want, just come with me to that room and take the test then."

I did and ended up making an A in that class. I also made an A in American History. The professor had a particular interest in the Civil War, its causes, how the two sides fought the war and its effects, which was like pitching to my sweet spot. After listening to Civil War stories since I was a kid, there was little I didn't know about this period of American history. When I sat for the test, it was a single question: Write an essay on the four causes of the Civil War and expound on them. I filled three blue books before time ran out.

The rest of my classes were another A and the rest Bs, which added up to a 3.6 grade point average for my first semester. A shocking development for me, par for the course as far as my family was concerned.

At the beginning of the first semester, I'd thought of rushing a fraternity, but when the great awakening occurred—grease monkey versus the world—I decided to focus on grades. This didn't mean I gave up on having a social life.

LSU was, and still is, the logical next step after high school for most kids in and around New Orleans. In my dorm were two guys who I knew from high school. They were trouble makers from the word go, and ended up at E. J. after they plumbed a water line into the gas line in the chemistry building at the high school they attended. Plumbers had to rip up the gas and water lines, which was also an accurate analogy for their attendance at that school.

One's father had been a member of the DKE (pronounced "Deke") fraternity when he was in college. DKE was an uptown New Orleans fraternity, and its members wore Polo shirts with little alligators and deck shoes. They tended to be tough on their pledges. Out of a sense of loyalty to his dad, my friend pledged DKE, but within a week or two he'd had enough and dropped the whole thing. It took him a while to call his father and tell him because I think he was more worried about what he'd say for dropping the fraternity than if he failed a class.

During the first semester, I hung with these guys. My roommate was another matter as he got more into partying and seemed dead set on failing out. Things just didn't work for us being roommates. After Christmas I decided to room with the ex-DKE pledge and my roommate moved in with a guy who was just as dedicated to getting loaded and ignoring the fact that he was in college.

Across the hall was a guy from Alexandria, Louisiana, and his roommate. Then there was a guy from Virginia who had a roommate from Amsterdam. The last of our merry group was a guy we nicknamed Stank. Past tense. He'd pledged the DKEs and they abused him, but he stuck it out until they rejected him, and he sort of fell in with us.

For me failure was not an option. I knew enough to get my work done before anything else. In high school, it was just easy. There were plenty of times I let the school work slide, but in my first year of college it was work first. A lot of the guys at LSU I'd gone to high school with were going to flunk out. I decided I needed to find some people who were going in the same direction as me.

My cousin—he was a year ahead of me and now back home at the University of New Orleans—pledged Phi Gamma Delta fraternity, known as Fiji at LSU, and told me they were a good bunch of guys. He dropped out of it during initiation when they asked him to do stuff he wouldn't do, but it got me to thinking. To be in a fraternity you had to maintain a minimum grade point average. Maybe I could find one that partied hard and got their work done.

A friend I'd known from youth group was a member of Fiji. We were more acquaintances than close friends since he went to a private school for high school, but we got along and he agreed to introduce me that spring to the guys.

"Do you guys have a spring pledge class?" I asked, and they said, "Sure."

Pledging in the spring was a little less formal than in the fall, though we would have to wait for the fall semester to be initiated. This didn't mean we got to just hang around the frat house. We still had to learn our place in the pecking order, which was the responsibility of our pledge trainer. I know, it sounds like training dogs or something. Our pledge trainer was from Monroe, which is a bit north and east from Winnfield. Today he owns a mortgage company.

Including me, there were seven pledges. My "big brother" was an electrical engineering major. We met at a beer bust that we made good use of. His running buddy was from Lafayette, a mechanical engineering major who had something like a 4.2 grade point average. The guy is hands down the smartest person I ever met, and he made it his job to break every rule on the face of the earth. Rules didn't apply to him if he could figure out a way around them. There were times when he was almost too smart for his own good.

Our pledge class was made up of a tall skinny guy from Baton Rouge, a dude from Lake Charles, one from Abita Springs who was a law enforcement major and the last guy who was a future friend and roommate, a guy I knew I would like the first time I met him. Like me, he wasn't what you would call a face man. When we first met as a group, we had to give our "Four Essentials," things that any college student should know about another. When his turn came, I took note. "My name is _____. I'm a freshman from Hattiesburg, Mississippi, majoring in nuclear proctology." He never cracked a smile, ever. I liked him.

As pledges, we had to do everything together which included cleaning the frat house, especially after parties, and doing any dirty work the trainers or upperclassmen came up with. We all looked up to the actives (the initiated sophomores, juniors, and seniors). I imagine it was something like grunts looking up to NCOs. They punished us and made life difficult at times, but they knew someday we would become them.

We had to know how to care for the frat, keep our grades up, and throw good parties. Now parties had to be more than a bunch of guys getting loaded. We had to get girls to show up, and to do that, a party had to be something. Exchanges with jungle juice, bands, grass huts, and a FIJI Island Ball. I took copious notes. In that spring of my freshman year I wasn't any closer to finding the girl who'd see me as her savior and save me from myself. But who cared, we had parties that girls wanted to come to. The rest was irrelevant.

Even so, in the midst of out-working and out-partying everyone, my routine of deep, painful crushes continued. The next on the list was one that Hattiesburg introduced me to. A Little Sister in the fraternity. She was beautiful in all the right ways and had no romantic interest in me whatsoever. I was like a puppy dog who kept running back for more rejection, though she may never have known how much I wanted to be with her.

Adding to my pain was the observation that quite a few of the girls at LSU used college as a time to be sexually promiscuous and experiment. I think some discovered they had powers over boys they never knew they had. They seemed to float around campus giving themselves to guys all around me, but never me. I heard more stories from the beginning of the school year through the spring of guys hooking up in the most incredible ways, but it was as if I lived in some sort of impenetrable force field.

And then this one girl came along. In the spring, I had a speech class and in that class was this girl. She was tall, wide, wore her blond hair in a bouffant, and was nice enough. I never gave much thought to her until one day my phone rang.

"Can I come over?" she asked.

"Uh, sure, I'll go down to the lobby and let you in."

By now, the brace was gone, but I still had to lean on the good knee and had a bit of a limp. When I opened the door, she was standing there wearing a long coat, a scarf wrapped over her head, and big sunglasses like she was trying to disguise herself. Kinda weird. We got up to my room, and the coat, scarf, glasses, and everything else fell to the floor, and we had voluntary, non-intoxicated, free sex. Then she left.

A few days later the phone rang. "Can I come over?" Now I'm not gonna lie. I felt like the only guy I knew who pined for a life altering relationship with the legs to go all the way to marriage, kids, and the rest. And yet my moments of passion were just that, moments. None of these occurred within a romantic relationship. The way I drank, girls looking for love and romance weren't interested in what I had to offer. As much as I wanted a relationship, I had to face facts that I wasn't relationship material. I wasn't looking for sex. I was looking for someone to fall in love with. This just wasn't her. But this was, well, unusual.

After several weeks she suddenly said, "I'm not going to come over here and do this if we're not going to go out together."

Wait, what? I looked at her. "You never asked me anything about going out." And the thought of actually going out never crossed my mind. I was busy, you know.

She frowned. "I'm cutting this off, and we're not going to see each other anymore."

"What? Why?"

"Because you don't ever want to take me out or go anywhere or anything." That wasn't true, I had just never thought about it. I mean why? But it made no difference to me. I would have gone anywhere. She got dressed and left. I saw her in class, but that was it.

The thing of it is, it was all wrong. I was supposed to be the rescuer, the cowboy, the reason for a girl's happiness, lust, and security. Not the guy she calls for a hookup dressed like the ingénue in a cheap thriller and then shakes off like a dusty coat.

I didn't feel good about these kinds of encounters even though as a guy the culture told me casual sex was a good thing. It was winning. Really? I felt kind of like a loser. It was nothing like what I wanted sex to be when I finally got to do it. Mom, in her infinite wisdom, had said, "Just wait for the right woman because when you're ready, the Lord will put her in front of you. When it happens, you'll know it. Trust me." She never said what to do when they landed in front of you buck naked.

After the Sam Spade ingénue hustled out of my room, I was back to normal. More in love with an idea, a feeling, a fantasy rather than a person. Ugh!

As with high school, I filled the sucking chest wound that was my love life with alcohol.

Most of my drinking was at the frat house and consisted of run-of-the-mill college binge drinking. Like the day my "big brother" and I were loaded and one of the goody two shoes paused in passing long enough to comment, "You two are just a couple of regular f**k ups." To which he replied, "Well, you have to get f**ked up regularly in order to be a regular f**k up." Such wisdom.

Then, late in the semester, Willie Nelson and Waylon Jennings played a concert out at the Baton Rouge fairgrounds. What a memorable experience. It was cold, some guys burned a small pile of car tires, I got really, really, really bombed, and woke up the next day in my dorm room wondering what the hell happened.

I was hung down, and my chest was killing me. It was also around noon on Sunday before final exams. My work ethic intact, I began to heat up water for coffee so I could try and push through my hang over and study. As the afternoon wore on, the pain in my chest worsened and my heart made a squishing rather than beating sound. Then the pain spread through my chest to my back.

"Hey man," I said to my roommate, "I think I'm having a heart attack."

He leapt up, grabbed another friend, and the two of them got me to Baton Rouge General Hospital. The ER doctor took X-rays and gave me his assessment. "You don't have pleurisy. But you need to see your doctor." And then they released me.

That night the pain was severe—the hospital didn't give me any pain meds—so when they opened the next morning I was at the campus infirmary where a doctor gave me a pain pill. A few minutes later the pain quit.

I looked up at him with great relief. "Thank you."

"Look, you have a pericarditis, inflammation of the membrane around the heart. At your age, it's probably viral. It is serious business. You need to go home and see your doctor." Viral? I didn't tell him about the whiskey or burning tires to keep warm.

I got a friend to bring me home, and right away, my family doctor admitted me to East Jefferson General Hospital. The treatment at the time was what the doctor called aspirin therapy to help reduce the inflammation, to which they added Quaaludes. I was fine with that.

For two days I was feeling pretty mellow. The aspirin did a good job, and the pain never returned. The Quaaludes did a better job of helping me not care about anything, so I took a Quaalude just before Johnny Carson came on the TV. He was a Fiji you know.

When I got out of the hospital, I was freaking out about missing all my final exams. Up to that last week, I had a 3.8 grade point average for the semester in which I took a ridiculous number of classes. Not taking my finals would have killed my hard work.

Dad brought me back up to school and talked to my professors. Of course I didn't tell them I got blackout drunk in cold weather the night before I came down with the pericarditis, and since they were decent people, they let me take my finals. I took three on one day and then the other three the next. I was still sick and my head a little mushy from the meds, but I managed to pull a 3.4 grade point average for the semester.

I don't know that my fairgrounds escapade had anything to do with the pericarditis, but I assumed that it did. This wasn't the first time drinking harmed my life nor was it the last. In my mind and heart there was a sense of restlessness that caused a push-pull battle between accomplishing goals I'd set for my life and the overwhelming desire to find peace through intoxication. The compromise I'd settled into early in my freshman year was the grease monkey versus the world. I would study harder than anybody else and party harder than anybody else. Getting sick and losing a few points off my grade point average did little to make me see with clarity the opposing forces of work ethic and alcohol.

I was making myself sick, and on some level I was aware of this, but denial is a powerful thing. I recovered my health and my grades did not fall through the floor so I called it a win for the grease monkey. Maybe Someone was looking out for me.

Abetting my denial was my roommate and friends in the dorm. By comparison, I was the responsible one. In the week leading up to final exams, a few of the guys decided they would just give up. They played golf, drank, smoked, played poker non-stop, and declared their intention to not take their finals. Too many viewings of the movie "Animal House." I couldn't believe they'd do that. Party, yes, but intentionally failing out of school was something I couldn't conscience.

I especially worried about my roommate. We grew up together; his brother and I knew each other from swim team. I knew and respected his father, we drank gin and tonics together in high school, and we lived in the same neighborhood. The final straw was when he showed no signs of going to his biology exam. His father worked in the biotechnology field, and many of his peers considered him to be at the top of his field. He'd given so much, and his son was blowing it.

He and the rest were in the study hall room on our floor playing cards when I went in and grabbed him by the arm. "You're going to take your biology test," I said.

He looked at me, then at my hand on his arm. "Flake off."

"No. You're going to take that exam."

"Like hell I am."

"I'll drag you out of here if I have to."

He tossed his ante into the pile of chips in the middle of the table. "Look, I'm going to flunk out, okay? My dad will kill me, but he's already pissed at me for dropping out of DKE anyway."

"No, you're going to take that exam."

He looked at me then at his cards. "I don't know, Frank."

"Don't do this, man."

He looked at his cards then the other guys. "Whatever."

I don't think he studied all that hard, if at all, but he did take his biology final and barely passed, which was enough to keep him in school. He ended up graduating and found a job working for the same biotech firm as his dad. I didn't save him. I just got mad.

I ran into him years later in New Orleans. He was with some friends, and I think it worried him I might say something about what we did in college. That was in the past and not something I wanted to dredge up either. My life had changed by then too. I said hello and asked how he's been and he said well. He told me he lives near the old neighborhood in Metairie and then we shook hands.

"Good to see you, Frank."

"Good to see you, too." I haven't seen him since.

#

With my knee healed, but not yet repaired through surgery, I went back off-shore that summer with a sandblasting and painting crew. I think it took about a day for me to learn that one of the requirements for working as a sandblaster/painter offshore is to have a criminal history. A DWI to these guys was small ball—most had been up for much harder offenses—but they could make me laugh.

We were based in Houma, Louisiana, which is about an hour and a half south and west from New Orleans and has access to the Gulf via a canal that feeds into Terrebonne Bay. The boat the company assigned us to looked like a beat up, rusted flatbed truck. The wheelhouse was stacked on top of the quarters above the ship's bow and behind that ran a long, flat deck where we kept pallets of sand, sand pots, air compressors, five-gallon buckets of paint, as well as assorted hoses, sandblasting guns, and paint sprayers.

I'm not sure if people know just how huge an oil rig is, but they dwarfed our rust bucket. I was a helper, which meant I helped set the pots, compressors, and hoses up, then fed the pots when they started to get empty. There were four, and each held five-hundred pounds of sand. When not hauling hundred-pound bags of sand and lifting them above my head to fill the pots, I scurried around tending lines and doing whatever anyone needed me to do. The guys who did the blasting wore heavy coveralls, gloves, hoods, and helmets, which in the summer heat and humidity, must have been unreal.

We'd sandblast for about half the day, then tear down the sandblasting rigging and replace it with spray painting rigging. If we tried to sandblast one day and paint the next we'd come back to a sheen of unpaintable rust. So, anything we sandblasted we painted, which meant I filled paint pots, tended the lines, scurried around some more, and then flushed and cleaned everything at the end of the day with jet fuel, (Methyl Ethyl Ketone or MEK). It was hard, hot, and dirty work. I did get to blast and paint some and only fell off the rigging once. I didn't hit any cross members on the way down, so I just dried off and went back to work.

There were three guys sandblasting and painting, the captain of our boat, another helper named Buck, a cook, and me. At each rig there were guys working on the rig and the company man—but we never saw much of these guys.

One job was on a production platform out in the Gulf. We offloaded our gear on one of the lower decks, then Buck and I set up the pots, compressor, lines, and the rest of the gear for the sandblasters. When we finished and they'd started work, Buck tilted his head—it was too loud to hear much—to indicate he was taking a break. Buck was a tall, golden-haired kid with a soft, blond mustache that he often toyed with. I nodded my head and watched him pull a pack of cigarettes from his pocket as he walked away.

He stopped near a twelve-inch sump pipe outlet that jutted up through the deck and was bleeding off natural gas. There must have been four or five large, red signs warning people not to smoke, but before I could yell anything above the noise of the sandblasting and the workings of the rig, he flicked his lighter and Poof! The lighter lit the gas into a flame spiking up from the end of the pipe.

Buck ran from the burning gas, and I yelled and waved my hands to get the attention of the guys sandblasting as well as our boat captain. Fear is a funny thing. In this case, everyone panicked. The guys shut off the sandblasters and threw them to the deck and ran over to me.

"We gotta get the hell out of here before the whole rig blows," one of them yelled. That's when we started moving like we had a purpose. A couple guys ran to where the boat lines moored us to the rig while the rest of us grabbed what we could and raced to the boat. Meanwhile, the captain was yelling into the radio at the company man in the office and control room about two decks above where we were.

The company man looked out the control room windows down to where we were then calmly walked outside and down the two metal flights of stairs. Nonchalantly he picked up a wide, flat, plywood board and pinned it on top of the sump pipe which put the fire out. Then he turned and looked at Buck and me.

"I don't care which of you idiots did this," he said as he pointed to the red do-not-smoke signs, "but don't do it again."

I looked at Buck. His eyes were wide. When the pipe flamed up it burned off half his mustache, and the other half looked like burned sugar. The unlit cigarette was still between his lips.

To tell the truth, it was kind of a tin-can operation. Not only was our boat a piece of junk, but it was often so overloaded that in rough seas we lost pallets of sand, pots tipped over and rolled around, and gear got messed up and spread across the deck. After one hitch, we were making our way in with six-foot seas. Not only did we lose a pallet or two of sand and the pots tipped over, but a rope washed overboard and got caught in one of the screws and seized up one of our propellers. It was already after dark and with just one propeller left, it would take forever to get in.

"Who wants to go under and cut that damn rope," the captain yelled.

I looked at him like he was crazy, but one of the sandblaster guys said he'd do it. The captain tied a rope around him and he went over the side with a knife. We were in one hundred fifty feet of water with a strong current going under the boat by the screws. And the sandblaster fellow was down there with a knife trying to cut through a big, thick piece of rope. He could have banged his head or gotten tangled in the rope and drowned.

He came back to the surface, and we pulled him back up onto the deck. He was beat from fighting against the current and trying to slice through the rope. Someone else with little sense had to give it a try. So, over the side I went. I tried my damnedest to cut that line, but I couldn't get it out of the screw to save my neck. It took us forever to get back to Houma to get a diver.

Before we headed back out, the company delivered a new cook to our boat. He looked like they had picked him off skid row the day before. His hair was gray and greasy, his beard looked like fleas lived in it, and he smelled like stale beer and vodka were seeping out of every pore in his skin.

We started out from Morgan City at night headed to Eugene Island, which is the name of an offshore block off the coast of Louisiana. A few hours after we started, I was in the wheelhouse with the captain when he asked, "Where the hell is that cook?"

I didn't know so I headed down to the bunkroom and yelled up to the captain to tell him he wasn't there or in his bunk.

"Well, go find out where he's at," the captain yelled back. "I wanna make sure he didn't fall overboard."

I poked around, and no one had seen him, and there was no sign of the guy until I climbed down into the engine room. "What in the world are you doing down here?"

He looked up at me with a big smile. "Oh, we're having a party."

There wasn't anyone else down there with him. "Really?"

His eyes were wide and he just said, "Yeah."

I went back up to the wheelhouse and reported to the captain that the cook was down in the engine room. Next thing you know we looked up, and he was standing at the door of the wheelhouse.

"Hey," he said, "I want y'all to come down to the engine room. They're having a New Year's bash down there."

I looked at the captain whose eyes were all screwed up. "What?"

"Yeah, a big bash. Lawrence Welk and his entire band is down there playing, and they've got a bubble machine going and everything." The guy's body shook from delirium tremors, and it was obvious he was hallucinating from alcohol withdrawal. "There's all sorts of people dancing, with the guys in tuxedos and the ladies, of course, in evening gowns, and it's all down in the engine room."

The captain looked at me then throttled down the engine as he turned the boat around on a gentle arc. "We're going to Morgan City so we can drop this sick sucker off."

#

I worked hard that summer, and as the start of college neared, a representative from the company called. "We could use somebody like to you as a foreman on one of these paint crews."

"I don't know," I said, "I got college and everything." There was no way I was going to be a foreman for a bunch of felons. No way!

"Well, if you want to quit college and be a foreman on a sandblasting and painting crew, you could start making good money right away."

I did like the money. When I came home after each hitch there was a check waiting for me. Since I was living at home, I could go out in Fat City or wherever and party until daybreak, then eat breakfast at Dirty Pierre's or the Pitt Grill. When I was due in Houma for the next hitch, I was drunk, fat, happy, and still had a bunch of money left in the bank.

I thought about the offer for a little while. A few seconds. I left offshore work because I didn't want to have to work that hard for the rest of my life. I'd also done well at school. I told the guy I appreciated the offer, but no thank you.

A week or so later Dad dropped me off up at LSU, and the grease monkey was back in the fight. I'd selected another heavy course load—I did this every semester of college—and remained committed to going through initiation at Fiji. Though I came to Fiji for the party, I stayed for the people. Many of my friends at the beginning of my freshman year were no longer in school, or our paths diverged and we didn't see much of each other. Most of the other students focused on either having fun or grades. There were only a few of us who approached both with the intensity that I did.

Fiji was a good home for someone like me. Not only were most of the guys committed to their grades and out-partying everyone else, but they were interesting people. We had a guy with a glass eye and his friend from Morgan City whose family owned some tugboats. After school, he captained boats. A guy from Baton Rouge, a forestry major, and a personality unto himself. Another's dad was a judge. One macho dude ended up working for a global engineering and construction company, and now posts photos of himself spearfishing in the Red Sea. Our president was a year ahead of me and went to the London School of Economics. But first he and the other seniors demanded that as fraternity treasurer, I exhaust the social budget by buying a last keg of beer.

LSU and the fraternity were a starting point for these guys. We fed on each other's energy, whether it was intellectual or having fun, though not all our fun was mature or what we would share with adult business colleagues. There was the time some guys turned off the lights in the back hall to light their farts. One of them lit his underwear on fire.

Then there was the fireworks battle. The upstairs versus the downstairs. Guys at the top of the stairs were shooting roman candles and whatever else they could muster at the guys downstairs and vice-versa. The cops pulled up out front and our FIJI president yelled, "Cool it!" A cop walked in the foyer, and there we were, holding smoldering roman candles behind our backs with gunpowder smoke hanging like a fog about three feet above the floor.

"There's reports of people shooting off fireworks around here," the cop said.

The president of FIJI shrugged. "There's nobody shooting fireworks around here, sir."

The cop pulled his belt up. "Hmm, I just want to be sure we aren't going to have a problem with that. Is that clear?"

"Yes, sir. I'll make sure of it."

"Good." Then he turned and left. We did cool it. For a while anyway.

And then there was the streaking, which meant wearing just ski masks at the 11:30 a.m. change of classes in the quadrangle as girls laughed, screamed, and threw their books in the air. A rather gigantic LSU cop once gave chase yelling, "Stop! Stop! Stop!" though there was no way he'd ever be able to catch up. The only danger was laughing too hard and not being able to run. In the end, all managed to escape and go on to well-respected careers in law, politics, and business.

At any rate, these were the kind of guys who belonged to Fiji and with whom I went through initiation. I'm not allowed to talk about what we did, but if you didn't mind ping-pong balls, buckets of ice, jockstraps, gray crickets, and burlap sacks, you'd be okay. All five of us slept in a closet with an ever-repeating tape of Monty Python sketches. It was sort of like a prisoner-of-war thing, but I now impress my kids with my encyclopedic knowledge of Monty Python. And we got to know each other well in the closet after being taken out to dinner ... at Poncho's Mexican Buffet.

#

All five of us survived initiation. I lived in a dorm known as *The Pentagon*, where I spent as much time as I could. Of course, there was a lot of horsing around and beer drinking, which drew me like a moth to flame, but I also looked up to and listened to the guys ahead of me. They liked to party, but most of them also seemed to know where they were going or at least had a sense of direction.

By contrast, I'd never settled into a major. I wanted something big. I just didn't know what. This is when I heard our frat president and another guy talk about a combined law and accounting program that prepared you for law school. Law school and following Dad into the legal profession seemed possible and large enough for my ambition or grandiosity. I switched my major to accounting, started wearing button down shirts with my blue jeans, and bought a pair of Wallabees.

Despite my more refined look, I was no less dedicated to getting drunk as much as I could and with a recklessness matched by only a handful of friends. Our loyalty to LSU football was absolute, and it would have taken an act of God for us to miss a home game. During my freshman year, I took up the habit of bringing a fifth flask of whiskey into the game as did the rest of the LSU student section. Of course I had another fifth for after the game. Each game was a big, loud party with our beloved LSU Tigers in the middle of it.

During the fall of my sophomore year, it was common for the guys to take a date to the game. I did what I could to find a date to each of the games. After a couple weeks of that, I got tired of going through the effort of trying to get some girl to tag along with me while I drank whiskey and whooped it up in the stands. I wasn't the only one going stag to the games, and we formed a tight little group of drunken football fans.

As the season moved along and the intensity of each game grew, so did my ability to get blind drunk. I vaguely remember when we played the USC Trojans, ranked number one in the country. LSU was unranked. It was a sellout crowd like always on a Saturday night in Tiger Stadium. LSU had USC beat in the fourth quarter with only seconds left. They punted to us, but there was a flag on the play, which gave possession back to USC.

We LSU fans believed that by making pure noise we could stop USC, and we did the entire game. It was the loudest football game I ever attended. As they moved the ball downfield, the volume and pitch increased until my ears rang from it, and I couldn't believe that USC's offense could hear themselves in the huddle, but they did and they scored. We got ripped off fo' sho'. After the game, USC's Coach John Robinson said he'd never come back to Baton Rouge to play again. Ever. And they really did get beat.

This was a hard game to forget, but the truth is there aren't many fourth quarters that I remember. I do remember waking up Sunday morning, always a bit surprised as if coming out of anesthesia, hung over, and wondering what happened the night before. I loved football, but drinking was more important. This was the beginning of not being able to stop once I got started.

Since LSU played throughout the South and further away on occasion, getting to away games was tough, but we didn't miss any when they played our arch rival the University of Alabama Crimson Tide. The Tigers were good, but Alabama was something else. Not only did some of the best people to ever play football run through their program but they had legendary coach, Bear Bryant. No matter where you sat in the stands, he was recognizable in his red and white hounds tooth hat, rolled up game plan held in his hands, and his intense flinty glare out at the field. We lost to the Bear every single time we played them. It was kind of depressing.

After our second or third loss, my pledge-brother roommate developed something of an obsession with Bear Bryant's hat. He wanted to steal it. In our junior year, we traveled with a bunch of other students overnight on a Thursday to Tuscaloosa, which was something of an adventure. We drank beer the whole way, and at some point had to hose the bus out because the toilet overflowed. Then as we went through Tuscaloosa a small, foreign-made car blocked the bus from making a tight turn. About fifteen of us climbed out, picked the car up, and moved it up onto somebody's lawn. Not a big deal.

That evening my pledge-brother and a brother who was a cheer leader went to check out the campus. For some reason he wore his cheerleading shirt. As they wandered around, the sun set beneath the horizon, leaving a halo of burgundy light. It was about 7 p.m. on a Friday, and there were only a few students milling about. Then they spotted the University's athletics department. A few lights were on, but it was otherwise quiet. The front doors were open.

They walked up to the second floor to Coach Bryant's office and the door was open just enough to let a soft, oblong rectangle of light into the hallway. They knocked.

"Hello, come in." His voice was deep and sure.

And there at his desk that was piled with papers and mementos was Bear Bryant. He looked up, saw the LSU cheerleading shirt and smiled.

"How are you doing, Coach?" one of the guys asked.

"Oh, good. You boys up for the game?"

My roommate spied it. On the sofa against the wall facing Bryant's desk was his red and white hounds tooth hat. There wasn't anybody around. You could just take it and run like hell.

"Don't you dare," the cheerleader muttered.

"Yes sir, we sure are looking forward to the game, Coach." Truth was their eyes were wide and humbled. To be in the presence of this man, a man who, even though he coached our rival, was beyond any contempt. It was overwhelming. He was and remains a legend, and though they walked into his office late on a Friday evening the day before a big game, he greeted them with respect and courtesy. The hat stayed where it was.

Later I heard about a guy who tried to grab the Bear's hat as the team was getting off a bus. It didn't go well. One of the tight ends ran the guy down and dislocated his shoulder. In all probability, it was wise not to monkey with Bear Bryant's hat.

A few years after meeting Coach Bryant, I had just graduated from law school and passed the bar when my roommate called me. "I got LSU-Alabama tickets."

The team that year was one of the best that LSU ever fielded, with guys like Alan Risher, Dalton Hilliard, Ramsey Dardar, Leonard Marshall, and Eric Martin. Still, I had my doubts. "No, I'm not going this year. Losing to Bama seven years in a row is too much, and I'm no glutton for punishment."

"Come on Frank. It's LSU versus Alabama and we've got one of the best teams we've ever had. Come with me. Get on a plane to Birmingham, and

I'll pick you up at the airport."

It didn't take much to convince me, and so that Saturday, yet again, I met up with our college buddies with a bottle of whiskey tucked in one pocket. Before the game, we tailgated like in times of old.

A few minutes later we filtered into the stadium. Our seats were near the Alabama band and it was a bright sunny Saturday afternoon so the sun reflected off all those brass instruments, and to be heard above the noise of the stadium, the band played as loud as it could. For a while I thought I would lose it, but the game started and it was great. I don't think Alabama made a first down the whole first half, and LSU ended up winning.

For some reason, the tunnel that led back to Alabama's locker room was right beneath the opposing fans section. For seven years, I'd watched in glum resignation as Alabama ran into the tunnel cheering their defeat of LSU. This time it was our turn to celebrate as the Crimson Tide marched into the tunnel defeated. Bear Bryant was the last of the team to get to the tunnel. He stopped for a moment, smiled, took his hat off, then shook his head and walked into the tunnel.

Bryant was already in bad health when that game was played, which might explain a little why we were able to beat Alabama for the first time in twelve years. Soon after, he announced his plans to retire at the end of that season and coached his last game on December 29, 1982, which he won. Afterward, a reporter asked what he planned to do with his free time, and he said, "Probably croak in a week."

On January 25, less than a month later, he died of a heart attack. Thank God we got to win one before he left this world.

In the back of my mind, I knew I had a drinking problem. Good grades and good times can only do so much to hide the truth. I loved each football game, but from the beginning, my anticipation for Saturday during football season was as much about the drinking as it was the game.

The truth of my relationship with alcohol began showing in high school, but by college my slip was well past showing. Every weekend began with getting drunk on Friday and staying at some level of intoxication through Sunday morning, when I began the sad ritual of homework and preparing for the upcoming week of classes.

Within this sad routine, there were also many instances when the truth was

was plain to see if only I'd looked. There was the time I mixed Ouzo with root beer because there was nothing else to drink. And then, the fact that every time I drank, I got drunk. There's an idiom that those in recovery use well past the point of cliché, but it's nonetheless true. One drink was too many and one hundred wasn't enough.

This hit home one Wednesday night when I asked my roommate to come out with me to a bar on Highland Road. We were Friday night regulars because they offered shots of bourbon—I called it Old Tennis Shoe—for a quarter. You could go there with five dollars and get plastered. But Wednesday was ladies night.

"Come on, man. It's ladies night."

"I have a test tomorrow."

"So?"

"I have to be back by nine or ten."

"Well, come on, then. I'll have ya back by ten."

He took in a breath. "No, you won't. There's no way we'll be back by ten. I know you. Once you start drinking, you can't stop. There's no way you'll leave that place until last call at 2 a.m."

"Aw, come on."

"No. I'm serious."

I knew he was right. When I started drinking there wasn't anything or anyone that could get me to stop. If I drank, I got drunk and not just a little drunk but sloppy, blackout drunk.

Then, on a cold November day as a sophomore just before class, Mom called to tell me that Poppy died. He'd been battling cancer and had endured repeated rounds of chemotherapy. The ravages of the disease emaciated his body so much that he looked like a prisoner of war. He was diagnosed at age sixty-eight, so he did get a few years of retirement with Ganny, but over the next year and a half the disease and chemo withered him away.

Though his death wasn't sudden or surprising, it was deep in its effect on me. I'd lost not just someone I loved but one of the two most important male role models in my life. As such, it also acted as an inflection point. In Poppy and Dad I saw the standard by which I measured myself, and that guided my belief in the man I was meant to be. Poppy's death gave me a moment of clarity, and I could see how far from the mark I was. It was also my first face-to-face confrontation with death.

At his funeral, I sat in the same pew where we have sat for a generation and felt everything I'd ever done wrong hit me. It was a deeper sense of guilt than I'd ever felt, and I thought, *Do not open your mouth to justify it because there is no defense.* Then the congregation stood and the organist played the first bars of the hymn "Holy, Holy, Holy."

I stood and prepared to sing the first lines.

Holy, Holy, Holy! Lord God Almighty!

Early in the morning our song shall rise to Thee;

Holy, Holy, Holy, merciful and mighty!

God in three persons, blessed Trinity! [20]

But as the congregation's voice rose as one, I was voiceless. My body shook and heaved as I wept, and not a note could escape my throat. I mourned his loss, but this was something different. I couldn't explain it then, but now I realize that I felt the very presence of God and that I stood before Him. I was speechless and undone, guilty and awake for the first time in many years. And when it was over I went right back to my old sleeping self. When I returned to college it wasn't as a chastened man seeking a higher purpose, it was still the grease monkey versus the world.

I know Dad worried about me, and I'm sure he saw me break down at Poppy's funeral. His call to suggest that I make it a regular practice to attend church shouldn't have surprised me, but it did.

"You've got nothing better to do, why don't you get up on Sunday and go to church," he said.

"I don't know Dad."

"It would be good for you and pick up your morale and everything."

I hated Sundays. Sunday meant I had to get sober, do homework, and get ready for a week of school to begin. When I was a kid, it also meant that Dad would walk out of our lives the next morning for the work week and I'd return to a routine that didn't make me happy and left me wondering what the point of it all was. Sundays meant the end of fun and the beginning of loss, which stayed with me even through college, law school, and into my career as a lawyer.

"No, Dad, I don't really want to do that."

He didn't stop trying, and I didn't stop not listening to him. I may have pretended it was a choice I was making based on some defensible merit, but the truth was there was no way I'd be able to stop drinking on Saturday nights and get up the next morning for church. Drinking was far too precious and necessary.

And so that's how college went for me. It was intense bouts of studying broken by intense bouts of partying. Every so often, Dad or Mom urged me to go to church, which I'm sure they equated with sobriety and living life closer to the established order of things. If I had wanted to, I don't think I could have done what they asked. I was too busy deriving as much earthly pleasure as I could grasp with my own two hands.

And I pined for love, whatever that was. In truth at the time, love was just an idea, a wish, a fantasy, rather than a reality, and in it I placed all my hopes that love could change me. It was wishful thinking. Each object of my affections was usually well out of my reach, but the truth was that I never found it because it doesn't exist. My fantasizing prevented me from learning that I must first learn to love God before another would love me.

The only thing that kept me from falling through the floor was my vow that the grease monkey would out-study anybody. I ended up graduating with a 3.4 or so grade point average. With my scores on the Law School Admission Test (LSAT), which I took in the spring of my junior year, LSU's law school accepted me.

Before I made my final decision about law school, I did some interviewing and even received an offer to work as a CPA for a whopping $14,000 per year. This was a lot for a starting salary back then. When I told Dad about the job offer and the possibility of going to law school he seemed to lean toward going to work rather than law school.

"Why are you trying to talk me out of law school?"

"Well, I just want to make sure you're not doing it just because I did it. It is not a lot of fun. You have to do it because you want to."

Of course, the effect of his words made me want to go to law school that much more. If you wanted me to do something, tell me not to do it. "Okay, but I think I want to go to law school."

He looked at me to size me up and see if I was serious or not, then said, "If you're going to go, just go."

Graduation was early in the morning on a Saturday in May. I woke up badly hung over. Mom and Dad were there, and afterward we went out to Don's Seafood, which was something Poppy would have liked.

My sister was doing post graduate work in English and went to England that summer. She had an apartment in Baton Rouge and a beagle named Melville—her dissertation was on Melville and *Moby Dick*—and she needed someone to watch the dog and her apartment. I was working in Baton Rouge that summer. Four years of college, a degree in accounting, and being accepted to law school meant little. The only job I could get was at Montgomery Ward's spin-balancing and mounting tires. I took the job, the apartment, and the dog.

My summer consisted of going to work, coming home, walking the dog, then drinking until I was loaded. It was a long, hot summer. Of course at the end of it, they offered me a job running the automotive department at Montgomery Ward's. *Really?* I was on my way to law school. I politely declined. Again.

Then law school started and it was back to the "me versus the world" attitude. The first day was orientation for the first-year students. I remember sitting in a large lecture hall as the dean of the law school stood and said, "Look to the right of you. Now look to your left. One of the three of you is not going to be here when this is over."

I looked at the guy on the right and then the left and said, "I don't know which of you two it's going to be, but it's been nice knowing you." It was just a statement of fact.

Louisiana Civil Law Systems was a first-year class taught by a man who looked like the Pope. He seemed pompous, bombastic, and was doing his best to bring to life John Houseman's character from "The Paper Chase." One of his favorite lines was, "You must read to understand ..." which he uttered like a Shakespearian thespian through a microphone that boomed his voice from the ceiling like the voice of God. I couldn't help but think why else would I read? Just for fun? And he'd walk through the aisles pratting on while everyone buried their head in their notes praying, *Don't call on me.*

My soon to be mentor and Admiralty Professor taught freshman Federal Civil Procedure. He was a solid, tough looking guy with a thick white beard and hair. Early in the semester, a student came to class late, walked in like it was no big deal, and took a seat. He ran him out of class. "You would never walk into a federal courtroom late. You can come back tomorrow. And be on time!" If I hadn't learned it yet, that's when I knew law school was real. And I was never late.

About the time the movie, "Star Wars," came out, we had another professor for freshman Contracts who we nick-named, "Darth Levander." Like all our professors, he loved to call on people when he knew they were doing their best to be invisible. I must have been fading in and out one day because he tilted his head, looked at me, and said, "What forms the basis of an agreement in a contract?"

I gave the pat, dumb answer, "It's a meeting of the minds."

He smiled. Just what he wanted to hear. "Have you ever met a mind?"

A few people snickered. I looked down at the top of my desk, and for the life of me I had no idea how to answer his question.

"Well, have you?"

Then it came to me.

"I think I just have."

There was quiet, waiting for his response. He seemed pleased with the answer and smiled. For the moment I was off the hook. But I was a glutton for punishment, and for the next two years I took every class he taught.

Going into final exams, I thought I was going to flunk out. In law school there is only the final exam. It is four hours long for each class, and the grade you get on that exam is your grade for the semester. That was it. My first final was in Civil Law Systems. We sat in a large lecture hall, and the professor passed the exam out face down, then he went to the front and said, "Begin."

I flipped the paper over and thought, *Take a minute and read through this.* As I mulled over the first part of the exam, a girl in the back row burst out in tears. "Oh God," she cried then ran out the door. That was the last we ever saw of her. Some people.

My last exam was Contracts, and it ran from one 1 p.m. to 5 p.m. on Friday. That entire week was nothing but an intense bout of studying and sitting for these four-hour-long exams. By that Friday, my brain was totally fried, and I wanted to get bombed. We had all thought this through, and I had a cooler of beer in the trunk of my car. With a few others, I sat in the parking lot slurping down beer right after the exam.

I learned quickly not to talk about exams afterward. The guy who always raised his hand in class always had the answer after the exam and did not hesitate to tell you how badly you had blown it. Inevitably "that guy" was wrong and flunked the class never to be seen again. So I learned to trust my gut.

This was the night of my sister's rehearsal dinner for her wedding that would be the next day. The drinking didn't stop in the parking lot, and like a hurricane over warm ocean waters, it gained intensity when I ran into my sister's fiancé's brother at the open bar. He'd finished his freshman exams for medical school that day, and we went on a tear, which ended for me with two bouncers tossing me out of the hotel onto the pavement. I had lost count at twenty-two gin martinis.

Dad gave me a ride back to my apartment, and the last thing I remember is collapsing into my bed. They say that gin will cause your hair to explode into split ends. That's how my head felt when I woke up to *boom, boom, boom.* Dad and my brother came to get me for the wedding.

"We've been calling and trying to wake you up. We have to be at the wedding in about thirty minutes," Dad said.

With some help, I put a tuxedo on and we made it to the wedding on time. I made it through the service without puking or passing out, but when we got to the reception, all I could do was sit in a corner nursing a bottle of champagne. Still, it was too much, and I slipped out of the reception and went back to my apartment where I slept from 5:00 that Saturday night until the next Monday. When I woke up, I packed my things and headed home for Christmas break.

This wasn't the first, nor anywhere close to the last time my oldest sister and her husband would have to deal with the intoxicated mess of a little brother that I was. Later, their oldest son would call the rattan chair in my Mom's den next to the television, "The chair where Uncle Frank lives" because they'd find me passed out there so often.

To be honest, my brain was fried. I was hungover, and hearing about all the test answers from the others guys made me doubt my answers, and I wasn't sure if I'd failed out of law school or passed. With my grade for each class dependent on a single final exam, I had no idea how I'd done. The wait for word that grades had been posted was painful.

There wasn't much for me to do. Just drink and twist in the wind. One night I was being melodramatic and asked, "Dad, what'll happen if I flunk out?"

He looked at me and said, "Well, I guess you'll do something else."

He was just so matter of fact about it that it came across as one of the most profound things he'd ever said to me. "This too shall pass" and "You'll do something else." Typical Navy pilot.

At the same time my drinking worried him. Most nights after we'd had our drinks and dinner, I'd go out for more. He'd say, "You shouldn't drive when you're drinking," but I'd just shrug it off. "At least wear your seatbelt." I'd head out the door leaving him and Mom to wonder what condition I'd come home in—if I made it home. The part of me that felt guilty was far overwhelmed by the need to keep drinking.

Then a friend called. "The grades are up on the Wailing Wall." The Wailing Wall was the name of the bulletin board where the law school posted grades. Those who didn't make the cut often walked away shaken, crying, and in a deep depression. They would wail. I drove up right away and almost couldn't believe what I saw. Not only had I passed, but I was one point from making the top ten percent of my class. Turns out that my friends who thought they had the right answers on the exam were the ones who flunked out. I should have listened to the advice I got from a second-year law student: "Never listen to the guy who always raises his hand in class. He's always wrong!" In Criminal Law, I scored the highest grade in the class. That should have been a hint that I could think like a lawyer. Or a criminal

#

I did as well in my grades the next semester and summer school. Then in my second year, a professor who taught admiralty and maritime law, among other classes, accepted me for a clerkship as a research assistant. For anybody else, I'd have been well on my way to a distinguished career in law, but I wasn't anybody else. I was drinking like an alcoholic because I was an alcoholic. I studied hard, but I never missed an LSU football game and getting bombed every Friday and Saturday night, plus maybe one or two nights during the week when the heat wasn't on. The studying and success that it brought didn't give my life meaning. It didn't calm the perpetual restlessness. Drinking was only a temporary salve to that restlessness, to the gigantic hole within me, but temporary escape was good enough.

It could also be fun.

My fraternity pledge-brother roommate also had graduated from LSU with a degree in computer science and found a job with a local hospital. We decided to share an apartment. He was responsible enough during the week, but on weekends we made good drinking buddies.

We also loved LSU football, so when the schedule called for them to go up to South Bend to play Notre Dame in September of 1981, there was no way we were going to miss that game. Also, due to the shortened season caused by the professional baseball players strike, the Chicago Cubs were in first place in the National League West.

Like any American, I know and love baseball, but unlike most folks, I didn't go to my first major league game until college. New Orleans was a football city, and the nearest professional baseball team was in Houston, about six and a half hours away. For a brief period during my undergraduate years, Mom and Dad lived in Houston as the result of changes with Dad's position at Shell. During summer break we went to visit them at the same time the Astros were to play a home stand.

My roomie said he wanted to check out one of the games and I said, "Sure, why not?" It was a doubleheader in the old Astrodome and during the first game, in about the fifth inning a fella named Ken Forsch was pitching when I took the last sip off my beer and leaned over. "This is the most boring game I've ever been to. Do you realize nobody has even hit the ball yet?"

His eyes widened. "Shut up, you idiot; the guy has a no-hitter going."

Forsch ended up pitching a no-hitter. How could I not opine that it was the most unentertaining thing I've ever seen?

"You idiot, you don't even realize what you've seen. People go their whole lives and never see a no-hitter, and you go to your first major league game and it's a no-hitter, and you're upset about it because you thought it was boring?"

"Yeah, that's why I don't like baseball."

I did like "Foamers" though. A Foamer was free beer if the Astros hit a home run on an odd or even minute, whichever was picked. During the second game after taking a leak, I heard a bat connect and suddenly there was a stampede. Being uninitiated, I figured it was a terrorist or a fire, so I ran too. Then we all stopped at the beer stand. And I learned about Foamers. What a great idea! Later some moron discontinued them. For safety reasons, no less.

When we planned the trip to go see the LSU/Notre Dame game and I suggested we catch a Cubs game in Chicago, he about fell over. I wanted to go because Dad, for some reason, was a Cubs fan, and I knew that they'd spent most of the last fifty years as the league's cellar dwellers.

We flew to Chicago on Thursday night and went to Rush Street, where we partied and went to a doubleheader at Wrigley Field on Friday. By the time the game ended we were bombed, but had to drive an hour and a half to South Bend where we stayed at a Holiday Inn with all the other fraternity brothers up for the game. LSU travels well.

We got up for the game, prepared our flasks, and I made sure I had our tickets. Dad got them from a friend of his at work who was an alumnus of Notre Dame law school. "These are the tickets. They're in the Notre Dame alumni section, so you all behave." Right.

We walked into the stadium with our flasks tucked away in the small of our backs. Shirt tails out, no problem. Then we looked up to our seats. At Notre Dame stadium, you enter at ground level then scale Mount Everest. And we had to pick our way through about a thousand Notre Dame alumni. Up we went, "Excuse me, pardon me, excuse me, pardon me, excuse me, pardon me ..." until we found our seats in and amongst people sitting shoulder to shoulder.

We sat down and proceeded with the customary pre-game coin flip to see who would go back down through all these people to the concession stand to get Cokes to mix with our booze. I lost. So back to, "Excuse me, pardon me ..." I got to the concession stand and asked for two Cokes. I expected to get two large cups with ice like they do at LSU and every other stadium on the planet, but instead the girl put two cans down on the counter. And they were warm.

"Can I have two cups?"

She smiled and put two tiny plastic cups next to the cans of Coke. Not what I had in mind.

"Can I have some ice please?"

"Can't. We need the ice to keep our 'pop' cold," she said with a heavy Midwestern accent. What?

Then I heard the LSU band start playing pre-game for the team's entrance onto the field, which is the greatest moment in college football.

"Excuse me?"

"We need the ice to keep our 'pop' cold." What? Pop? Who is Pop? This did not compute.

"Never mind," I said to her and grabbed the cans with the cups on top and turned to head back into the stadium.

That's when I met the security guard. "Hey, you can't bring cans in. You've got to pour those in the cups."

I looked at him. "Are you kidding me?"

"Nope."

I poured the coke into the cups, which filled them to the brim and stepped back into the stadium where it was ninety-three degrees, bright, and sunny at eleven-thirty in the morning. "Excuse me, pardon me, excuse me, pardon me ..." I made my way back up Mount Everest and handed roomie a tepid, rapidly warming cup of Coke.

"What is this?"

"That's your Coke. Shut up."

We started drinking, the game got going, things got exciting, we dipped deeper into our flasks and we started to have a good time. Toward the end of the first half we had a good buzz, Notre Dame was up by a few touchdowns— each Notre Dame score was met by a round of polite hand clapping by the alumni, like at the opera—but LSU had the ball. A few plays later, LSU drove into the end zone and amid this throng of Notre Dame alumni we jumped up, waved our shakers, and hooted and hollered for our team.

As we yelled and carried on, I looked down over the heads of a thousand people and there, looking back up at me was the LSU law school associate dean who had graduated Magna Cum Laude from Notre Dame. From there, he attended LSU law school where he was on the Law Review and at the top of his class. As dean, he was the bearded epitome of the stern, don't-be-an-ass law school professor. And he taught my Federal Courts class.

He rose and looked me dead in the eye.

"Oh, crap."

Then he turned around and sat.

On Monday morning, he walked into the classroom and got himself straight. Before he started, he looked at me and asked with a grin, "Did we have a nice time in South Bend?"

"Yes, sir."

Then he proceeded to grill me as he went through a hypothetical case that involved the tortured trip of two drunken LSU students through multiple states and jurisdictions, breaking multiple laws, and committing every tort on the face of the earth. Plus a few crimes. It was hell at the time, but we got a good laugh out of it later.

When I think of this story, there's a lot to not be proud of, but at the time it was fun. It made for a good story. However, this was more the exception than the rule. Once I started drinking there was no stopping, which meant intense hangovers, an inability to take full advantage of my time at law school, and worse.

During my third year of law school, I went down Highland Road to a place called the Hog's Breath Saloon with my little brother in the fraternity. We got into drinking Long Island Ice Teas, and in quick order I'd downed four of them. I ordered a fifth, then went outside to the car to get a pack of cigarettes.

As I walked back to the bar, a guy who'd just pulled up on a bike—he had the leather vest, boots, the whole deal—asked me for a cigarette. I'd been fiddling with the pack in my fingers and it dropped to the ground.

"F**k you, man," I said and bent to pick the cigarettes up. This was the second time I said that. You would think I would have learned.

My fingers fumbled with the cigarette pack as the guy teed off and kicked me in the face with the toe of his boot. The boot busted my nose, cut me bad, and I heard blood hitting the ground, Splat, like a cow pissing on a flat rock. I bent over and pulled my hands to my face. The guy got on his bike, kick-started it, and I heard the deep muscular revving of the engine as he pulled out of the parking lot yelling, "F**k you!"

Blood covered my face, and I couldn't see a damn thing, but I pulled myself up and started to head back into the bar. At about the same time, my friend ran out. "What happened to you, man?"

He drove me to the emergency room where they checked my nose and stitched the cuts across my face and just above my eye. Then he drove me to my sister's house. I walked in smelling of booze and my face a bloody mess. She was married and pregnant with their first child, and they had to take care me. It was only Friday afternoon. It wasn't even dark outside yet.

The next Monday, I had to bring slip opinions or some other materials to my professor's office. Basically, we read every case that came out of every appellate court in the state and wrote little blurbs for a newsletter. I may have learned as much from reading those cases than my classes. It was a plumb assignment for the student he selected.

"What happened to you?" he asked when I entered his office.

"I got into a fight."

He didn't frown or smile or anything, just looked at me with his eyebrows furrowed. "I hope the other guy looks as bad."

"No, actually not."

In the fall of my senior year, I had him for Torts. (Civil wrongs, not the little cakes.) Despite showing up at his doorstep a bit hungover and a lot beat up, he liked me (I think) and I liked him. He knew I had worked offshore, and as an admiralty and maritime law expert—he taught the class—I think he respected how difficult that work is. He also had his eye out for guys with blue collar work experience, which made me believe he had a soft spot for people who know what it's like to work for a paycheck.

Early in the semester I was asked to go through William Prosser's book on tort law and put together a review of the Louisiana cases and materials. Years later that research evolved into a successful book on Louisiana tort law. Nice to know that I played some small part.

Probably the best thing about being his clerk was that I got a key to the law library. That meant that I could get in early before the other students. When the associate chancellor of the law school opened the school every day at seven in the morning, I was already there.

"You should have been a farmer instead of a lawyer," he would joke.

One weekend my professor wanted my material from the week delivered to his house on Saturday morning. I showed up hungover around midday on Sunday.

"You didn't bring these over yesterday," he said.

"No, I didn't. I'm sorry."

He frowned, took the manila envelope, and shut the door.

# # #

The spring of my Junior year in law school, we had Moot Court, which involved making an oral argument to an appellate court. My scheduled oral argument fell right after a tryst I had with a newly divorced mother who had moved in next door. She invited me over for dinner. She had a small child, and I should have known better.

The night before the argument, I developed an itch more intense than working with fiberglass insulation. Dressed in a suit, I stopped at the Campus Infirmary to get tested.

"Yep, you have the clap," the doctor announced. Somehow he found it amusing. "But don't worry; some antibiotics and you will be good as new. Bend over and count backwards from twenty." The syringe was huge. I counted.

I started to get up.

"Oh no, not yet. We have to do the other side too! Start counting."

My buns were so sore I could hardly walk, or rise to address the appellate court. They say that you are to imagine the judges naked to calm your nervousness. Well, I didn't have to imagine anything! I had my own secret, which I found amusing like the doctor. And in that wrongful search and seizure argument, I had no problem conveying that my guy got screwed. And so had I. Literally. After the vote, I won that case and figured that under the circumstances I might just make a pretty good lawyer after all.

# # #

The summer after junior year, most students worked as clerks for law firms with which they are seeking permanent jobs. I landed a clerkship for half the summer with one of the top firms in New Orleans. This was the first time I ever wore a suit and the first time I worked in an office with professional people. They intimidated the hell out of me.

On a few occasions some of the heavy hitters of the firm invited me out to eat lunch, which terrified me. I had no idea what to talk about, and it was like I had some sort of "social anxiety disorder." Or maybe it was because I was hiding the real me. I could barely bring a glass of water to my lips because my hands shook so much. To say the least, I felt like a boy among men.

For the second half of the summer, I clerked for what was primarily a maritime law firm. When I interviewed with them to get the clerkship, they noticed on my resume that I did some work with the professor. The legal community knew and respected him for his work in admiralty and maritime law.

"You must want to do maritime law?" one of them asked.

The truth was, I didn't. I was set on oil and gas. I'd taken every corporate, tax, oil, gas, and mineral rights course known to man, and even though I clerked for an admiralty professor, I didn't have any desire to do admiralty and maritime litigation. They just assumed I did, and I didn't have the confidence to say no.

The first deposition I attended involved a maritime collision case between two lawyers known for their obstreperousness. They would become known as, how should I say, two of the more colorful members of the local bar. One could be blusterous to the point of frustration. The other carried a pistol that he waved around when exiting his car to show that he was armed. When Hurricane Katrina hit he was made famous for sitting on his front porch, shirtless, with bandoleers strapped across his chest, holding two pearl-handled revolvers and drinking Pimm's Cups. By the end of that one deposition I thought, *I don't think I want to do this for the rest of my life.*

The thing about clerking the summer before your last year of law school is that you are trying out for jobs with the firms you clerk for. I was sure I'd get an offer from the oil and gas firm, and I wanted to work for them. I could have interviewed at other firms but, I thought, *This is what I want.* I also didn't think they wouldn't make the offer since my grades placed me within spitting distance of the top ten percent of my class. Alcoholic or not, the grease monkey all but won the war when it came to studying.

Summer ended, I went back up to Baton Rouge, and then in February I got a call from one of the senior partners. "I'm passing through from Lafayette to New Orleans. I want to have lunch with you."

Ugh, not another lunch, I thought, but what could I say?

At lunch my social anxiety kicked in, and he said, "We can't give you an offer."

"What? Why?"

"Well, one of our junior partners raised the issue that your dad is general counsel for Shell, which is a client, and if we give you an offer it would look like nepotism."

"Well, I think it would be nepotism if he worked for you guys."

He took a deep breath. "No, but he works for one of our clients and so, you know, we think for appearances; he doesn't think it would be right if we offered you a job. Sorry."

I walked out of that lunch wondering if this had more to do with the fact that I drank too much or something else. It just seemed weird.

Either way I was out of luck. I went to my professor and asked, "What am I going to do?"

"Let me talk to someone and see what he can do." He had ties with a firm that did work for Lloyd's of London.

Well, he didn't have anything, but he knew of a guy leaving another large, New Orleans maritime firm— that did a lot of marine insurance work—to start his own firm. He might be interested.

I went down and interviewed a week or so later. When I met him, he reminded me of my pediatrician when I was a little kid. He was about five-feet-five-inches tall with dark hair combed back and a real pleasant kind of personality. He smoked a pipe, and as I learned later, he loved to drink bloody bulls, which is a mix of vodka, tomato juice, beef stock, Worcestershire sauce, hot sauce, celery salt, lime juice, and lemon juice. Sometimes they're garnished with okra or a pickled green bean.

He was also an ex-Navy guy, like Dad, and I think he had a sense that I didn't yet fit in with the New Orleans lawyer mold. I was more of a blue-collar, roughneck kind of guy still, and it seemed like that was good with him.

I felt comfortable with him—no anxiety, or at least not much—and after a bit he said, "You're in the right place. The job's yours if you want it."

"Yeah, I do," I said.

This is where things got interesting.

Chapter Seven

Jimmy was a true character and a fitting start to my legal career.

The office was in a relatively ornate, granite-block building in downtown New Orleans about a block from the federal courthouse. Jimmy tended to wear gray suits, though sometimes blue, with loafers that had little tassels hanging from them. In his office, he sat behind a partner's desk, which was an antique—he always did like antiques—with hand carved inlay and a leather top.

He kept shoe polish in one of the bottom drawers, which he used whenever I or anybody else talked to him about a case. He also smoked a pipe. Both he and his office smelled of fragrant pipe tobacco and shoe polish. Real uptown. On my first day he let me know exactly where I stood in his eyes.

"You see that copy machine out in the office?" he asked.

"Yes, sir."

"I charge clients ten cents a copy. I'm going to make more money off that copy machine than I'm going to make off you."

That might have turned out to be a true statement.

"I want you to read this book." He handed me *Dress for Success*. "You're a lawyer, look and act like one. Now, come with me."

I think one of the reasons Jimmy hired me is because I had worked off-shore. He had been in the US Navy and his practiced focused on admiralty and maritime law, which meant I had some hands-on experience. I knew the law, and I knew what it meant to work offshore.

But it also meant that I had little knowledge of working in an office or what it meant to act like, sound like, or dress like a lawyer. Dressing had never been my strong suit. I was just too self-conscious, and if I got in the trick bag of judging how I was dressed, nothing was ever right. I hated shopping for clothes, particularly with my mother and sisters. What they thought was popular was just not what cool guys wore. A leisure suit? Really? You wouldn't catch me dead in a disco bar. But just what I should wear tied me up in knots.

In retrospect, I always measured my insides by other people's outsides. I'd be drunk, spouting off, and someone would ask indignantly, "Just who do you think you are?" Good question. My response, "I don't know, who do you think I think I am?" Seriously, I had no clue. So I tried not to think about how I dressed. It just caused neurosis and pain.

Next thing I knew, Jimmy and I were browsing through an uptown men's clothing store looking for a couple suits. "Look, you need a blue suit for a jury trial, and you need a gray suit if you're trying a case to a judge," he said.

He went on to add that I should only wear white and blue shirts with a red tie. "Though you can get away with a blue tie, if you want." I needed a black belt to go with black shoes and a brown belt to go with brown shoes.

I bought the whole kit, which included a maroon tie with little white spots. A couple years later, a partner of Jimmy's said to me, "If I see you wearing that tie one more time, I'm going to rip it off and throw it in the trash. You wear the same damn thing every day." He was half right. What he didn't know is that I had three of the exact same ties in my closet at home. Like I said, I was never a style guru.

Learning to dress was the least of my problems. Law professors gave me a topnotch legal education, but it was Jimmy's secretary of many years who taught me what I needed to know. Back then they weren't called paralegals, we called them legal secretaries. She was the best and knew far more than me about the real-life practice of law. I didn't even know how to get to the courthouse.

"Honey," she said to me on my first day. "I'm going to have to watch you like a babe in the woods." She was right and any time I had a question—not just about where the courthouse was, but about anything else—I went to her.

At the time, the maritime law bar in New Orleans was second in number only to New York. Jimmy had left one of the larger and more prosperous

New Orleans admiralty law firms to start his own firm, focused primarily on marine defense work. For example, if a company's workers were injured or experienced blowout or something else that needed their expertise, they could handle the matter in-house or farm it out to an outside law firm. In the '70s and '80s, working offshore was a dangerous business. People were severely injured and killed. And despite safety advancements, it still happens, as the BP oil spill of 2010 has proven. Stuff happens. This was not lost on Jimmy. The stakes were high.

Jimmy had connections with London Underwriters through New York, who sent work our way as well as other clients. Pretty much, all defense lawyers were careful not to let associate lawyers cultivate relationships with the client. Clients have been known to follow the lawyer they like.

Jimmy's relationship with his old firm ran deep. Somehow he was related by marriage to a senior partner. The partners in that firm were typically of the bluest blood, uptown New Orleans, and old wealth. Most were members of the Boston Club and the Mardi Gras Krewe of Rex. The partners were not amused when a group of associate attorneys loosely formed the "Not S.O.B." club. (Boston spelled backward.) A chart of how these firms of the time were interconnected and related would look like the family tree of European royals. At one time, there was even a rule that you had to put your suit coat on if you ever left your office

A big chunk of the work we did was for a maritime insurance brokerage firm that selected defense counsel on risks placed through the world-famous Underwriters at Lloyd's of London, which itself really isn't an entity, more like an association of underwriters. An individual or company can place insurance through Lloyd's for just about any risk you could imagine. Lloyd's then would go out and create a portfolio of insurers and companies that would take a percentage of the risk and then charge a premium to insure it. Then the various underwriters would subscribe to a Cover Note for their percentages of the risk and the insurance policy would be written and issued. That's the simplified version.

We also represented the American Bureau of Shipping (ABS), which is a vessel certification society with surveyors that approve vessels and rigs and help set standards for safety in the shipping industry. One of the first cases I worked on was February 15, 1982 while I was still at LSU Law School—the sinking of the *MODU Ocean Ranger*—an offshore semi-submersible drilling rig that sank east of St. John's Newfoundland with eighty-four crew members on board. There were no survivors. ABS had classified the rig on construction and everyone was sued.

After graduating in 1982, even though I had a job, I hadn't passed the bar exam yet. I wasn't officially a lawyer. One of my Fiji brothers had graduated from LSU, then went to Loyola Law School and clerked for the same firm I had clerked for, from which I had hoped to get an offer. He got hired, I didn't. But we both started work that summer and began studying for the bar exam, taking a review course at Tulane Law School. The exam was in the air conditioned Superdome where we froze our butts off despite it being late August. It took some time to grade before our scores were released, but I passed, and in late October of 1982 the Chief Justice of the Louisiana Supreme Court swore us in with a ceremony at Tulane. I was finally a lawyer, and maybe I could out-earn the copy machine. My Fiji brother and I went to lunch uptown at Delmonico's on St. Charles Avenue to celebrate. Predictably, I got loaded.

After passing the bar, I worked for Jimmy and rented an apartment in a complex at the end of West End Boulevard on Lake Pontchartrain near the New Orleans Yacht Club. There was a swimming pool, a great view of the Lake, and Fiji brothers living there as well. Across the levee in West End Park was Deanie's Seafood, where we used to go eat with Ganny and Poppy when they came to town. The restaurant sat on pilings over the lake, and they had every concoction of seafood you could want, which included a shrimp remoulade loaded with fresh horseradish. (I learned to duplicate it when I was a kid, and Mom had me make it for her bridge parties. The ladies loved it, and I got outside requests. But I never gave up my secret for the remoulade sauce and won't here either.) Deanie's was also the place where I greatly expanded my vocabulary as a young boy. Then there was The Bounty, more of a watering hole party place open 24/7 and other bars. I could just walk or crawl home over the levee.

Not long after I joined the bar, Jimmy's father-in-law died. A doctor who had founded his own clinic, he had made a lot of money. My boss was appointed as the lawyer for the estate in the will. Jimmy was smart, but he didn't know what to do with an estate. He knew I had taken successions and trusts in law school, so he told me to handle the thing. I finally got the estate closed and told myself this was the last time I'd do anything like that again. In later years, I would handle one divorce case, and only because there were dueling allegations of infidelities and hot tub videos. I never did get paid, and quickly learned to stick to what I knew.

Working for Jimmy was a real lesson. No one in my experience knew more about marine insurance than he did. It was common back then—before computers—for law firms to have a library, and Jimmy's firm was no exception. There were the American Maritime Cases as well as several books detailing U.S. and international maritime laws and things of that nature, which wasn't all that unique.

What was unique was the decor. He had thick, wooden tables made from old, wooden-ship hatch covers that had big, brass bands on the ends and indentations on either corner. Brass bars ran across them as handles. Wooden duck decoys were everywhere. His father hand-carved most, if not all of them. Jimmy used to stand in the library admiring them, holding a pipe to his mouth, wearing wing tip shoes with little tassels, and smelling of shoe polish. He spoke with a little bit of a lisp and told me about them with a quiet admiration. "They are antiques," he'd say, and then he described the breed of duck and how he used to duck hunt at a private club on a lease near Pointe à la Hache.

Often his lectures on duck decoys came after lunch. He'd come into the office in the morning and dictate his correspondence, which his secretary took down in shorthand as he shined his shoes. Then he'd finish shining his shoes, light his pipe, do some work, wander into the library, and ask me or the other associate lawyers for updates.

After a few hours of this it was time for lunch, which was a big deal. He either went to the Bienville Club, which was members only, or sometimes Antoine's in the French quarter. He had his own waiter and loved to take clients—especially those from New York—to Antoine's and order chocolate covered oysters. They'd sort of look at these things, which are fried oysters covered in a dark, beef sauce like a demi-glace. They're super good, but if you'd never had them and you thought it really was a chocolate sauce, they probably didn't look that great.

Jimmy would have two or three Bloody Bulls at lunch and come back to the office with a reasonable buzz going, which meant he couldn't get much work done. His secretary would pour him a Tab and a cup of coffee which he took with cream and Sweet and Low (yuck!). She then gave him the letters she typed, he signed them and then lit his pipe, talked on the phone, and whiled away the rest of the day. There were plenty of exceptions to the routine, and

Jimmy could get rather exercised when negotiating settlements or when cases moved in unpredictable ways.

#

Despite Jimmy's somewhat genteel work schedule, he was an ace with maritime insurance law, so we were in the mix for any big cases that came our way. By contrast, if a big defense firm had offered me a job, I would have been the most junior of the associate attorneys relegated to carrying a partner's briefcase. Instead Jimmy took me under his wing. The result: I gained valuable experience and learned the real-world practice of maritime and admiralty law from the inside out.

Several cases we took related to coal-carrying ships. At the time, coal miners in South Africa and Australia were on strike creating coal shortages in Taiwan and mainland China. The soft bituminous coal of Ohio and surrounding areas could not be burned in the United States because of the high sulfur content. But you could burn it in China (no EPA), which spawned long-term coal supply contracts with the Chinese. Our ships loaded coal in Myrtle Grove, Louisiana, for transport to Taiwan.

As far back as the 1800s, everybody knew that coal would spontaneously heat, that oxygen will react with carbon and oxidize, which creates an exothermic reaction. So coal needs to be packed down or it will catch on fire.

The coal was transported down the river in open hopper barges. It got rained on. And being dumped in piles with no packing, there were openings where air got into the load. At one point someone took aerial photographs of fleets of barges on the Mississippi, and they looked like Christmas tree lights. At the loading terminal, the barges were off-loaded to ships with conveyor belts that again dumped the coal in piles. The ships then closed the hatches and sailed.

When the ships reached the Panama Canal, the temperatures in the holds started to rise. The captains looked at the cargo regulations for coal, which stated that some deep mined coal had methane in it. The solution to cool the cargo, they thought, was just to force-air-vent the holds, which made the problem worse. After clearing the Panama Canal, the temperatures continued to rise at an intense burn. The ships put in at Long Beach, California, where they asked their Port Captain what they should do. "You've got to cool it off, so open the hatches," he said. Mistake number three. We nicknamed him, "Open Hatches," as he created floating barbeque pits.

The cargo was offloaded after hot spots were extinguished and spread out over an abandoned World War II airfield to cool, which happened to be where Dad did basic training. Each cargo hold had sulfur and heat damage that had to be fixed before the ships could reload the coal and sail with thermocouples inserted to track the temperatures and a covering of inert nitrogen. ,

On arrival in Taiwan, there was a cargo shortage by tonnage and a loss of heating or Btu values, plus damage to the ships. We represented the Chinese cargo underwriters, filing suit in New Orleans federal court under maritime law for the cargo damage, and with New Orleans at the center of this fiasco, just about every law firm in the city got involved. And Jimmy threw me into the middle of it. I was a first-year-out-of-law-school newbie taking depositions with the most experienced, respected, and talented maritime lawyers in New Orleans. It was an incredible opportunity and learning experience.

While many of our cases were like the coal ships, we had another that was a bit more personal and closer to home. At the time, the Greater New Orleans Bridge (now the Crescent City Connection) had three lanes, two lanes moving in opposite directions and a third middle "emergency lane" that carried traffic in either direction during the morning and evening rush hours. This arrangement worked well unless an intoxicated driver crossed the middle lane and hit another car head-on. And in New Orleans, with Bourbon Street, this didn't take long.

One Saturday, a drunk driver hit our clients, a family, head-on. The impact killed the father, broke the mother's hip, and paralyzed their young daughter. The driver of the other car was killed and carried the state minimum required insurance, at that time $10,000, which didn't even come close to covering the medical bills. I don't think Jimmy had ever handled a plaintiff's case of this nature before and it showed.

We sued the state for not installing a median barrier to prevent crossover accidents. We also sued the other driver and her insurer hoping to hold the state liable for the whole as a joint tortfeasor, the law at the time, as there was no real insurance and she was deceased. We did our best to pressure a settlement, but as we moved forward, it became clear they would take the issue to court. And as we neared the court date, Jimmy's nerves started to get the better of him. He was not a trial lawyer, and I could sense that standing in front of a jury scared him to death.

On the day of the trial, Jimmy had to give an opening statement for the plaintiffs. There are limits placed on what an attorney can tell a jury, and in this case, one of the big ones was not to state the amount of insurance carried by the drunk driver. It's a huge "No-No" and would cause an immediate mistrial. Before we even got to the courthouse Jimmy was a nervous wreck.

In his opening statement, he looked at the jury, eyes wide and said, "Ladies and gentleman, this is a case on behalf of this family because on the date in question this intoxicated young lady crossed the center line on the Greater New Orleans Bridge and hit these people head-on, killing the husband, breaking the wife's hip, and paralyzing their young child.

"And the reason we are here is because the offending driver only had ten-thousand dollars' worth of insurance." Wait, what?

Everyone in the court room was thunderstruck. The attorneys for the insurance company immediately moved for a mistrial, and the judge granted it. We had invested a significant amount of money into this case as well as time. I have always wondered whether Jimmy really wanted a mistrial to get him off the hook because he was so nervous. I will never know. Our firm was fired. I learned right then that it took a different breed of cat to be a plaintiff's lawyer.

And me? I didn't know who I was supposed to be. I was a lawyer, but beyond that I didn't know what life was about other than getting drunk and continuing to seek my version of true love, whatever that was. My dad always said that you won't really know how things work until you reach age thirty. He also said that you cease to be embarrassed at age forty because you don't care what anyone else thinks. He was right. Again.

There was one good thing. For the first time in my life, I had a decent salary, so I bought the Trans Am of my dreams. Baby blue, T-top, 5.0 liter V-8. She was sweet. And I went on some epic drinking binges. There was the Bounty, Deanie's, Sportsman's Paradise, and others where I could sit and drink until they kicked me out at closing time. On Fridays and Saturdays, especially after football season, I didn't have anything else to do. There were times when I came into work late and hung-over. Jimmy would say, "Come on and get some coffee, then come into my office." I sat down with the coffee as Jimmy polished his shoes. "You went out last night?"

"Yeah."

And he'd kind of laugh. I'm not sure that he knew when I got started, I couldn't stop. I think he just ascribed it to youth and assumed I'd grow out of it.

At about the same time, I met this girl. She was from Opelousas, which is in southwest Louisiana, Cajun country and worked in the makeup department at D. H. Holmes, a fancy upscale department store. She was a Creole beauty and had an extravagant way about her. But she felt like she wasn't good enough for me. That surprised me because I often didn't feel I was good enough for most people, especially good looking women. We kind of dated for a bit. Several weeks passed without seeing too much of her, and I asked what was going on.

Her face flushed and her eyes wandered from mine. "I took a pregnancy test and it was positive."

My chest tightened. "You're pregnant?"

"No—"

"Then what—"

"I didn't want to upset you or hurt your career or anything so I got an abortion."

"You didn't say anything or even ask me what I thought?"

She started to cry. "No, I just thought it was the right thing to do."

I took her home, then drank until morning.

"Come into my office," Jimmy said when he saw me slink into the office in the early afternoon.

I sat down and he started polishing his shoes. "You were out drinking last night?"

"Yeah, but there was a reason."

"Well, out with it."

"This girl that I was dating found out she was pregnant and she went and had an abortion."

He stopped brushing the shoe in his hand. He was stunned. So was I. His eyes softened as he looked at me. "I can't believe that." We sat in silence for a moment. "I'm sorry. I don't think I'd have been able to come to work if it had happened to me. You okay?"

Among his quirks and personality traits, there was a gentlemanly sense of kindness within him. I'll never forget that.

#

The hot coal cases were big and complicated with multiple sides advocating for their interests in ways that made the whole thing a convoluted mess. But there I was in the middle of it, learning the difference between what my professors taught in law school and how real-world lawyers practiced law. The differences were stark, and I honed a set of legal skills I never knew existed. I often used that great legal maxim impressed on me by my mentor, "There's more than one way to skin a cat."

I also learned that alcohol and legal work go hand-in-hand if the work doesn't suffer. Just like school.

During the odyssey that was the coal cases, we traveled to Long Beach, California, to take depositions. We stayed a week and took the depositions in a conference room at our hotel. We'd work for the day, the length of which depended on the depth of inquiry for that person or entity we grilled under oath, then at night we went down to the bar for a few drinks then out to dinner. I was getting drunk just about every night.

The Coast Guard commandant took a few days to interview, and one night we got especially liquored up. I felt like crap that morning, my guess is the others did as well, so at lunch we ran down to the pool for a dip. We lost track of time and were about to race back to our rooms to change back into our work suits when one guy said, "Hey, the Coast Guard guy seems cool enough. Let's just go back and finish in our bathing suits."

The rest of us kind of shrugged and off we went. When we entered the deposition room, the Coast Guard commandant smiled. He didn't care that a bunch of New Orleans maritime lawyers came to depose him in their swimsuits. The only people who were put off were the two straight-laced guys from a defense firm that never went with us to dinner, much less swimming at lunch, which will just have to go unnamed.

"We want the record to reflect," one of them said, "that there are counsel that are inappropriately dressed at the deposition."

We couldn't have cared less. Neither did the commandant.

On our last night we decided to go up to Hollywood, but before we left, I got started with three 151 rum and tonics. I don't remember a thing from that night. Nothing.

The next morning when I woke up, I had that shaky feeling that I'd done something stupid. None of this was a new sensation. I pulled some clothes on and went down for breakfast, where I ran into one of the guys.

"I feel like warmed over dog crap," I said.

"Yeah, I can imagine."

"I don't remember a damn thing."

He cocked his head and looked at me. "You don't remember the ride down Sunset Boulevard in the convertible?"

"No, what did I do?"

He shook his head. "You don't want to know." I believe it must have been lunar in nature.

I didn't press him to tell me, and none of the other lawyers said anything. Some of these guys knew my family and others were up-and-coming lawyers at prominent law firms. It's one thing to toss a few back, but it's another to get blackout drunk and cross the line with your behavior. I was deeply embarrassed.

The writing on the wall was clear and unambiguous to everyone but me. My drinking and behavior when I drank was becoming progressively worse.

#

We had one other plaintiff's case, a knee injury to a seaman under the Jones Act. We were in settlement negotiations when late on a Friday afternoon, Jimmy received a call from the opposing counsel with an offer. The trial was set for the following Monday morning.

Jimmy's secretary answered the phone. "He is unavailable right now, may I take a message?" The other lawyer was a jackass. He said he would hold. She tried to get him off the line, but he wouldn't budge. "Do you know where Mr. Hanemann is?" she asked. "I think he's in the bathroom," I said.

There was a mid-office conference between his secretary, three lawyers, and a paralegal about whether we should breach the sanctity of the restroom to tell him the jackass, uh call, was holding. We flipped a coin. The paralegal lost. Into the bathroom he went coming out a bit shaken. "Jimmy's not happy."

A minute later, Jimmy came into the office area, looked at us, went into his office, and closed the door. A few minutes later he walked out of his office and announced, "I want a firm meeting, right now!"

The corners of his lips were a little crooked and his eyes narrow, but I could tell he was trying hard not to smile. With great aplomb he announced, "From now on this law firm's policy is that I am never to be disturbed when I'm in the bathroom taking a crap!" He looked at each one of us. "There are two exceptions. You can disturb me if they've pushed the button to launch nuclear missiles, or if the president has appointed me as a federal judge. That's all. Back to work." We all burst out laughing, including him. And the case had been settled, favorably.

It was a little while after that episode when our paralegal asked if I'd like to go out for dinner and drinks with him and his wife. It wasn't an unusual thing for us to go out—by now I knew that drinking in front of colleagues was a risk—but we did like to get together from time to time. Then he said, "We know this little place off Veterans Highway where there's a waitress you might be interested in."

I said yes and met her that night. I asked when she got off work and did my best impression of Joe Cool—you know, one of Snoopy's alter egos—and it sort of worked. She came over the next day, a Saturday. She'd brought a little bag for the night.

"Ooh, I want to go swimming in the pool," she said.

She darted into the bedroom and emerged wearing a leopard-skin print bathing suit that barely covered her. "Come on, Frank."

It was Saturday, I'd been out drinking Friday night, was drinking most of the day, and I just said, "No thanks." She frowned a bit and left for the pool. I watched from the balcony.

When she came back in, she was soaking wet. "Frank, let's go into the bedroom ..."

I took a sip off my drink. The LSU football game was playing on the radio, and it was a tight third-quarter. I hesitated. Decisions, decisions.

Her eyes narrowed. "Frank, come on."

"Alright."

We went into the bedroom, but, well, let's just say there were problems. And not with me. So I bailed. "I'd really rather just listen to the game now."

She didn't say anything, but I could tell I hurt her feelings. I turned up the radio and freshened up my drink. She sat in the bedroom for a few minutes, but when she emerged her clothes were on and her bag packed. "I'll see you later," and she left, for good. Que sera, sera.

The game ended, I can't remember who won, and I sat in my chair drinking until I passed out. When I woke the next morning, I was still in the chair drunk and hung-over at the same time. I made coffee, then fell back into the chair more or less in another world, thinking about my life. It was as if I led a double life. During most of the week, I was Frank the relatively reliable lawyer. On some weeknights and every weekend, I was Frank the hopeless drunk making a mess of every relationship and aspect of what it meant to be a human.

For some reason, maybe to go out and get a bloody Mary and breakfast, I got dressed and drove my Trans Am down Lake Avenue toward Veterans Highway. I was an emotional wreck, which my being drunk made worse. Next thing I knew, I plowed into the rear end of a car stopped at a traffic light.

I waited for the police with the woman whose car I hit, convinced that the cops would arrest me. Instead, they wrote me a ticket for careless operation and drove me home. The police towed the car to the dealership rather than the pound. I had insurance, and they settled with the woman for the limits on the policy. The police should have hauled me off to jail, but for whatever reason, I got a break. Maybe Someone was again trying to tell me something. Again. I guess I wasn't listening.

One night, when I was drinking most of the night in a bar off Veterans Highway, for some reason I decided I wanted fried chicken, so I got in my car and drove to a Popeye's Famous Fried Chicken with a drive-thru window. It was Saturday, and I'd been on my usual weekend bender and saw no reason to stop. I just needed a little fuel to keep going.

I pulled into the drive-thru, music cranked, drunk, and impatient for some chicken. The car in front of me wasn't going fast enough, so I eased up on them, and kissed my bumper against theirs. Then I hit the gas and pushed whoever it was forward past the window. Worked like a charm. I smiled at the girl taking orders, who looked like she didn't know whether to run or smile back and ask how she could help me. Hey, I was hungry.

Of course the people whose car I pushed didn't care for what I did and called the police. Good thing they didn't leap out of their car and beat the crap out of me. The police pulled into the parking lot, and I started spouting off some nonsense, I don't remember what. I don't think I even made any sense.

Well, they looked at me, then each other, and didn't arrest me. Under the watchful eyes of the two cops, I exchanged insurance information with the other driver while I waited for my order of two huge boxes of chicken, four orders of onion rings, biscuits, and everything else. I could have fed the family at one of Poppy's reunions at Saline Lake.

"Hey buddy," one of the cops said to me, "there's no way you can drive. Is there anyone you can call to pick you up?"

I called a friend of mine who lived in the same apartment complex, and he came with his girlfriend. I rode with him, and she drove my car home.

The next morning I woke up with the usual blinding hang-over, and there was chicken all over my apartment. And biscuits. And onion rings. "Hey, I don't know what the hell happened last night," I said to the same friend on the phone. "There's chicken all over the place."

"Man, we came back and partied down by the pool, and you just kept walking around saying, 'Hey man, you want some chicken?' You had so much chicken you didn't know what to do with it." Hmmm...well, I said, "Do you want some chicken or not? Cause I've still got plenty!"

Then in the midst of being a progressively bigger drunk, I found my way to another woman I couldn't have. This one was pure gold.

I'm not sure why, but after the failed attempt with the waitress, the paralegal's wife said she had another girl she thought I'd be interested in. She was blond with high cheekbones, sort of a Farrah Fawcett look, which was my poison as far as women went, and tall with a full figure. She also had a young son from a previous relationship and, guess what, she tended bar. A match made in heaven if I ever saw one. I agreed to meet and immediately developed my usual infatuation. It was pretty much the beginning of the end for me.

In the fall of 1984, a partner at one of the defense firms involved in the hot coal cases called me and asked if I wanted to come to work for them. Apparently, they liked my work. I thought about the offer for a bit and worried that Jimmy would see leaving as an act of disloyalty. After all, if I'd worked for any of the other firms in the coal cases, I would have been a junior attorney doing research with little if any profile. But Jimmy believed in me, gave me significant responsibilities—especially for such a new and inexperienced lawyer.

In the end I said yes. This was the chance to work for a much bigger firm, and by then I was ready to make the move. And it was more money. I didn't say that?

I went to the interview and got the "offer" such as it was. "We will pay you XXX dollars, now all you need to do is go resign. Don't worry, we do this with everyone who already has a job." When I got back to the office I found Jimmy in the little pantry where we made coffee and so on and said, "Um, well, I'm leaving and I'm giving you my two-week's notice." To me this was no different than giving notice at West Esplanade Shell or my offshore jobs, but the look on Jimmy's face told me this was a bigger deal.

"Come into my office."

I made the mistake of going into his office.

"Look, I know how these things work. They make you come in and resign your position before they actually make you an official offer."

My face flushed. This was not supposed to be this difficult. He looked up at me and stopped shining one of his shoes for a moment. "Who hired you?"

"Well, I don't need to tell you that. It's none of your business."

"Oh, it makes a difference."

"I don't think it makes any difference."

"It does."

"All right." I told him. I didn't have anything to hide. It was his old firm. He smiled. "I figured that's who it was."

And they represented the time charterers in one of the hot coal cases. Theoretically this could be a conflict of interest—a lawyer can't work for two competing parties in litigation—but even so, I could just not work on that case. These things were usually worked out.

But Jimmy wasn't going to make things easy. He filed a motion to recuse his old firm from the case because of the alleged conflict of interest. And it hit the fan. The senior partners got involved. It was a mess. And the "offer" was put on hold. I guess technically there was no conflict as I never formally took the job. So I was just swinging in the wind, a man without a country. Or a job.

To say the least, the situation worried me, but it also gave me time to think. In particular, I wasn't all that enamored with defense work. This wasn't standing up for the little guy who was wrongly accused of some crime or foul, but defending large, wealthy corporations from the all-too-often little guys they hurt.

We had one case with a guy working offshore who was injured by a crane operator when he set a load down on him. The lawyer that represented him just didn't know what he was doing. He fired out pleadings and paperwork randomly, and I never knew what was coming next. The practice of law attempts to be orderly and predictable, but this lawyer was neither. When it came time to take the crane operator's deposition—we defended the company he worked for—the injured guy's lawyer didn't bother to ask the crane operator if he had ever been fired before or involved in any other accidents. This is basic law 101 stuff.

We knew the operator had hurt other guys, been run off other jobs, and cited for safety violations. Because I represented the company, I couldn't say a word of any of this. And he wouldn't either, unless asked the right question.

We offered to settle the case, but the other attorney turned it down. The case went to trial and we zeroed the plaintiff. He recovered nothing, nada, zero. The other lawyer was so incompetent that the judge ordered a new trial. With a better lawyer we reached a settlement. Just think how a lawyer could do representing injured workers if he actually knew what he was doing.

About the same time of my legal limbo, I went golfing with Dad and one of the lawyers I worked with. I was drinking as we worked our way around the course and went on a rant about how defendants (a.k.a. wealthy corporations and their insurers) cover up evidence, lie, and pull all sorts of stunts to avoid accountability to people who get hurt.

"You know, with all these companies all it means to them is a dollar," I said, "and there are real human beings getting hurt. I talk to these insurance adjusters, and it's all about is money, and they don't give a damn about the working guy who gets hurt."

As general counsel for an oil company, I'd just unwittingly described what I thought of my dad's job. It was unfair. My dad had been around the block a few times, and he always took the human side into account. I'd forgotten this, but my friend hadn't. He was pissed at my disrespect.

"Frank, listen to me. Your dad is one of the best men I know. You've got no right to stand out here like you are disrespecting him, no right."

Anger burned from his eyes, but Dad had an expression of equanimity. I may have hurt him, but he was cool and patient as he always was with me. "It's all right," he said. "He's just blowing off a little steam."

To resolve the motion to recuse, there was a big conference with the federal judge handling the case. All the lawyers attended, including me because the judge ordered me to appear.

I sat in the judge's office, which was adjacent to the conference room. I felt like I was waiting outside the principal's office or for Dad to come home after I did something stupid, but worse. My career and reputation were on the line.

At one point the door opened as a guy walked out of the room and I heard the judge say, "I don't care if I ever hear his name again!"

That's it, I thought, *I'm never going to practice law in this city again, ever.*

After about an hour they came out with a deal. They agreed I could go to work without the firm having to recuse itself if I didn't work in the maritime and admiralty law section of the firm. I couldn't even speak to the lawyers until the case was over. Instead, they put me in the business section beneath a senior attorney that looked like Doc Brown from "Back to the Future," but with more outlandish hair and round glasses. He was a nice guy and brilliant, but I knew nothing about the type of cases he was handling.

They stuck me in an office—which was huge—about as removed from anybody as I could be. While I was getting the biggest paycheck of my life, nobody seemed to notice or seemed to care if I come in four days a week or five. On top of it all I was disillusioned with defense work and forced to practice outside my area of expertise. I was miserable. But my circumstances were just an excuse. I was a drunk in love with a bartender.

I could not get her out of my mind, and I believed, rightly or wrongly, that if only she would fall in love with me, all would be right with the world. Unfortunately, she liked me just enough to follow her around like a puppy dog. She was nice, funny, flirted all the time, I drove her to work, helped with her son, bought her furniture for her house, lent her money, and helped her get a car. And yet she didn't want to get romantically involved with me, which makes me the idiot.

And, I was drinking, a lot. I would play the how-much-sleep-do-I-really-need and how-hung-over-can-I-be-for-work game. I'd drive her to work, sit at the bar ogling her, and drink with the rest of the guys who liked both the booze and the way she looked. I'd promise myself I would leave at ten and be home in bed by eleven. As ten approached, I'd leave at eleven and in bed by midnight. As I rationalized sitting at the bar all night, I'd weigh the inverse relationship between how late I drank and how hung-over I'd be the next morning. By the time the clock struck two or three in the morning I'd start rationalizing in reverse: I could be an hour late followed by two hours, three hours, and finally they won't miss me.

The alarm would go off at the same time it always did but I'd turn it off and sleep until noon. If I was up to it I got dressed and went to work, but as often as not I called in sick.

As 1984 faded into 1985, I was doing a lot of drinking, and I was in love. Unfortunately, I was the only one. Both she and her son came one night to my parents' house for dinner. When I was in the kitchen with Mom she asked, "Do you ever date anyone that doesn't have a kid?"

"Well, it's not like I'm sleeping with her or anything." Which was true.

Mom and Dad were polite, but I'm sure they thought, Here we go again.

I knew she was using me. And I didn't care. Kind of like Oscar Wilde says, "The only thing worse than being talked about, is not being talked about." The only thing worse than getting your ego stroked is not getting your ego stroked. I was one sick puppy.

On one of her nights off we went to The Bounty to see a band play. She drank tequila shots, among other things, and got messy drunk. At about five in the morning, I loaded her into my car to take her home, but she passed out on the way so I brought her to my house.

We pulled up in front, and running through my head was something her friend had said. "You know, why not one night when she gets really bombed just bang her and then you'll get it over with."

What the hell kind of friend are you? I thought. "I don't want to do that. I want it to be the real deal." And these days it would be called rape, which it is. While deep down I may be a sensual insect, I could still make Dimitri Pavlovitch proud and do the honorable thing.

In my driveway, the first light of morning was glowing on the eastern horizon. When I opened the car door, she just sort of poured out into the front yard. I tried to pick her up but she folded in half. I was afraid the neighbors were all looking out their windows, wondering what the hell was going on. It wasn't far from the yard to the front door, so after an internal debate, I just grabbed her by the ankles and dragged her across the front yard, up the porch, and into the foyer. I hoped the neighbors didn't think I had a body or something.

I went to the bathroom and came back to find she'd thrown up. There was green tequila vomit all over the floor. *Great.* I got a few paper towels and cleaned her up as well as I could. As I stood and looked at her passed out on the floor, I gave up. True love was never going to be in the cards for me.

I sprayed her down with a can of Lysol and went to bed. When I woke up she was gone.

One thing about being an alcoholic, behavior is a difficult thing to change. Despite my epiphany, I still wanted and obsessed over her, which led to some uncomfortable interactions. The longer I sat at the bar and drank, the harder it was to watch her flirt with other men. This was part of the shtick of being a barmaid. She'd flirt with the old men to get them—get us—to buy more drinks, give bigger tips, and buy her drinks, which we would gladly do.

But I hated watching her sweeten up the other guys, and the drunker I got, the more it pissed me off until I mouthed off to her. "You don't own me and it's not like we're going out or anything," she said to me more than once. Other times she said, "Man, once you get going, you can't stop." That was her way of telling me I was in a sick condition.

Sometimes my anger and jealousy led to fights, which led to me being bounced out of the bar. Finally, the owner said he'd had enough. As I walked into the bar on a Friday night, he grabbed my arm and said, "Look, you can come in here, but you can't drink."

This wasn't the first place that had kicked me out. Many other places had already banned me for getting drunk and picking fights with the biggest guy in the bar. Most of the time, once I got the guy riled up, I talked my way out of it, and we'd end up spending the rest of the night drinking. It was recreational in nature. It was a game to me, but who wants that kind of crap in their bar? No one.

During the day when I made it to my job, I also worked for one of the firm's other partners in the business division. We had a case that involved some damage to tanks at a refinery, several of them. Each was a separate claim.

The partner I worked for wanted a colored folder for each of these cases. We started with red, blue, green, orange, and so on. As we kept going we had fuchsia, pink, chartreuse, you name it. Finally, we ran out of colors.

"Look, I'm sorry but you could buy the biggest box of crayons, and we still wouldn't have enough colors for this." The whole thing was driving me nuts. "I know you want all these different colors, but, I mean it really is kind of stupid. Can't we just number them?"

That didn't go over well. But that wasn't the clincher. I was thoroughly confused and disillusioned. I knew that I had emotional issues with this girl, and for the first time I admitted to myself that I might have a drinking problem. *Might*, mind you. I needed help.

I had always been truthful with people. Always will be. So I decided to just go to the partner working on the tank damage cases and tell him the truth. I told him that I was having women problems and that I thought that I had a drinking problem. I was going to get help. I will never forget his response. After thanking me for telling him the truth about what was going on, he looked at me and smiled, "Don't worry, we are not vindictive people."

The next week, a partners' meeting was held. On Good Friday, Doc Brown called me into his office. "You need to resign." I knew what it meant.

"What if I don't?"

"If you don't, you're going to be fired."

I didn't know what to do. I said, "Okay," and just walked out of his office. I don't think I waited more than five minutes to call Dad. "I just got fired."

"You're kidding."

"No, it's sort of a don't-let-the-door-hit-you-in-the-ass situation."

"Wow."

"Yeah, he said I either resign or they're going to fire me."

Before this, Dad and I had gotten together more than a few times for lunch, including when I worked for Jimmy, and he knew my drinking was causing problems. Several times he asked, "Why don't you try just having two drinks then calling it a night?"

Who does that? I mean, really, who does that? "Okay, I'll try."

"Maybe you just shouldn't drink." Not what I wanted to hear. Then my dad asked if remembered a friend of his— the one who got the Notre Dame tickets where I made a drunken scene in front of my Notre Dame alum law school professor.

"Yeah, I do."

"He goes to a recovery group. He's a great guy, and one of the best lawyers I know, but he was a mess when he drank. He'd do stuff when he drank and he'd wake up in Taiwan or Singapore or some other place overseas and have no idea how the heck he got there or why he was there. Maybe you ought to try to quit, too."

"Maybe. I'll think about it."

But on that Good Friday he sounded worried. "Don't do anything rash." I guess he thought I might try to hurt myself or do something stupid. "Come over for Easter and I'll see you then."

I went across the Lake to my parents' house in Covington and arrived happy to that see my older sister and her family were visiting from their new home in Columbia, South Carolina. They'd recently moved after her husband found a new job there. With them was my nephew who was about four years old. I settled into "The chair where Uncle Frank lives."

When I sat alone and drank, it was like entering an alternate universe where I could wallow in alcohol and the hopeless pain of romances that went astray. I was too dumb and stupid to see that a moody, often angry, cigarette-smoking guy in tortoiseshell glasses, who was a sloppy drunk didn't make an attractive prospect. I had the law degree and that was it.

That Easter I kept it together enough to enjoy seeing Lee and her family, and in a quiet moment Dad and I talked. The gist of it was that maybe I should think about getting help. I knew I needed to do something.

Chapter Eight

Coincidence?

Think about it, there must be higher love
Down in the heart or hidden in the stars above
Without it, life is a wasted time [22]

—"HIGHER LOVE," STEVE WINWOOD

One of the signs and symptoms of alcoholism, especially when the disease has progressed, is a susceptibility to moments of grandiose thinking. After being fired, I was a man without a country. A lost sailor, set adrift in a too-large boat with a too-small paddle, seeking his North Star. I knew I wouldn't be able to find much defense work and good riddance. Who wants to be a corporate stooge sticking it to the little guy? I'll just do something else, something big and heroic, or so I thought.

And then in drunken despair, when the grandiose thinking gave way to depression, loneliness, and truth, I didn't know what to do or what I could do. As far as I knew, I was now a pariah of the New Orleans legal community. I was ready to return to work offshore.

I talked with Dad and he said, "You can always do paralegal work or insurance work or something. There's a lot you can do. You can find a job and make a living you know." The subtext that I heard as he spoke was that my law career ended when they fired me, though maybe that isn't what he meant, just what I heard.

It was spring of 1985, and without a job I drank and stewed and fell deeper into the hole I was digging. In the afternoon, I'd pick her and her kid up and drop him off at the babysitter's, then drop her off at work. I couldn't go in without the owner bouncing me out of there, so I'd go home and drink or go to another bar. Around two-in-the-morning I'd pick her up and we'd go to a bar which was open 24/7. This is where all the waiters and bartenders and cooks and so on would go when they got off work. The sun would come up, and we would go get her kid, I would drop them off, then go home and pass out.

What I didn't know was that coal case was still chugging along and causing problems. Actually, Jimmy was causing problems. He sent the Chinese underwriters a bill that they refused to pay.

"Well, then," he said (of course, I heard this second hand), "I'm not going to work for you."

So, he withdrew and sued the Chinese for his fees. And just by coincidence they hired a lawyer that I knew from my college days at LSU. He settled the fee dispute and then took over the remaining coal cases.

Walter is a bit older than me, was the president of Fiji before I was an underclassman, and he left the firm from which I was dismissed way before me and the coal cases to start his own firm. He was partnered doing plaintiff's work with another LSU graduate from New Iberia, who had also been routed through a large defense firm. Beyond our brief and casual acquaintance at LSU, we met at a Tulane/LSU football game, where Fiji alumni ended up partying in their hotel suite after the game. They were foolish enough to let word get around that they were having an LSU/Tulane party, and a gang of us barreled our way in.

Walter is as smart as a whip. In high school he was on *Prep Quiz Bowl*, a televised quiz show for teams of high school students, and in college and law school he earned just about every honor there was. As a lawyer for the big maritime defense firm and then on his own, he'd earned a topnotch reputation. And he is a political animal.

On top of all that, his Dad was a Bar Pilot (compulsory pilots who captain ships from the Gulf up the Mississippi and are paid very well), and his grandfather a ship's captain. Maritime law flows in his blood.

When he interviewed for his first legal job, the dry witted partner inquired, "So, your dad is a Bar Pilot?"

"Yes, Sir."

"And you want to practice maritime law instead?"

"Yes, Sir!"

He put down his folder and frowned. "Sorry, we only hire smart people around here." He was just kidding of course.

Walter called and told me he had boxes of documents from the coal cases sitting in his office. "You were involved in the coal cases, and I noticed you took a lot of the depositions. Do you want to come over just on an hourly basis and work on these cases?"

I didn't have to think for even a second. "Yeah I do, but wouldn't there be some sort of conflict?"

"I checked with the Chinese, and they will waive it."

"When do I start?"

I was back to balancing my drinking and work life, but I committed to making it work.

A few days later, I walked into Walter's office on the ninth floor of the old Barnett Furniture building. It was a beautiful office, and when Walter saw me, he said, "We need a place for you to sit and a desk. Let's go out and buy a desk." He took me to Hansell-Petetin and paid for a nice, sturdy, lawyer's desk.

As we walked back up to the office, he turned to me and said, "You know, the best thing that ever happened to you was leaving that firm. You might think it's the worst thing that ever happened to you, but it's the best thing that ever happened to you. Some of the best lawyers I know used to work there. Including me."

Then Walter told me how he left. He and a couple other lawyers decided they would leave their respective firms and form their own firm. They agreed to give notice on Good Friday, so Walter went to the partner he worked for and said he's leaving with these other guys to form their own firm.

The other guys did the same at their firm on the same day. Once word got out though, their firm launched a full-court press to keep them. This culminated in an Easter Sunday meeting with one of Walter's partners-to-be and his half-brother, who was also his partner.

Monday morning they called Walter. "We're not leaving."

"What? I already went in and told them."

"Sorry."

Walter explained the situation. The partner Walter worked for looked at him. "No, that's all right. Stay, if you want."

Walter knew he could be believed and trusted. But he had other doubts.

"Do you think the other partners would hold it against me?"

"What do you think?"

He thought for a moment. "I can't take that chance. I'm leaving." And he did starting his own firm focusing on plaintiff's work. After a short while he brought in Mike from his LSU and Tulane law school days—the two were sharp students and not afraid of a little trouble.

I started working through the boxes of depositions and documents related to the coal cases and a few days later met Dad for lunch. "Look," he said. "You are getting a second chance. You really should watch your drinking."

I knew he was right, but resolve on my own and try as I might, I just could not stop once I started drinking. And my obsession with the barmaid didn't help. My ego needed stroking. The drinking and irrational emotional thinking were tied together, but I didn't know that then. So during the week, I'd tell myself, "I'm not going to drink today, I'm not going to drink today ..." and I would make it through the week white-knuckling it until the weekend. This lasted from May or June of 1985 through Christmas. Weekends were another story. And of course, I had to go on vacation, right?

In late summer of '85, the barmaid and I took a trip to Cancun, Mexico. I should have died. First, the chartered plane had mechanical problems, so we had to sit for hours in the New Orleans airport and wait for repairs. All there was to do was drink. Then I drank on the plane, in Cancun, and had a faint recollection of a Tequila gun that ran the length of some bar. Just pull the trigger and fire a tequila shot into the mouth of some lucky, or unlucky soul at the end of the barrel. Which was apparently me.

Night turned to morning and a day on the beach with little umbrellas and volleyball all day long. The movie *Top Gun* was out so we were into it, but the next day I should have died from alcohol poisoning. We found a boat to go to Cozumel snorkeling and I drank every orange, purple, cola, you name it, Mexican soft drink I could find. I was sunburned, dehydrated, and delirious. The ferry back was so packed with people and animals that it was a floating news story just waiting to capsize. And I wouldn't have cared. I made it back alive. Broke, but alive.

In August of 1985, Walter asked me to come to his office. "Look, Mike and I have worked up a compensation formula for you to work here on a full-time basis as an associate lawyer."

I made it, I thought. Then I heard the formula. I got a base salary of thirty thousand dollars, but out of that they deducted my overhead, which included a legal secretary, phone service, rent, paperclips, etc. Beyond my salary and overhead, I'd get a percentage fee for the cases I worked on. And that incentive did it for me. Nothing like a good carrot. And I was hungry.

The fee percentage was the same to me whether I brought in the case or not. But because firm cases usually meant another lawyer's involvement, for which he got some credit, the fastest way for me to earn any significant money was to bring in my own work. As Walter said, "You eat what you kill." Then again, he also said that I needed to "justify my existence." That was harsh, man. But true.

It was nice to have a little freedom and responsibility handling my own cases. The firm also began to grow as our work expanded. Within a few months, we hired two clerks. With an actual office of two partners, an associate lawyer, two clerks, and a handful of legal secretaries, Walter decided it would be a good thing to have an office Christmas party. For me this was a worlds-colliding moment.

We loaded into a limousine bus and drank our butts off as we rode around New Orleans. Mike and Walter wore pirate hats with patches over an eye, and I joined in with the craziness. We went across the lake to Annadele's Plantation for a big Christmas dinner, and then went past Covington and stopped by Mom and Dad's for a quick how-ya-doin', followed by a Men's Club, and then the French Quarter at Pat O'Brien's.

When we got to Pat O'Brien's, I was blackout-drunk. The next Monday, Walter pulled me aside. "What were you doing at the party?"

"What?"

"A friend of mine came up to me at O'Brien's and said, 'Hey, do you know this guy?'"

I was wearing an overcoat, walking around like the dirty old man played by Arte Johnson on *Laugh-In* and going up to women and asking, "Tickle your ass with a feather? Ha, ha, ha ..."

"It's the punchline to a joke," I said.

He told me I was also using my old college pickup line: "Wanna go out for a pizza and a screw?" It worked maybe once out of a hundred times. Well, not really.

I would feign surprise. "What's the matter, you don't like pizza?"

"Do you remember I had to get you out of there because of that?"

I didn't.

Then Christmas came. I like Christmas, and as my life was spinning out of control, it offered a moment of peace, of remembering family and what it was like to be a kid when I believed that life had a certain purity to it. On Christmas Eve, I was driving the barmaid to work, "Silent Night" was on the radio, and I was overcome with a warmth that emanated from my heart.

I looked at her, then back to the road. "You know, it's times like this at Christmas when I think there is hope for the world after all."

She looked at me like I was out of my mind.

I tried to straighten up my act, but I just couldn't. During the week I was okay mostly. But Friday would hit, and I'd tell myself I was going to stay out for a while and then go home at a reasonable hour, like a normal person. After a couple of drinks, I was like Don Birnam in *The Lost Weekend*. Saturday morning came, the sunrise breaking over the eastern horizon, and I was drinking screwdrivers for breakfast. Then I crashed for four or five hours, got up, nursed my hang-over for a bit and started the whole thing again.

I'd spend Sunday wondering what in the world happened. If I was across the lake at Mom and Dad's, it was just as bad with me passing out in the chair where Uncle Frank lives.

Then there was the night on Bourbon Street with the frat guys. We had been at Pat O's, and I was drinking *Pete Specials* made with crystal clear liquor. I lost count at five, and walking down the street, I realized I couldn't feel my legs. I was leaning against a light pole holding it up, when a woman of the night approached, grabbed the end of my belt, shoved her hand down my pants, and commenced to proposition me. I was anesthetized. All I could do was call for help. "Help! Help!" A pitiful sight. And a comical one at that. My buddies were across the street rolling in laughter. When it became clear I wasn't going to pay, she gave up.

Toward the end, I had been "banned" from most bars. The Swamp Room was last on my list, but that didn't last long. One night I put ten dollars worth of quarters in the juke box and played "The Asshole" song twenty times. You know the song, "Were you born an asshole? Or did you work at it your whole life? Either way it worked out fine, 'cause you're an asshole tonight."[23] After playing ten times, the bartender walked over to the juke box and jerked the plug out of the wall. He only had one word for me, "Asshole!"

If you've ever wondered how a guy with a good career and money ends up drinking in low life bars, this is it. I was running out of places that would let me walk through the door, because once I got started I got balls-out drunk, and at some point I'd piss people off enough to get tossed for good.

One Friday evening when I was trying to stay sober, I went to my Trans Am parked behind the office and it was gone. Vanished. I checked with the security guard. It hadn't been towed. I laughed at the only logical conclusion because I just couldn't believe it. It had been stolen. I called the police and filed a report.

The next morning the phone rang. It was NOPD to advise that my car had been found in New Orleans East and to respectfully ask me if I could come and identify the remains.

The thieves stripped the car bare. The yard man smiled. "You want to tow it somewhere? Or just take a check for the salvage?" I was despondent because I carried only the minimum required liability insurance on the car having canceled the comp and collision. I just couldn't afford it with my driving record. I was without wheels. What was I going to do?

I went that Sunday afternoon to the local Dodge dealership with the salvage check and found a used Dodge 600 K car that maybe, just maybe, I could afford if they would finance it. I didn't want to call Dad to co-sign but would if necessary. Then the most amazing thing happened.

I took the car for a test drive. Turning back into the dealership with the salesman, I heard the squeal of brakes, a loud boom, and the salesman and I were shot out of a cannon. We had been rear ended, big time.

The dealership said they would deduct thousands off the purchase price once repairs were made because the car had been wrecked. The next day I felt like someone had injected Novocain into the middle of my neck. The phone rang, and an insurance adjuster offered me three thousand dollars for my injury. I grabbed it, then called the salesman and got him three thousand and took a one-third contingency fee. The price of the car had been magically reduced by over half. Pretty cool. Maybe Someone was looking out for me after all.

The barmaid and I managed to maintain a sickly symbiotic relationship. I obsessed over her, raged at her flirting with the other drunks, and got tossed out of bars. She ignored my romantic desires, used me for rides, money, booze, and anything else I could make available to her. She was, in the vernacular of the time, *A Material Girl*. Periodically, I'd tell myself I'd had enough and vow never to let her use me for anything again, but like the good, inebriated drunk I was, it never lasted.

Then a friend of hers came over from Florida for a visit. Normally she'd party with us, find some guy with a pile of cocaine, and disappear for a week. This time we partied, but she had tickets to a Stevie Nicks concert in Gulfport, Mississippi, and like a good boy I let myself get talked into driving.

We left around noon on Saturday, got drunk, saw the show, and then spent more than an hour searching for my car in the vast field that was the parking lot. Settled in the car, she then whined, "I need to see my parents over in Florida. It's not far."

I'm not sure how many last straws I had, but I muttered something about this being the last time. We headed off to a place three hours away in the northern part of the Panhandle. We got to the trailer house her parents lived in at about four in the morning, slept for a few hours, and woke to her mother making us breakfast. We ate and then she said, "Okay, I'm ready to go back home."

My head ached. I was hung down big time. But I drove the five hours back to New Orleans. On the way home I said to myself, *Self, this is b*ll sh*t. I'm not going to be used like this anymore.* Though I'd said this many times before, I kind of meant it this time.

#

In the spring of 1986, I woke up hung-over to the phone ringing and ringing. "Hello?"

It was Walter. "I've been trying to reach you to find out where the hell you are and why you're not at work. Do you know what time it is?"

I looked at my clock. "It's noon. I'm sorry Walter. I'm not feeling well, but I'll be in in a minute."

When I got to work, Walter and Mike called me into Walter's office. "Look, this is your last chance"—missing work was still part of my routine— "We know you went out drinking and that's why you didn't come in this morning or any of the other mornings you disappear on us. What if you missed a court deadline for us? How the hell would that look? What would it say about the firm? We can't have it, we just can't."

"I'm sorry, Walter. If I had court, I would never do this. You know that."

"Well, this is your last chance. Either you do something, or we're going to have to act."

"Okay, it won't happen again."

#

Trying to stay sober was like a dishonest toddler learning to walk. "Did you fall?" "Hell no!"

I drank intermittently, and when I did, heavily. And though the shine had worn off with the barmaid, I wasn't quite all the way done with her, yet. It was during one of these not-quite-done, dishonest-drunken-toddler moments that I woke up Saturday morning to the phone repeatedly ringing.

At the time, the firm was representing some switchmen and other employees in a labor dispute during the divestiture of AT&T. These guys believed the company wrongfully terminated their jobs. The case was brought to us by a New Orleans city councilman, and we were suing on behalf of our clients in federal court. We had a meeting scheduled with the switchmen—that Saturday morning. Why did it have to be on a weekend?

I picked up the phone. "Well, where were you?"

"Walter, I'm sorry."

"My office, Monday morning."

Later I learned that Walter spoke with a psychiatrist about me. "Look," he said to Walter, "if you guys aren't really going to let him know that this is it, then you're just enabling him and you're not helping. If he comes in late or oversleeps, or whatever, you have to lay it down for him. No more excuses."

Monday morning, Walter called me into his office where he and Mike were waiting for me. His body, usually relaxed and easy going, was stiff and closed. "This is the last time. If you mess around and do this again and don't come in, you're fired—"

"I'm sorry."

"—and I will destroy you and make sure you never work in this town as a lawyer again. Ever! I mean it!" He was pissed. And I was scared to death. He meant it. Every word.

Years later, Walter told me he felt horrible doing that. After I had left his office, Mike told him he was harsh. Walter replied, "Yeah, I feel bad for being a jerk, because I like Frank, but I had to draw a clear line for him."

Hearing Walter say he would end my career was like a bomb going off. I considered him a friend and mentor. I looked up to him, so to hear him say he would destroy me, well, he had to be pissed and at the end of his rope. I was at the end of mine. The barmaid was another failed fixation, and because my free time was generally consumed with drinking, there wasn't much else. Friends had fallen by the wayside or reached a point where they were fed up with me and moved on with their lives.

I was stuck in a state of suspended maturation. I was neither growing nor moving my life toward any larger goal than getting through the next day. Alcohol consumed everything, and made me blind to the larger world that existed beyond my own selfish desires. I was so blind that after Walter's threat, all I could think was, *What's the point? I mean, seriously, if this is it, what's the point?*

I'd made money, tried wine, women, and song, but what's the point to it all if in the end all I do is make myself and everyone who knows me miserable? *If this is all there is,* I wondered, *and it's all fleeting and meaningless, maybe I ought to just stop fighting, let alcohol take me, and checkout because, what's the point?*

Thank God for Mom and Dad.

I met Dad for lunch at Kolb's and told him what happened. Dad was angry about it, unusually angry it seemed. What I didn't know is that Walter already spoke to Dad.

"Frank, you need to do something and go to a recovery group. That's it. There's no choice."

"I am." I was defeated. Either I got busy trying recovery, or I got busy slowly dying from alcoholism.

"This isn't going to go away on its own, you know, so maybe it's time to reach out for some help. You could speak to Pastor Malsbary down at the church."

"Okay, I'll talk to Pastor Malsbary." It had never occurred to me to seek out our church or faith for answers. It wasn't that I'd given up on faith, I believed in God, but I saw God as a passive force, if anything at all, and church as something I did with family on Christmas and Easter. (Yes, I was a *Cheaster.*) The rest of the time, Sunday morning was too valuable for giving it up for church.

Reverend Malsbary was the pastor who came to our house so many years ago and sat with Dad and a glass of scotch for the evening. It felt like that one conversation was enough to get Dad back into the rhythm of church, but I'm sure there was more to it than that. Since then, Reverend Malsbary was a friend and something of a guiding light. Dad found comfort with him and in his faith, and he wanted to share that with me.

When they first connected, the church was a smaller building, just in its first years, surrounded by empty lots and a crushed-shell parking area. When I went to meet with Reverend Malsbary, the church was larger, almost beautiful in its design, and landscaping and the area around it was in the process of being built up. In fact, Dad had served as an Elder. There was an elder on the Session with him, last name was Berry. Elder Berry.

I sat with my hands folded in my lap, unable to look Reverend Malsbary in the eye. "I'm having this problem." Then I explained the drinking and the barmaid and that there was a history behind both. Neither was new behavior. "What do you suggest?"

He was quiet for a moment, perhaps letting some of the emotion ease. "We have Alcoholics Anonymous meetings here at the church."

I looked away.

"But maybe you ought to go see a counselor about why you have all these feelings and why you drink so much. You seem kind of confused." He paused again to gauge my reaction. "He's a pastoral counselor, which means he's an ordained minister, and he's got a doctorate in psychology from Princeton."

Afterward, I called Dad and told him what he said.

"You going to go?" he asked.

"Yeah, I think so."

"Well, don't worry about the cost. I'll pay for the appointment."

And so, a day or so later, I was sitting in his office. He was a laid-back guy who looked like the dad from *Calvin & Hobbes* with dark hair, tall, glasses, and a congenial personality. In the waiting room, there were these little pamphlets, "Are You an Alcoholic?" with test questions. I could only pass if I cheated. Not good.

"Tell me, what's going on?"

I did something of an emotional brain dump of everything. Drinking, chasing the barmaid, the firing, Walter's ultimatum, anxiety, depression, the feeling that my life was off the rails and that I didn't know how to deal with any of it other than to try and drink it away because that's the only thing that stopped the world from spinning too fast. I laid it all out and then said, "You know, the world is just totally against me." My focus was completely outward.

He looked at me, and there was the tiniest hint of a smile in his lips and eyes. Not an uncaring sort of expression, far from it. More like he saw through me. "You know what your problem is?"

By now I was totally worked up and that little hint of a smile didn't help my mood either. "No. That's what my Dad is paying you fifty dollars an hour to tell me. What is my problem?" My voice was raised.

"Your problem is, you don't know what your problem is."

"What the hell are you talking about?"

He leaned forward in his chair. "Why don't you do this? Next time you go out, I want you to have two drinks and just stop."

"You gotta be kidding me. Why would I do that?"

"Can you do it?"

I knew I couldn't just have two, but said, "Okay, I can do that."

I went out that night, a Friday, making darn sure that I had no work the next day, had two drinks, then proceeded to get plastered.

The next week I went back.

"Did you try what I said?"

"Yeah."

"How did it work out?"

"How do you think it worked out? I got bombed."

"So, you can't control the amount you drink once you start?"

"No."

"Maybe you ought to go to a meeting?"

At John Calvin Presbyterian Church, they had AA meetings on Tuesday and Thursday nights. At the Tuesday night's meeting, there was a professional athlete who had started a young people's meeting. I was twenty-nine years old, I still felt pretty young, so I went.

It was in the preschool room, so the chairs were made for little kids, and we sat with our knees up to our chests looking foolish. In my mind, I may have failed the two-drinks test, but I wasn't ready to give up yet. I went to the meeting to prove I didn't need to go to the meeting.

It is read before every meeting and I will never forget the first time I heard it. *How It Works* from pages 59-60 of the *Big Book Alcoholics Anonymous*:

> Rarely have we seen a person fail who has thoroughly followed our path. Those who do not recover are people who cannot or will not completely give themselves to this simple program, usually men and women who are constitutionally incapable of being honest with themselves. There are such unfortunates. They are not at fault; they seem to have been born that way. They are naturally incapable of grasping and developing a manner of living which demands rigorous honesty. Their chances are less than average. There are those, too, who suffer from grave emotional and mental disorders, but many of them do recover if they have the capacity to be honest.

Our stories disclose in a general way what we used to be like, what happened, and what we are like now. If you have decided you want what we have and are willing to go to any length to get it, then you are ready to take certain steps.

At some of these we balked. We thought we could find an easier, softer way. But we could not. With all the earnestness at our command, we beg of you to be fearless and thorough from the very start. Some of us have tried to hold on to our old ideas and the result was nil until we let go absolutely.

Remember that we deal with alcohol—cunning, baffling, powerful! Without help it is too much for us. But there is One who has all power—that One is God. May you find Him now!

Half measures availed us nothing. We stood at the turning point. We asked His protection and care with complete abandon.

Here are the steps we took, which are suggested as a program of recovery:

1. We admitted we were powerless over alcohol—that our lives had become unmanageable.

2. Came to believe that a Power greater than ourselves could restore us to sanity.

3. Made a decision to turn our will and our lives over to the care of God as we understood Him.

4. Made a searching and fearless moral inventory of ourselves.

5. Admitted to God, to ourselves, and to another human being the exact nature of our wrongs.

6. Were entirely ready to have God remove all these defects of character.

7. Humbly asked Him to remove our shortcomings.

8. Made a list of all persons we had harmed, and became willing to make amends to them all.

9. Made direct amends to such people wherever possible, except when to do so would injure them or others.

10. Continued to take personal inventory and when we were wrong promptly admitted it.

11. Sought through prayer and meditation to improve our conscious contact with God as we understood Him, praying only for knowledge of His will for us and the power to carry that out.

12. Having had a spiritual awakening as the result of these steps, we tried to carry this message to alcoholics, and to practice these principles in all our affairs.

Many of us exclaimed, "What an order! I can't go through with it." Do not be discouraged. No one among us has been able to maintain anything like perfect adherence to these principles. We are not saints. The point is, that we are willing to grow along spiritual lines. The principles we have set down are guides to progress. We claim spiritual progress rather than spiritual perfection.

Our description of the alcoholic, the chapter to the agnostic, and our personal adventures before and after make clear three pertinent ideas:

> (a) That we were alcoholic and could not manage our own lives.
> (b) That probably no human power could have relieved our alcoholism.
> (c) That God could and would if He were sought." [24]

When I left, I knew I was screwed. It was like everybody was talking about me and none of it sounded good. Of course, they weren't literally. Each person told their story, or some portion of it, but in each of their stories, I heard my own clear as day. Yep, AA had messed up my drinking for good. But these words kept echoing through my head: "That one is God, may you find him now!" and "God could and would if He were sought."

Later that week, I had another session with my psychologist.

"How did it go?"

"I don't know." Little did I know that there was a spark, a path revealed in that meeting. I wanted what these people had, I just wasn't sure I believed that they were real.

"Are you going to go back?"

I thought for a moment, maybe looking for a way out. "Yeah, I guess."

He leaned back. "I have a little test I want you to take." He picked up a piece of paper. "It's a personality test, only takes a few minutes," he said and handed it to me.

When I finished, he scored it and in a calm voice said, "Well, not much of a surprise, but you are clearly a Type A personality. You do everything balls out. You've always done everything balls out, which includes drinking. You just need to redirect that energy to something that's more constructive rather than destructive—"

"Okay."

"—because you're an adrenaline junkie and you're not happy unless things are messed up and in upheaval, and if things get too peaceful, you'll just do what you have to do to mess them up again because you like the chaos."

And he kept on calmly reading me the riot act. "And as part and parcel of all that, you have this notion in your mind that you want some blonde goddess that will just bow at your feet and do everything that your heart desires."

That's pretty much it, I thought.

"If you want to crawl out from under this life, you need to start thinking about channeling this stuff into ways that are more productive."

Over the next few weeks, I kept going to the Tuesday meeting. My reward was two, deeply cathartic moments. The first, in front of a room filled with strangers, was saying for the first time in my life, "My name is Frank, and I'm an alcoholic." And that was the first big paradox: You have to give up to win. You have to stop fighting anything and anybody. I wasn't cured, but for the first time I admitted what I knew to be true all along. The second, admitting I was powerless over alcohol, and my life had become unmanageable.

"I think, too," he said at one session, "you drink to snuff your fear because you don't know where your life is going."

I didn't.

"And you think your life is dependent on other people and institutions." It was, wasn't it?

I had pumped gas, put up with customers, and put up with bosses out on a rig. Yeah, I had also acquired a colorful vocabulary. Like the sayings I learned from Hank, a roughneck from Oklahoma. I never did catch Hank's last name because of something about outstanding warrants for grand theft auto. Wouldn't be prudent for him to tell. But I digress. I had always identified with the working man and just did not like defense work. It made me feel dependent and miserable. Maybe I had a problem with authority.

I said as much, and he responded, "You probably need to go into business for yourself."

I wasn't so sure about that. I got the general notion. But going it totally alone? That seemed, well, lonely.

Dad said Walter was a good man. He had never steered me wrong. Walter was from out in Chalmette, and he grew up underneath the smokestack at the Kaiser aluminum plant. We used to play Chalmette in football, and I never looked forward to the guaranteed post-game headache.

During Hurricane Betsy as a kid, Walter had listened to a TV station reporter who was on the phone with someone in Pilot Town, down where the Mississippi empties out into the Gulf where his dad worked. In an instant, the voice on the phone turned to static, cut out, and the announcer said, "We've lost Pilot Town." I remembered that moment. It was like the hurricane blew Pilot Town away and Walter sat there believing he had lost his dad. A few hours later, his dad walked in out of the storm and to Walter with the wind and rain pounding outside. It was as if God had resurrected his dad from the dead. He had been through the storm.

Then, when Walter was old enough to work, it was in a shipyard in Chalmette, not summers at a club somewhere with soft hands. He knew what it meant to work for a living and what a working man goes through. I could sense early on that we had the same passion.

Until he suggested I work for myself, I hadn't seen that getting fired from the large firm I had previously worked for had opened a door. Of course, I had been told that several times, but I just didn't see it. Today I am thankful that I was fired. It was true. I said, "You know, I think I'm in the right place. Quite frankly, the nature of our business is to eat what you kill." I had already been told those were the rules.

"Maybe leaving defense work wasn't such a bad thing?"

"Maybe not."

"But, the reason why is a problem."

I nodded.

He smiled. "Sometimes, the worst thing that can happen to you is the best thing that can happen to you. It's true in your job, and you might think that going through recovery is the worst thing to ever happen to you, but it could be the best thing that ever happened to you."

Unfortunately, I wasn't done with selfishness quite yet. But it was a start.

# # # #

I wasn't healed, and the skies didn't break in some sort of Hollywood ending. In fact, I was up to my ass in debt, believed I was one screw up away from Walter ending my legal career, and in an office where you eat what you kill, and I wasn't killing much. I had no idea where my next client would come from. But, I'd get up in the morning and sit out on my little balcony with a cup of coffee and a cigarette and look out into the street. That was my daily, one-day-at-a-time routine. I got a base minimum salary from the firm that I managed to cover and in a pinch I'd call Dad and ask him for a few bucks, but I could make it through each day without drinking. I was on the proverbial "pink cloud," and though I had found a spiritual solution to my drinking problem, I was only waltzing. Steps one, two, three, a-one, two, three. And I was going round and round on one and two. My life played back in front of my eyes in short clips. It was scary. But to quote Socrates, "An unexamined life is not worth living." I had never seriously looked back and examined mine. All I could do at the time was sneak an occasional peek.

As difficult as my life was, it was one of my most peaceful and meaningful times. I was going to meetings four or five days each week, as many as I could get to, reading the AA *Big Book*, and learning about myself, God, alcoholism, and what it meant to be sober. Of course, my initial question was whether I was an alcoholic to start with. After all, I wasn't on skid row, didn't drink every day and didn't have to, and could go days or weeks at a time without drinking. One of the pages in the *Big Book* stood out:

> But what about the real alcoholic? He may start off as a moderate drinker; he may or may not become a continuous hard drinker; but at some stage of his drinking career he begins to lose all control of his liquor consumption, once he starts to drink.[25]

That was me! I always drank like that! Suddenly my roommate's words as a junior at LSU rang through my head. "Once you start you can't stop." I could have had a *V-8!*

I had reached the point where one was too many, one hundred not enough. And once I danced that tune, I was defenseless against the first drink. I had an obsession: One day, somehow, I would be able to learn to control my drinking. I had to be relieved from that obsession, and I was told that the only remedy was a spiritual one. My defense from that first drink must come from a higher power. I knew what the God thing was about, or thought I did, but I really had no clue. I believed that there was a God, now I just had to see that I wasn't Him.

This was the hardest piece because it meant overcoming my own nature, my own need to fight, my own ego and belief I could do it on my own. I was still the high school kid who if you wanted me to do something, tell me not to do it.

As I look back, I had been living a common AA joke. I walked down a corridor and looked to the right where there was a door that was locked, but there was a key in it. Whatever was in that room couldn't get out unless I let it out. And there was a sign on the door that said, "Don't F**k with the Gorilla." Of course, I would open the door and mess with the gorilla and it would beat the ever-living crap out of me. And then after I healed and sufficient time passed for amnesia to set in, I would believe the plausible lie. "That Gorilla ain't that bad, is he?" Something inside me made it impossible to walk past that door and that sign. I needed help learning to leave the Gorilla alone.

So, I went to meetings, waltzed through the first three steps, and kept repeating, "I will not drink today, I will not drink today ..." It was working.

The worst of it was after work on Friday afternoons. I'd grip the wheel and just repeat my mantra over and over. When I got home, I kept up with the mantra and then got to a meeting as soon as I could. Saturday morning, more mantra and another meeting. Saturday night, same thing and then two meetings on Sunday, too.

Over the course of a few weeks, I made friends at these meetings and we started hanging out at Shoney's or any other all-night place that served coffee and let us smoke. There was the wife of a former LSU player from the glory days, a Boston salesman named Clark (pronounced "Clock") who talked like,

"Pahk the Cah in the Bahn." It was a real cross section of the people who end up in New Orleans for one reason or another. We'd sit, talk, tell jokes, tell stories, and just stay sober together. And I replaced bar hopping with meeting hopping. It's amazing the people you meet. I knew a lot of them from my past life.

Summer came—this was 1986—and I thought I could start to live my life a little bit outside of the program. So, I went to my old bar—I swore up and down to the owner I was in recovery—sat at the bar drinking diet Coke, and talked to whoever was there. I got bored fast and left. There was nothing to do and drunks are, well, just not pleasant. I mentioned it to one of the guys—he became one of my sponsors, I had more than one—and he said, "I don't think that's a very good idea, but you can do it if you want."

I went back again, and again it just felt wrong. I mean, there I was sitting in this bar with a bunch of guys with nothing going on, I'm not drinking, so what the hell am I doing? Then I remembered something my friend had said, "You don't go shopping for underwear in a hardware store." He was right.

A few weeks before Walter's last, last warning, I was drinking in a bar spouting off about the cases I handled, how much money they were worth, and how much money I was going to make. It was an epic episode of grandiose thinking. I was in mid oration, and it was about three or four in the morning when an old drunk at the end of the bar said, "Shut up!"

There were three other people in the bar, and we looked at him. "Who the hell are you?" I said.

He looked up from his drink. "If you're such a hot shot, what are you doing in this sh*thole?" An accurate assessment.

When you are right, you're right. I needed to stay out of the holes.

Summer became fall, and while I hadn't had a drink since Walter's second last chance and was "working the program"—the ultimate cliché—I should have been worried about having a defense from the first drink. It all was still force of will that kept me from falling through the floor, but I was doing it. And I was really wrestling with this God thing.

I had to ask the question from *The Who* in reverse. The questions, "Who are *you*?"[26] didn't ask who I was anymore, it asked who God was. How do I relate to Him? I had to relate, have a relationship, or I was done. The thought was scary. In my chair in the morning, there were moments when I sensed God's presence, but they were fleeting. And what about the things I had lost? Time? Money? And the things that I wanted, like love? I was still confused.

I prayed like hell.

One night, at the "Young People's" meeting, a group from a thirty-day in-patient rehabilitation program at a local hospital walked into the room. This wasn't unusual—this meeting was close to the hospital and part of the program—but what was unusual was one of the women I didn't recognize. She was about five feet tall with poofed up blond hair. She wore a vest over a tight halter top that pressed her breasts in a way that revealed her cleavage, and her lips were ruby-red. Large, hoop earrings dangled from her ears, and she wore a leather bracelet on one wrist. She was, in every way, a locked door with a sign saying don't mess with the gorilla. If I was defenseless from the next drink, I was also defenseless from the next babe. I suddenly realized that there were gorillas everywhere!

She walked straight to me, like I had a sign on me. "Hey man, what's up?"

Out of a sense of self-preservation and survival paranoia, for the first time in my life, something inside me screamed, "Run, just run like hell!" Fighting all my instincts, I said calmly, "Not much," and walked away repeating in my head something to the effect of, "Leave that one alone, just leave that gorilla alone ..."

#

Somewhere along the line, I managed to pull in a new client whom I could genuinely feel good about helping and whose case may even have provided me with a modest boost in my income. He was working to offload a ship when a piece of cargo gear failed, and a broken cable injured him. Before the accident, the American Bureau of Shipping (ABS) inspected the cargo gear, which meant I had to get the inspections from the ABS as well as conduct depositions in New Jersey.

I issued a *Subpoena Duces Tecum* to the ABS and requested to take the deposition in early December. When the ABS's lawyer responded, I was pleasantly surprised to see that it was one of the female lawyers I'd worked with at Jimmy's. We were friends, platonic only—she saw the better half of the double life I led. I flew up to New Jersey for the deposition. The plan was to take the deposition, then the next day I'd fly down to Columbia, South Carolina, to have an early Christmas visit with my sister and her family.

After the deposition, totally spur of the moment, three of us lawyers got into a cab and headed to an Italian restaurant. When we sat down we started telling war stories, which got us all laughing. When someone ordered a couple bottles of wine for the table, it seemed as natural as walking and breathing.

When a glass was set in front of me and red wine poured into it, I didn't blink. The scent of the wine, the restaurant, talking, all of it seemed so ordinary and normal. I was six months sober, but after the first sip, I was off and running—with no thought or fight whatsoever. I had been waltzing through recovery. But something wasn't right, it just hadn't clicked. I had no spiritual awakening, and so I had no spiritual defense against the first drink.

After dinner, it was snowing outside. Christmas lights were lit. It was festive. We stopped and picked up a bottle of bourbon and from there things got a bit blurry. The next thing I knew, a couple stewardesses poured me out of a plane in Columbia, South Carolina, and I staggered with my sister to her car. It was the same old story, here's Uncle Frank, wasted again, and landing in their orbit like some sort of drunk and annoying asteroid. The next morning, I woke up on the couch with my nephew staring down at me. My body hurt—really hurt. I had gotten unused to this hangover business. I walked into the kitchen for some needed water.

"Hi, Frank," my brother-in-law said as he leaned back against the counter eating a bowl of cereal. A cup of coffee rested on the counter next to him. "Need some coffee?"

"Yeah, you know it."

"What happened to you last night?"

I felt nothing but shame. And I was really scared. Six months of work, of sobriety, gone. For the first time in my life, I truly felt powerless to not pick up that first drink. I'd known for a long time, too long, that I was powerless against every drink that followed, but I thought force of will, desire to be better, to do better, fear of losing my career, fear of dying drunk and alone, all of it would keep me safe from the first drink. It was a lie.

I looked at him. "I don't know what happened, I really don't."

We ate a quiet dinner that night, then Saturday I boarded a flight for New Orleans. I made it home and then went off to my regular Saturday night meeting where they gave me a "24-Hour Desire to Stop Drinking" sobriety chip. I was back to square one. I was ashamed. I was also terrified that on Monday Walter and Mike would find out I slipped.

Sunday morning, I woke up and sat in my living room with a cup of coffee and was just sort of bewildered as to how or why it ever happened. One minute I was having a nice dinner, and the next I was a drunk. The AA *Big Book* was on the table next to my chair where I left it before leaving. Usually, that thing went with me everywhere I went. I opened it to the chapter titled Bill's Story. In it, he discusses wandering around Winchester Cathedral as a young, American soldier just off the boat in Britain and soon to be sent to the Western Front during World War I. An aged tombstone catches his eye:

> *Here lies a Hampshire Grenadier*
> *Who caught his death*
> *Drinking small cold beer.*
> *A good soldier is ne'er forgot*
> *Whether he dieth by musket*
> *Or by pot.*

Bill then writes, "Ominous warning—which I failed to heed." [27] After much suffering, all caused by alcohol, Bill is able to get sober, and upon reflection, he sees that his higher power, God, drew him to that stone so many years before when he was a young man as a warning. I think that all alcoholics who find their way to recovery and sobriety have a story (often stories) where they encounter a vision of warning of their future self if they kept drinking. We all share the same sad fact that due to ego, blindness, addiction, we failed to heed the glimpse into our future.

And I thought of the times my sister helped me or accepted me into some part of her life when I was drunk and suffering emotionally and physically. There was her rehearsal dinner, where bouncers threw me out onto the street, and the following day, when I could not celebrate her marriage at the reception. Then in law school, when I showed up at her doorstep bloody and reeking of booze after a biker kicked me in the face. To show up like that again at her home, with her husband and children, my young nephews, the shame of it was more than I could take.

I can't go on like this, I thought. At the same time, I didn't know how I slid so easily from recovery and sobriety back to a pitiful and humiliated drunk. For the six months of my sobriety, I thought I'd found peace and calm, but as I sat with the Big Book, I realized I hadn't found true peace or calm. My life was better as a sober person, but it was also filled with the anxiety and white-knuckle fear of falling back into my old life. I only had my own will and determination not to drink, but obviously, I am imperfect.

Is this all sobriety has to offer? Once again, I thought, *If this is it, just take me out. I quit.* I felt like I had a hole in my gut and the wind just passed through.

In my slip, I'd proved what the *Big Book* says when it explains that an alcoholic "will be absolutely unable to stop drinking on the basis of self-knowledge." [28] I also knew that it was the first drink that would get me drunk. I'd already admitted and believed I was powerless over alcohol once I started to drink and that I'd reached a point where there was no self-control over the amount I drank. I drank to get drunk; I saw no other point to drinking.

I had gained six months of sobriety, but that was all. And yet, in each meeting, I saw and witnessed people who'd found peace. These things worked in them, but why not me? What else was there that I hadn't tried? Just as I'd known for years that I was an alcoholic, but lived in denial, I maintained a willful ignorance of a second truth. Sitting in the quiet of my living room, I read, "The alcoholic at certain times has no effective mental defense against the first drink. Except in a few cases, neither he nor any other human being can provide such a defense. His defense must come from a Higher Power." [29]

I'd proved this as well. Just like the story of the guy who thought a little whiskey in his milk would be okay, I had accepted a glass of wine with no thought. And this terrified me because it meant that this would happen again. It was like living life with the sword of Damocles hanging over me, ready to fall at any minute and destroy me. How many more episodes could I survive physically and emotionally? How many before others lost all faith in me?

I had to do something. On a shelf was the Bible Mom and Dad gave me years before. It was bound in black leather and all but unopened. It wasn't that I doubted God or lacked belief in His existence. I didn't believe He wanted anything to do with me.

The *Big Book* says, "Deep down in every man, woman, and child, is the fundamental idea of God." [30] And there is the story of the man who tumbled out of bed to his knees and was overwhelmed by a conviction of the presence of God. "When we drew near to Him He disclosed Himself to us." [31] Maybe this would work, but I had no idea how.

Then I opened the Bible and looked for something about peace and hope. I went to the book of Romans for no other reason than it sounded like it was ancient. I didn't know anything about the Bible. I flipped through and came to chapter 5 and started reading. "Therefore, since we have been justified by faith—" I didn't know the true meaning of faith at the time—"we have peace with God through our Lord Jesus Christ. Through Him, we have also obtained access by faith into this grace in which we stand and we rejoice in hope of the glory of God. Not only that, but we rejoice in our sufferings, knowing that suffering produces endurance, and endurance produces character, and character produces hope, and hope does not put us to shame, because God's love has been poured into our hearts through the Holy Spirit who has been given to us" (verses 1-5).

It seemed odd to me that we should rejoice in our suffering, but as I thought on this passage it dawned on me that it is one of the greatest paradoxes. I had to give up and lose to win. I had to quit fighting alcohol altogether and turn it over to something else. I had to let go and let God. I had to get out of my own way.

I read on, "For while we were still weak, at the right time Christ died for the ungodly. For one will scarcely die for a righteous person—though perhaps for a good person one would dare even to die—but God shows his love for us in that while we were still sinners, Christ died for us" (verses 6-8). I began to weep and sob uncontrollably. Christ died for me. It's hard to capture the intense emotions of this moment. It shook me to my core and for the first time, I experienced truth emotionally and viscerally as opposed to just intellectually.

When Poppy died, and the choir and congregation in Winnfield sang "Holy, Holy, Holy," I could not sing for the sobs coming from me. I have since realized that it wasn't sadness at his passing, although I was sad, it was because I was standing in the presence of God, something so much bigger than myself, and believed I was meaningless and unworthy. For all my sins and ability to sin with ease and comfort, I was guilty as charged.

The weight of God's presence, love, and forgiveness in my humble, little apartment overwhelmed me. All my iniquities and secret sins were set before God as if I had died and was standing before Him in judgment. It was the same as when Poppy died and I faced the certainty of death at his funeral for the first time. But this time, I knew that God loved me enough to send His son to suffer and die for my sins before I even came into this world.

Prostrate on my knees and weeping, I prayed directly from the *Big Book,* "God, I offer myself to thee to build with me and to do with me as Thou wilt. Relieve me of the bondage of self, that I may better do Thy will. Take away my difficulties, that victory over them may bear witness to those I would help of Thy power, Thy love, and Thy way of life. May I do Thy will always." [32]

It wasn't in church or a recovery meeting that I came to God. It was alone on the floor of my apartment. There had been signals. God was made known to me through my family, the church, those who had extended friendship and grace and through the stories and experiences of other people that reflected the love of God. Looking back, I could see how God worked in my life.

By all rights and privileges from the things I had done, I should have been dead. But for some reason God had brought me to this point. Was I to believe that there was no reason for it? And what of love, the thirst for justice, the innate knowledge of what was right? These things could only have come from God. I just don't give myself that much credit to believe that they came to me just on my own.

One could call these *Signals of Transcendence*. God showed himself through each, but I was unable to see them, to receive the signals. I got hints, such as the joy of Christmas with my family as a kid, the order and protection of my family and siblings, the pangs of conscience at doing wrong, the desire to rescue and save others, as well as through the example of calm, love, and goodness set by my mother and father.

But this experience, in my small apartment, with God was real. God was present through Jesus Christ, and I was changed. When I finally got up, it actually physically felt like God had lifted a rock from my shoulders, and I have never again had a serious urge to drink. Sure, there are times when I think how nice it would be to have a glass of wine with a special meal or to sit with a drink after work, but these are fleeting thoughts that run into the hard truth that I never drank like that, ever.

More importantly, the obsession was lifted. And as time went on, I no longer had the resignation to succumb to sinful urges. Instead, I had a desire and the ability to not sin. In Latin, it is *posse non peccare*. I could live life in the moment, one day at a time, seeking God's will, not my own weak and flawed inclinations and desires. It worked, and it is still working. For thirty years I lived wondering what it would feel like if I smoked this, drank this, ate that, took this? I have spent the past thirty years finding out what it feels like to quit drinking this, smoking this, drugging this, or eating that. The process in reverse.

After all these years, I know these things are true, not just because they are written in the Bible, but because they are true. I have lived it. I once thought it impossible for me to change, to be freed of the desire to drink, but God did it. I didn't do it by myself because I was unable. It was God that changed my heart. That I could change, that I live a life that is not devoid of pain yet is peaceful, is a gift from God. And what I do with my life is my gift back to God. To receive this gift, I had to let go of my ego and will. I had to accept that I am a child of God, not the other way around.

And if God is in control, he's in control of everything. Once I accepted His help and got out of His way, that's when my life changed. It was all of God and none of me. That's why I believe what I believe. Jesus Christ saved me as if He physically plucked me from the path of a speeding bus. I don't know how else to put it. I just know what I know.

And it has been my experience that people who develop a personal relationship with God make it. They can change, I've seen it many times, and learn to live a life that is happy, joyous, and free. God shows up big time at recovery meetings and elsewhere where the need is great. God shows up where the rubber meets the road, where there is poverty and extreme turmoil and where there should be despair and hopelessness, places where you would not expect to find Him, but He is there. You just need to look for the signals because He is always informing us of His presence.

Now that I have kids, I can sometimes sense that they don't believe what I am telling them or what they hear in church and at school. And I tell them, "I wouldn't expect you to believe it just because it's written in a book. I didn't believe it either when I was your age just because it was written in a book." I know, they must learn the truth of it through experience, but I can provide them with the clues and hints they need to be able to see the signals when they are ready.

I smile when I say this. After I told Mom of my coming to faith she said, "I knew you would, but not because I told you so or it's written in a book, but because it is truth, and I raised you to look for the truth."

Posse Non Peccare

Chapter Nine

The Pink Cloud

Christmas of 1986 went by like a blur. I spent the holidays going to meetings—I did well over ninety meetings in ninety days—hanging out with my sponsors (I knew I was a handful so immediately got more than one), and concentrating on not drinking. Throughout, I got a lot of advice and shared a lot of my story. To help me figure out how to live life as a sober person, one of my sponsors told me in no uncertain terms, "You have to change your playgrounds and your playmates." The force with which this edict was uttered foretold how such a change would be difficult, but important.

Obviously, recovery became my most important new playground and the friends I met there my playmates. Some of them were people I recognized from the bars I used to frequent. "I was wondering when you would get here," they would say, a greeting I would later use as others would appear in the meeting rooms. At another meeting, after telling a bit of my story, an old timer came up to me and said, "You're lucky you had a high bottom."

"What do you mean?"

"You're young—" I was thirty at the time—"and you didn't wait until you had to drink all day just to stop shaking and hallucinating. This disease will take you lower than you ever thought you could go." While I appreciated the sentiment, such thinking was dangerous for me. I had to remember why I got there. So I would latch onto portions of the *Big Book* like, "If, when you honestly want to, you find you cannot quit entirely, or if when drinking, you have little control over the amount you take, you are probably alcoholic." [33] In light of my history, this description fit me to a tee.

I may have had a high bottom, but I beat myself up over the time I thought I'd wasted, the lost professional progress, and inability to find a true love, never mind even understanding what that is. And truthfully, I was blessed by not having gotten entangled in marriage much less children.

This led me to recognizing yet another paradox. Everything that happened to me before I fell to my knees and accepted the truth of God, occurred for a reason. It beat the fight out of me so I could see with clarity for the first time in my life that I needed to completely rely on God for all things. When I exercised my free will, I screwed it all up, but now that I'd surrendered and given my will and life to His care, I felt more than just hope. And because I had absolutely nothing to do with it, I knew God was sovereign. I was at peace.

When I explained this to some friends over coffee at a café, they smiled and said, "Welcome to the pink cloud." It was totally normal and boring, yet just being "normal" was amazing.

It was the little things.

Like if I was sober and at home in bed before midnight (nothing good happens after midnight), I didn't wreck my car or get arrested. I didn't get thrown out of a bar. I didn't get my face slapped by a beautiful female for being sober, kind, polite, and respectful. If I showed up and worked, surprise, surprise, I got paid! And if I didn't get bombed and spend all my money, I wasn't broke when the bills came due. I could not only get to work, but be engaged with my work. I represented my clients to the best of my ability and not only did I get paid, but I got more clients.

I was leading a "normal life" like all the regular people out there I knew, which was totally new to me.

One concern I did have was how other people would react when they found out I didn't drink anymore and that I was in recovery. I don't know why I was concerned. Nobody cared if I drank or not. There were those who said they'd believe it when they saw it and seemed to think I couldn't change, but time proved them wrong. And they didn't miss me a bit.

There were also those who did care. Mom and Dad noticed a change in me, as did Walter and Mike. Though I'd been sober up to my slip, which had been a definite improvement, what they saw after that Sunday morning in December of 1986 was a changed man. I brought Walter a copy of the chapter in the *Big Book* titled *To the Employer*. It states that the employer of an alcoholic who understands and works the program will end up with a loyal and dedicated employee for life. I intended to see that prediction come true.

I must admit, Walter looked skeptical, particularly with his last chance speech still fresh in his mind. Indeed, talk is cheap. But I assured him that I understood that the proof would be in the pudding. I had to work, and I had to bring fees into the firm. That's what I was there for and that's why I burned so many late nights studying. I was there for a purpose. And proving it by doing it was all right by me.

With my sobriety, it was now time to live my purpose without the limitations of my ego and belief that I knew better than anybody else, especially God. So I let go. I trusted God. This meant doing the work as well as I could and listening to my internal sense of right and wrong. When I did these things, I started to get good results. The entire role that I was to play changed. I no longer took responsibility for everything, only those things I could control. I played my role as an attorney searching for the truth, nothing more, nothing less. And the fear disappeared over time. In all of this, I see God's hand at work, and for thirty years I've justified my existence and proved the *Big Book* to be right.

I broke up with the barmaid. It was short and sweet, particularly because it was a one-sided deal anyway. It was like breaking up with myself really. A few months later, I did ask a young woman out who I knew from drinking in a bar she happened to own, where I discovered that I knew her as a kid. She had gone to first grade with my little brother, was an entrepreneur, had her life together and was rather cute. I'm not sure why, but I called her.

"Yeah, yeah," she said, "I'd go out with you."

"Well, I'm in recovery and don't drink anymore."

"Okay."

"I just thought you should know."

"Sure, it's all right."

We talked some more, and she mentioned she and a friend were going up to a party in Baton Rouge and that they'd be meeting her friend's husband up there. He was flying in from a business trip or something. We drove up in my car, and she and the friend had a couple drinks to loosen up on the ride, but nothing serious.

We got to the party and soon after, the friend's husband arrived at the house. I guess they must have not seen each other for some time because they got hot and heavy right in the living room. You know, *geez*.

The rest of the night everyone stood around drinking and talking and being "normal" with alcohol, whatever that is. Seemed to me everyone got drunk, they just quit early like a bunch of light weights. The friend and her husband seemed to have fun, my date enjoyed herself, but I got bored.

I drove back to New Orleans with the three of them that night and dropped the two love birds off at their place then took my date home. When we pulled in, I said, "Look, I really like you, but I don't think this is going to work out. I'm dealing with some things and I think we're on two different wavelengths here."

Her face seemed to drop and she just said, "Sure," and stepped out of the car. I drove off and left her standing on the street. I don't think she understood where I was or what I meant. Maybe she thought I accused her of drinking too much or something, but that wasn't it at all. I wasn't ready and she just wasn't the one.

For the most part, I minded my own business. I went to meetings, attended church every Sunday, and worked on cases. I made more friends through the program, and after meetings we haunted coffee houses talking about life, sobriety, and football. I also routinely met with my sponsors, and that spring I started my Fourth Step. This required making what the *Big Book* describes as a "searching and fearless moral inventory." To say the least, this is an emotionally difficult process. That is why it is the step that is the most detested yet the most necessary. You have to own it before you can clean it up.

I was as meticulous in my search and writing as I could be at that time. This was really the first time I'd ever gone back over my life and examined where I came from, my sins and transgressions, and how each affected me and the people around me. I wrote about fear and insecurity, loneliness and feeling unloved, as well as the anger and rebellion I used to overcome those feelings.

For the first time ever, I stared myself straight in the eyes rather than looking past the problem. I met the enemy, and he was me. This process helped reveal all the feelings and emotions I'd covered up with alcohol, which reflects an interesting and true concept of the program. Alcoholics stop growing emotionally when they stop feeling. This was true of me.

This process also taught me that feelings are just feelings. They come and they go, and life is not just how you feel in a particular moment, but how you manage those feelings and accept that they are a creation of my mind and influenced by my own character defects. I don't have to act or react to each one. I can be as happy as I choose to be.

Looking back, I remembered living on Melody Drive and being afraid Mom had abandoned me that one day, which stayed with me for two decades. There was also the fear of being small and getting hurt playing football and my refusal to even put my wrestling uniform on at one meet. I was stuffing down with alcohol my insecurities, fear of being alone in a crowd, and the fear that I would never find love, and within that, that I was unworthy of love. And I read how perfect love casts out fear. So I cast it out.

Drinking had exaggerated my character defects and halted my emotional growth and as such led me into a continuous downward spiral, where each failure or transgression confirmed what I believed I already knew about myself. I was not worthy of goodness and love because no matter how hard I tried, I caved and failed. It was classic guilt. Why set these standards for yourself that you know you would never be able to meet? Failure was certain. I became pessimistic. *Non Posse, Non Pecarre.*

The secular world just rocked on like God didn't exist, so you could do whatever turned you on. I sought happiness in worldly things—sex, drugs, and rock and roll. And for me it was mostly just the drugs and rock and roll. Two out of three ain't bad, right? I always had this nagging feeling though that there had to be more to this life. There just had to be. It took me crashing and burning, slamming against the ground, and total capitulation to finally surrender and realize that what I needed, what would give me true happiness was not of this earth.

There is a quote by C. S. Lewis—author of *Mere Christianity*—that hits the nail on the head for me. "If I find in myself a desire which no experience in this world can satisfy, the most probable explanation is that I was made for another world." [34] I had stepped into that other world.

Some folks in recovery call this *The Fourth Dimension.* Some call it seeking to walk daily in God's will. Anyone who has a heart changed by God to seek His will, not theirs, has it. It is variously referred to as *The Narrow Road, The Road Less Traveled.* But it is not just living life on life's terms, although that is part of it. It is more than that. It is living life the way you were created to live it. It is living life God's way, with victory over sins. Not successive defeats. One day at a time, one moment at a time. Always going slow, following the signs, seeking to know God.

Living the AA program opened my faith. I could see that God had made Himself evident in many ways in my life. The beauty of nature and His creation. The love of parents, siblings, family, and friends. How God provided a way for me and many times rescued me. The ability to think, to reason. For the first time, I saw God in everything. And for the first time I felt loved despite all the terrible and humiliating things that I had done. Why? Because God sent His Son to die for me. It changed me. It was transcendent. And by doing my Fourth Step, I could see how it all fit.

As I looked back over my life I realized that the last time I felt I had it together was in sixth grade when my team won the parish championship. It wasn't that we won—that was most certainly good—but how it reflected the boy I was compared to the adolescent and man I became. That was when I stopped growing emotionally. I had to go back and start over. And so, as I wrote and reflected, I wanted that feeling back, the feeling of being right in the world. I wanted to stay in the Fourth Dimension.

I took my written fourth step and confessed it to my sponsor and my pastor. Then I burned it. The admissions were embarrassing, humiliating, and true. It was also the most freeing experience I've ever had.

###

Since the fall of 1986, I'd managed to avoid my old fixations and behaviors around women. The first test was the babe who came to the meeting at John Calvin. She was blond, beautiful, and exactly the kind of girl I would become infatuated with, but I walked—to my mind, ran—away. The second was the girl I went on a date with up in Baton Rouge. By then I was listening to God and letting Him take charge. The result was that I recognized I wasn't ready for a relationship, and perhaps she wasn't the right woman for me.

I didn't see my Baton Rouge date again for many years, but after the young, wild-looking blond made it through treatment, she continued coming to the Tuesday night meeting. I was friendly, as I was with everyone, but at the same time she made me nervous. It's hard to explain, but I knew she was nothing but trouble.

Within a short while, she became part of the group that went out for coffee after meetings and sometimes hung out socially. We talked, and I came to learn she grew up in Harahan, Louisiana, and that she had a young son named Nicholas from a marriage in Dallas that went bust and left her a single mother. She had an apartment and worked three jobs bartending and waiting tables.

Throughout the spring, summer, and fall of 1987, she kept showing up, we chatted, I was still nervous, and we forged a friendship that felt casual with few expectations. It wasn't the biggest thing in my life—that was God, sobriety, and work—but it was a nice thing. Then in mid-December she came up to me after a meeting and said, "You seem like a nice guy, I think it would be a good idea if you asked me out."

So, I did.

To this day I tell people she asked me out, because I had no intention of getting beaten up over a nonexistent relationship. She tells people I asked her out, which I suppose is technically correct. This wouldn't be the last time I had to interpret a statement by her. Today, "the grass needs to be cut" means please go cut the grass. "We're out of milk," means please go get some milk. You get the picture, I'm expected to be a mind reader. I have intuitively learned to interpret statements by women that used to baffle me.

I asked and she said yes, but because she was working so many shifts, taking care of Nicholas and everything else, we had to set our date for three weeks from the time I asked. And so we went about our business. There weren't any phone calls late into the night or anything like that. It kind of felt to me that she saw it as just another day, maybe it'll happen, maybe it won't. And amazingly to me that is how it was. It wasn't long before I started to get the familiar feeling that maybe she was going to blow me off. Then, two days before our date, she called. "Hi, it's Lee. Look, I can't go out Friday night. Something's come up."

"Okay."

"But let's reschedule it." That was a bit of a surprise.

We did, but that was another three or four weeks off. Again, I thought, *Yeah, right, like that's going to happen.* So I went back to minding my business. *My business* at that time was still meetings and work.

The four weeks went by, and the night before our date she called. "We're going out tomorrow night, right?"

Actually, this time I had forgotten.

"Are we supposed to?"

She paused. "Yes."

"Okay, I guess we are."

It was mid-February of 1988 when I went to her apartment to pick her up for our first date. The weather was relatively warm, and she greeted me in a short spring dress with high heels. *Mercy!* She was a total knockout. The sight of her stopped most of my brain functions. We chatted while she grabbed a jacket and walked out to the car.

I took her to Tony Angelo's, an Italian restaurant since destroyed by

Hurricane Katrina, and then back to her place for coffee. As the night wore on, my nerves settled, and we talked and laughed. Nicholas was at his grandmother's, and we made out on her couch for a little bit. Then it was time for me to go.

Riding high, it felt as if I'd reset the clock. This was our first ever real date, and after that night we started going out, like boyfriend and girlfriend. And I couldn't help but look around and ask the question "Why me?" But I sure wasn't going to look a gift horse in the mouth.

#

Around the time Lee and I started getting to know each other in the fall of 1987, a thought occurred to me. If the last time I felt whole was in sixth grade after winning the parish championship, maybe I could connect with that time again. I knew the guy who coached the juniors at Girard Playground, my old team, and so I gave him a call to ask if he needed a hand.

"Absolutely. I could use some help on the offensive line."

I think he already knew what I was going through, but I laid it out for him, and he didn't bat an eye. He knew I loved football, could coach it (probably), and believed me when I said I wanted to do something to help his players. We only had thirteen kids on the team so there were two rules. Nobody could get hurt, and everybody had to make their grades at school. The practices began at six in the evening—Girard had lights—which meant I could leave work and drive straight to the field.

What I found each night with those kids was a rebirth or a regeneration. It was an opportunity to do more than teach the game I had loved so much, but to be of service. When I quit as a kid, I left behind the discipline and structure that may have led me to a different path. Coaching brought that back and offered the opportunity to maybe steer a kid like me toward a better life, or at least give them something they could take pride in. And it was a lot of fun.

By the summer of 1988, I was sober, my career was moving forward, coaching gave life a renewed sense of purpose, and I was in love for the first time in my life. Seemed like everything I had hoped for was coming true.

I think it was June when I brought Lee to meet my parents, sort of the last stop on our way to the eventual. As expected, they were happy to see me happy, but there was some concern. In part, I think they viewed my sobriety as being a welcome, but relatively new thing. Truthfully, I don't think they understood it. But they couldn't deny what they saw with their own eyes. By moving so quickly, I think there was concern I might jeopardize the progress I'd made.

I remember telling them about my spiritual awakening and that with it I'd come to Christ and found sobriety. I also tried to explain what it was like being on the pink cloud.

"Well, yeah, that's really good," Mom said. There was hope in her voice that finally her son Frank believed all that she'd tried over so many years to teach me. But she and Dad had heard grand plans before.

There is an old saying about bacon and eggs. "The chicken is interested, but the pig is committed!" So I took the next step, which was taking Lee and Nicholas to the Fourth of July family reunion in Winnfield. No boyfriend of girlfriend was ever made to endure the family reunion unless a marriage proposal was in the offing. You could set your watch by it.

I think it was a week or two after that Lee and I were at her place hanging out. I had already been through the mental process of working up the nerve to ask her to marry me. I talked to Dad, who said that there is just no "perfect" time for these things. "Sometimes you just have to take a deep breath and jump." Well this would be a leap.

Nicholas was five and about to go into first grade, and I said to myself, "Self, you can't just sit on a fence, not with a boy around." I knew what had to be done.

I said to Lee, "Let's take a walk."

"It's raining."

"We'll grab an umbrella. It'll be romantic."

"We're just gonna get wet!" But she capitulated. Maybe she sensed something was up.

It was past midnight when we stepped out into the street and the steady rain. I put my arm around Lee as we walked from street light to street light, huddled under a pie pan of an umbrella. Soon our pants were drenched and I stopped.

She looked into my eyes, questioning my actions. I kissed her. Her lips, neck, ears. The umbrella dropped and my arms went around her. She was just the right fit. I pulled back and looked her in the eyes. She had no idea what was coming. We were soaking wet, but it didn't seem to matter.

"Will you marry me?" I asked.

She dropped her eyes, nuzzled into my chest, and began to cry. *I blew it!* I thought. *She's going to say no.* Then, at that moment, without any questions or pondering the long-term ramifications, she jumped and said, "Yes! Yes, I will marry you!"

What a relief! We kissed again in the light of the street lamp. The rain continued to drench us, but we couldn't have cared less.

Some people will tell you getting engaged is a foolish thing to do for people with just over a year of sobriety. Newly recovered alcoholics should not make big life decisions like this. But you know, I still had a bit of that *if you want me to do something tell me not to do it* in me and so did Lee. We weren't going to listen to what anyone had to say anyway. We never listened before, so why start now?

One thing we did listen to was a suggestion to receive premarital counseling, which we did with Reverend Malsbary. With Nicholas' dad out of the picture, he and I talked about what it would mean for me to step into the role of not just stepparent, but being his dad.

"Frank, I'm sure Nicholas doesn't realize what it is that you're doing for him, but when he is grown up, he'll come to realize it, and he's really going to appreciate that you committed to being his dad and giving him the guidance and unconditional love that every child deserves."

"I'm good with that. This is where God put me, and with Lee He's given me what I was looking for."

What I have never said (to anyone, until now) is that Nicholas was God's gift back to me for the child that I had lost. And I would do it again in a heartbeat.

The first test of our relationship came when Lee said, "You've got to quit smoking with me. I am not going to have more children and smoke." In high school, I broke up with one girl because she asked me to quit smoking. So this was a litmus test. I'd already quit drinking, and in AA they say, "First things first." So quitting smoking is not even on anyone's radar screen. There are bigger fish to fry. So at most meetings, you'll see a group of smokers taking last puffs before the meeting and then lighting up together right afterward.

I knew that I would quit nicotine at some point in my life—it was, after all my first addiction and drug—but I had decided that if I was going to quit smoking, I was only going to go through that misery once.

"I don't know."

"I found a program. Insurance pays for part of it and we pay for the other part and it's an FDA approved program." I agreed. I later came to know the phenomenon of being snared by the words of your mouth.

We made an appointment for a few weeks out, and I didn't think too much about it after that because I was busy preparing for a trial. As the date to quit approached, I was getting ready to try this case smoking two or three packs of cigarettes each day. So on the phone the day of the appointment when she called to remind me, I said that I didn't think this was a good time for me to quit. Being so busy and all.

She didn't miss a beat. "Okay, I'll just go without you." Was this some sort of a test?

In a pig's eye! I thought. "Never mind, I'll meet you at the clinic."

The doctor injected us with a drug—probably Chantix, but I can't be sure—and gave us Scopolamine seasickness patches to put behind our ears, which would kill all sense of taste and smell. This was followed by another injection, of what I do not know, and a prescription for a mild muscle relaxant.

I'd always said if I could make it without a cigarette for the first twenty-four hours, I would be okay. The problem was that I could never make it for more than a few hours. That first day flew by without much of a craving for a cigarette as I was so drugged up. I remember fiddling with my fingers a lot, but I made it. The next day went about the same, but after a week we both started to feel a little irritable and had a fight over something so ridiculous I can't remember what it was.

It was enough, however, to make Lee mad at me for a few days. I spoke with her mother to ask what was going on. I wanted advice, but instead she said peremptorily, "Well, if you can't get along after you quit smoking, maybe you just shouldn't get married at all." Oh yeah? Really? These people knew how to push my buttons. But I politely said, "Thank you," and hung up.

I immediately called Lee and said for the first time what I was bound to repeat more times than I can count. "I'm sorry." She softened, said she was sorry too, and the two of us smoothed things over and were back on track. Whoever said love means never having to say you are sorry was just flat wrong. You had darned well better be ready to say you are sorry. A lot. And even when you are really not!

We set the date of our wedding for December 10, 1988, almost exactly two years after my spiritual awakening and our improbable meeting. Lee asked her best friend to be her maid of honor. After I stopped drinking, I had made amends to some of my old fraternity friends. It was good to rekindle those friendships as the most common reaction was, "I'm glad you stopped because I couldn't stand to be around you. You were such an asshole." What could I say?

They were right. But a best man?

The more I thought about my best man, the only person I knew who placed his confidence in me when I had no confidence in myself was Walter. He was a fraternity brother from LSU, drew a firm line in the sand when I needed it most, and he continued to believe in me as a person and lawyer. When I asked him, he seemed a little uncomfortable, and I worried I'd imposed on his good nature, but he agreed and I've been thankful for that ever since.

After my sisters married their husbands in December, Mom swore she would never again take part in a December wedding. But John Calvin Presbyterian Church was decorated for Christmas, it looked beautiful, and she seemed to take pride in being the mother of the groom for a change. The wedding was small, Lee was gorgeous, Reverend Malsbary performed the service, and the reception was held at a hotel in Metairie. We provided hors d'oeuvres and champagne. If someone wanted a hard drink, the hotel bar was available. And of course the Winnfield crew was there in full force.

We spent our first married night in the hotel's honeymoon suite with leftover hors d'oeuvres, football on the TV, a hot tub in the room, and I had a sexy new bride. Everything I had ever fantasized about God made come true, but only after I gave up trying to make it happen under my own power. I was the most blessed man ever. Now it was sex and rock and roll. Yep, two out of three ain't bad.

I'd managed to save a few coins for our honeymoon, which we spent in the British Virgin Islands. We stayed in a little bungalow on a small inlet with a beautiful white sand beach. We snorkeled and sailed and ate wonderful meals with sparrows and greenfinches flying above our heads. The thing I remember best was a hammock on a pathway near our bungalow. At night, beneath a canopy of stars with the gentle rolling of waves, we'd lie there together, quiet, gentle, in love and at peace with the world. Well, sometimes we were quiet.

The first of what would be a series of homes for us was a small apartment off Kent Avenue in Metairie just behind a busy Mexican restaurant. Not really the ideal either of us had in mind. Before long, we found a three bedroom, red-brick, one-story house in River Ridge that reminded me of the house I grew up in on Melody Drive. Our intention was to be there just long enough to put some money away to get a bigger place and start filling it with kids.

To hold up my end of the bargain, I approached my work with a strengthened sense of purpose. My life was no longer just about me. I was responsible to two people, one a young boy, and I wasn't about to let either of them down. One of the first things we did was have Nicholas baptized. As I walked down the aisle holding his six-year-old hand, I don't know who was more frightened, him or me.

I went to a lot of noon lunch meetings downtown. You'd be surprised at how many lawyers I got to know. I got a lot of good free counsel. One friend I looked up to was a senior partner of a large defense firm who has passed away since. I'll never forget something he said to me early in my recovery. I was ranting and raving about some case in which I thought I was being treated unjustly—I guess I had something of a persecution complex—and this fellow listened politely until I finished. Then he addressed me in a friendly manner with a smile and said, "Frank, don't take yourself so seriously, nobody else does." He had just taken a pin and burst the bubble of my ego. And he was absolutely right. It wasn't about me at all. It was only about getting to the truth. And that took all the pressure off.

And I also got my first big plaintiff's case from a friend who had really referred the case to Walter, but I got involved and handled it. A man in Natchez, Mississippi, had just started driving a log truck from the woods to a saw mill across the Mississippi River in Ferriday, Louisiana. He was a middle-aged fella and had experience with trucks, but not much experience toting logs.

The loggers had stacked the timbers on the truck as high as they could get them in a pyramid then wrapped chain binders over the load to hold them down. When he got to the mill, a foreman pointed to where he was supposed to park his truck and said, "Pull over there and pop your binders."

Being new to this kind of work, he wasn't aware that under OSHA the mill was required to position a forklift against the load as he released the chains to stop any logs from falling. When he popped the second binder, a large log rolled off and crushed him dead. He had a wife and three teenage sons.

I drove back and forth between Metairie and Ferriday and Natchez taking depositions. As the case developed and it became clear it was going to trial, I started practicing my closing argument. I had a blue Dodge at the time, and while I drove I talked to myself and rehearsed different arguments with the intent of drawing from the jury as much emotion as I could. People probably stared at me thinking I was nuts because I'd often be pontificating in my car with tears streaming down my cheeks. I thought, if I can't make myself cry, how am I ever going to make anyone else cry?

We tried the case, and finally it was time for my closing argument. I stood, addressed the judge, then looked into the eyes of the jury. "This man was blessed with three sons and they were blessed to have him as their father. But there will come a day when one of those boys will bring a girl home to meet his mom and he's going to say, 'Gee, I wish Dad was here to see this.' And the day is going to come when his beautiful bride is going to walk down the aisle and he's going to look and there will be an empty space in the front pew and he's going to say, 'I wish Dad was here to see this.' And the day will come when that young man will hold his first child in his arms and he will look up and say, 'Dad, I really wish you could see this.'" By the time I finished, there wasn't a dry eye in the court room.

After I delivered that argument and we waited for the verdict, I remember thinking about the social anxiety I used to suffer at the firms I worked for, when I couldn't hold a cup of coffee steady. That anxiety never entirely went away, but here I was, a young lawyer on my own, in a suit from J. C. Penney, and this man's family dependent on me. I was nervous at first, but to represent these people, working people, against insurance companies and their lawyers, well, I can fight for a guy and a family like that. I was zoned in, and it was like I was in sixth grade again.

When the verdict came back, we won, and we won big. I finished up what I needed to do in Ferriday and then hopped into the blue Dodge to drive back to the office. As I drove, I remembered Walter telling me when I left to, "bring home the bacon."

I hit New Orleans and stopped at a grocery store then drove to the office, walked into Walter's office, and threw a pound of bacon down onto his desk.

He smiled. "What is this?"

"That's bacon."

"Bacon?"

"Yeah, you said bring home the bacon so here it is."

Winning that case cut me free. I took whatever came in the door, tried to help as many people as I could, and never worried about getting paid. And it just clicked.

One of our next cases came when Sister Mary Battaglia called Walter from the Desire Street Clinic located in one of the most dangerous urban neighborhoods at the time. It was also the site of one of the worst lead poisoning outbreaks with kids testing at high lead levels. We went down to the clinic, spoke with some of the mothers, and got involved in a class action seeking damages related to lead paint ingestion. Ultimately, the case settled, but it stretched from early 1989 when we reached out to those mothers until 2016.

I have learned this many times, but it bears repeating. Good lawyers take cases for the juice, not the money. It is always about something bigger than themselves. It is about right and wrong and the meaning of justice. And we have many times confirmed what we have known all along. When we stand by our sense of right and wrong and work to the best of our ability, we succeed professionally, financially, and spiritually. I love being a lawyer, something I don't know that I would have said before 1986.

I could tell war stories all day about cases. Like my law professor at LSU said, "Truth is stranger than fiction," although I didn't believe him at the time. There was no way that all the weird things we read about in the law books could happen again and get any weirder, right? Think again. Here's just one.

I had a case against the City of New Orleans when my client from Arkansas (slightly intoxicated) rolled his truck into a guy's front yard losing his left ear and suffering massive brain damage. The four lane boulevard he was driving on came to a bridge over the London Avenue canal, where the left lane continued over the bridge, and the right lane peeled off to the right and turned into a residential street. A sign with two arrows to show that the lane separated was mowed over so many times that the city just stopped replacing it. The guy in the first house on the street got tired of people knocking on his door at 2 a.m., so he painted the curb at the separation of the lanes with orange paint he bought at Home Depot, to no avail, then asked the city if he could put one of those concrete barriers in front to his house to keep cars out of his yard. The city said no, a concrete barrier might cause injury on impact. They suggested instead a dirt berm. Of course, this just launches the vehicle airborne, but no one thought of that apparently.

While deposing the homeowner, he recounted how just before daylight after my man's accident, the police returned searching his front yard with flashlight beams. He asked what they were doing. "Looking for the man's ear." Oops. "I saw my dachshund in the yard chewing on something after the accident!" Yes, it was my man's ear!

My client was also a member of the Hell's Angels and had tattoos all over his body. Swastikas everywhere, which was going to be a problem in a jury trial in Orleans Parish, which is over 80 percent African American. I deposed his treating neurosurgeon who saw him in the ER. My first question was, "Do you remember treating this man?"

"Oh yeah, I will never forget him. The very first time I saw him he was on the gurney, massive head injury, covered with a sheet, his bare feet sticking out. As I walked in, I couldn't help but notice he had two words tattooed to the bottom of his feet. 'F**k You!' But I treated him anyway."

The brain damage made my guy a gentle giant, an accidental frontal lobotomy. So I asked him one day, "Do you really have 'F**k You!' tattooed to the soles of your feet?"

He smiled, "Yep. We had to do that in the Hell's Angels."

"Why?" I asked.

"So when the coroner put the toe tag on us we would get the last word."

"Good thing the ER doc didn't listen."

# # #

In the winter of 1989, we found out that Lee was pregnant. Mom and Dad were elated, as were Lee and I, but I also realized my life was about to get more complicated and expensive. After a few cases, we were able to get rid of Lee's ancient black Datsun and buy a new four-door, red—Lee's favorite color—Honda Civic.

I kept driving the blue Dodge even though Nicholas—whom we found out had ADD—had been bouncing the seat up and back until it broke. I had to put a four-by-four behind the seat to prop it up, but it still looked like I was in a low-rider. One day later on, I asked Nicholas to close the trunk and he was strong enough to slam the thing so hard that it threw the trunk lid off center, just a hint of things to come.

So I was driving the old clunker while my wife had the nice new car just like Dad used to do. I had made sure that we could afford the mortgage payment without Lee having to work when we bought the house. My wife was not going to have babies and have to work. My Dad had taught me better than that.

Of course, Lee anguished over leaving her job. All women want families and careers. They discuss it in their secret underground meetings that they have when all of us husbands are asleep. They just have a dilemma not being with their children and being at work. So, we husbands try to do our best to be sure they don't have to work after having kids if they don't want to. But it is a no-win for us too. Truthfully we miss our kids as much as they do when we are working or on the road instead of being at home. So, don't accuse us of being out there working having fun instead of being at home. But we do it because, well, that's our job. And for you guys who stay home and let the wife work, whatever floats your boat. I just know for me, my wife ain't working because she has to.

And while I've stepped in it, I might as well track it around some. Wives have a saying, "Just let him think he's in charge," like they are really in charge. Well, I've got news. We husbands and Dads just let you think you are letting us think we are in charge. We play along, but we really are in charge. So there.

Which brings me to another subject, the secret to a good marriage. You ready? Sex. I can't give you a direct Bible quote for that other than that is what marriage is all about. And if my wife said it would turn her on if I stood buck naked on my head in the corner wearing chaps and six shooters spitting nickels, then *Yippee Kay Yah*! You get the picture. And pick a day, particularly if you have kids. Just find a door with a lock. Tuesday has always seemed to work for us. I mean, nothing good usually happens on a Tuesday, so why not? For years I have been in great moods on Tuesdays. No one can figure it out. Let 'em keep guessing.

But here's the point. For me anyway, sex wipes the slate clean, like getting flashed with that light by Kaye in *Men in Black*. Amnesia. As a great aunt told my Mama, "Don't go to bed angry, and don't discuss finances before breakfast." And my experience is that it is impossible to stay mad at someone you are sleeping with. It just can't be done. I can't even remember what I was mad about. Like hitting reset. God made us that way and it was for a reason. Use it.

Like all women in pregnancy, Lee reached a point when she started nesting, which meant turning the third room in the house into the baby's room. She bought a crib, toys, and furniture, painted and decorated. She also bought Nicholas a book about the biological changes a pregnant woman goes through so that he could follow along with everything. One of the pictures showed the child in utero with a description of the uterus, amniotic fluid, and so on.

Then Lee decided she needed to do something to increase her energy. "I feel like I want to be in good shape after I have this baby," she said, "so I want to start riding my bike."

"I don't think that's a good idea at eight months pregnant. What if you fall off?"

Nicholas was sitting at the kitchen table eating cereal. He never looked up, "Don't worry, Dad. If she falls off, the baby will be protected by the idiotic fluid." I started to worry, just a little. Spencer entered the world on August 1, 1990 after we watched the ramming scene from the movie Spartacus, and I experienced love in a new and powerful way.

Life kind of kept bouncing right along. Lee was happy to be at home with the kids, I was happy to work and provide for them, and I would like to say that we had no more and no less than the normal anxieties, challenges, and joys of any young family. But because I don't know what a normal family looks like, I can't say that for sure. The following summer, Dad retired and he and Mom moved back up to Winnfield. The camp on Saline Lake was still in the family, and this time it was my turn to bring the family up for the reunion. It was warm and good for us to be together. At some point each day, I took Spencer for a nap and lay with him on my chest humming him to sleep.

It took a little while for our next son to be born. Lee had a miscarriage. It was rough, but on January 16, 1994 during the fourth quarter of the NFC Championship game between the Green Bay Packers and Dallas Cowboys, Sam came into the world. I remember because Lee made the OB/GYN and I turn the game off when she went into transition.

# # #

We went to church and Sunday school at John Calvin Presbyterian. Dad had been an elder, so now that I was a father, I became the first second-generation elder.

Then during Sunday school, something odd happened. In the background was the campaign for the U.S. Senate between Mary Landrieu, Democrat, and Woody Jenkins, Republican and very prolife. Personally, I am prolife, so that's generally how I vote nationally, but I split on all the other issues mostly toward the Democrat side being a trial lawyer. Truthfully, sometimes I feel like a man without a country. I can't vote half-and-half. Lee is also prolife, so she leans to the Republicans. Walter, who other than my family is the most important person in my life, is a dyed-in-the-wool Democrat, prolife but not a "one issue" person. This left me in the middle between Lee, who wanted Jenkins' signs all over the yard, and Walter, who left a pile of Landrieu's signs on my desk every other day. I tried to be Switzerland, but it was an uneasy neutrality. I was glad when that election was over.

Lee had been visiting other churches and wanted to make a switch. She felt that the Presbyterian Church (USA) was too far on the liberal side. While I agreed, I didn't want to let go. I grew up in that church after all.

One morning at Sunday school taught by a lay woman, who was also an elder on the Session, with debate over the campaign swirling in the background she made the following statement, "I think what you believe about abortion is a personal issue that the Bible doesn't say anything about."

That's when I agreed to visit another church.

Lee had found Grace Presbyterian, a Presbyterian Church in America (PCA) church, nearby. As I understood it, back in the early 1970s the Presbyterian Church split over a range of spiritual and governance issues, and the PCA was born. I agreed with where the PCA fell regarding the governance issues, but I was most interested in its stand on traditional Christian theology and adherence to the Westminster Confession of Faith.

Anyway, Reverend Richard Davies had this one-hundred-fifty-member church off Clearview Parkway that Lee visited and said I should just come and give a listen. I went and it was the first time I'd heard expository preaching in which the minister works through the Bible verse-by-verse. Dick was working through the minor prophets and had gotten to the Book of Malachi. After the fourth Sunday, I went to him and asked, "Why do you keep picking on me in the back row?"

He laughed. "Why? Somebody's talking to you?"

"Yeah. Every time you say something, it's convicting me."

"Well, I think you're being convicted by the Word of God."

"Yeah, I suppose the truth is hard."

"That's why most people don't preach like this, but we go verse-by-verse because every verse is here for a reason and if it is hard news, it's hard news, but people need to hear the hard news." We switched.

I was kind of getting used to this living on faith business, so I wanted to start tithing but had some debts that had me hogtied. If I tithed, I might not be able to handle the bills. So I got an idea. One of the deacons of the church worked for our bank, so I worked with him to collapse some of my debt into one low interest loan so that I could tithe as Poppy instructed me to do as a kid. "Ten percent of the gross," Poppy admonished, "not what you make after taxes. God deserves His due." And so, I began to give to God ten percent of everything I made. And I have never worried about money since.

#

Lee and I seemed to hit a groove with a new son every two years or so, and we didn't have much of a desire to stop. Well, maybe I did. I suggested birth control, but she wouldn't even consider taking "the pill," much less anything else. No estrogen therapy for her. So being a good husband, I decided to try to take things into my own hands, so to speak.

A few nights later she sauntered out of the bathroom, romantically dressed, eased up to my nightstand, and picked up a packet. One eyebrow went up, "Trojan? Really, Trojan? What am I supposed to do, act surprised and say, 'Gee honey, I wonder what's inside this thing'?"

And then it hit me. I had bought a condom from a company with probably the worst marketing department on earth. A company that named its product, a condom, after a bunch of guys that got together and said, "Okay, here's the plan, we all hide in this big thing and when we get inside, we all jump out and charge!" What a terrible name! I surrendered and decided to fly without a net, like the trapeze act, The Flying Zucchini Brothers.

Now I don't say this to be crude. Rather, this was a test for us, really for me, on whether we were going to trust God in our marriage or not? The Bible says that children are a blessing from the Lord. They are like arrows. Blessed is the man whose quiver is full. Don't get me wrong. I had nothing against doing a lot of quivering. But I had my reservations. My doubts. But Lee didn't and I shouldn't have either. So our attitude from then on was that we would take and love what the Lord gave us.

Then in the early morning on Monday April 8, 1996 just after Easter Sunday, after the movie The Ten Commandments, Fletcher was born. Dr. Hevron was a little late on this one. The head was out, and the resident and I were about to turn the shoulders when he came running in. I figured about one third of the baby was already delivered when he got there, so as I paid cash up front, I was due a refund. Being a Tulane graduate though, he wouldn't even entertain the notion.

Lee wanted each birth to be natural, which meant taking Lamaze classes. This was coaching on a different level. We took the class with each pregnancy because I'd trained myself in college, law school, and with each case to immediately forget everything the moment the exam, class, or case ended. It was called a brain flush. To get me focused on having another kid, I had to go to Lamaze class.

When Lee became pregnant yet again, this time with Jackson, I was off to Lamaze class with the same instructor who had taught each time. I made it through Lamaze once more and then on October 12, 1998 after Hurricane George's drop in barometric pressure almost sent Lee into an early labor, Jackson was born. We were at the same hospital where the Lamaze class was taught. While I stood next to Jackson's bassinet in the nursery inspecting his dot (I always put a dot with a Sharpie on their foot and neurotically followed them into the nursery so they wouldn't get mixed up with someone else's kid), the Lamaze teacher noticed me and asked, "Since you've been through it a few times, do you mind coming and talking to a class I'm teaching in a few minutes?"

Next thing I knew, I was standing in front of five or six pregnant couples explaining that I always knew when Lee was going through transition—the toughest phase of labor just before pushing—because she threw up. "That means its show time and you're about to have this baby."

A terrified looking guy in the back raised his hand. "I have one question. Does it hurt?"

"No, not at all. It won't hurt you one bit." He still seemed concerned.

#

Life opened to me and for the first time, I could see, truly see. Meaningful love, children, and a sense of direction and expanding curiosity about God were greater rewards than I could have ever asked for and gave life the sense of meaning and purpose that drove so many of my past anxieties and the desire to placate that emptiness with alcohol.

It was also during this period of my life that Uncle Frank's health began to fail. Uncle Frank's life was something of a mixed bag. He liked to sit out on his porch with his Bible and leaf through it. He also had to file for bankruptcy for the store. After that, he sold his house and moved back into the old home in town. Then there was some hoo-rah-rah over a bill Uncle Frank owed Uncle John at the car dealership that Dad got all mad about, but went up and paid.

Uncle Frank's retirement consisted of golf most days and drinks with Aunt Martha. The two of them never had kids, and their social circle was rather small, so I assume it may have been a lonely retirement. Then he was diagnosed with cancer. He had a colostomy, bag and all, which was later reversed. It was pretty painful.

Then he was diagnosed with liver cancer. The doctor told him it wasn't possible to operate, but they could do chemotherapy. Uncle Frank had planted a pile of garlic, onions, and shallots in his backyard garden, and I don't know quite where he got the idea, but he ate as much of them as he could stand. Raw.

He also decided to start chewing tobacco rather than smoke his unfiltered Camels. After a few months, he went back for a scan and to meet with the doctor. "We don't understand what happened, but whatever you're doing, keep doing it because the tumor is about a quarter of the size it was on the last scan." So, he went back to chewing tobacco, shoveling down raw onions and garlic and sitting on his porch reading his Bible. Eventually the cancer caught up with him, and Dad called me to say that Uncle Frank's kidneys were shutting down. I drove up to Winnfield, and when I got there, Uncle Frank was swollen up and died a little while later.

Like every other, Uncle Frank's funeral was held at First Methodist Church. And as at every funeral, when the choir started singing "Holy, Holy, Holy," tears poured from my eyes. But this time was different. As with Poppy's funeral, I felt the deep and moving presence of God, but I also reflected on Uncle Frank's life, the golf, whiskey, choices he'd made, conflicts with Dad, and what to me seemed to be a lonely life.

I looked around the church, my cheeks moist with tears, and the question that passed through my mind was, *Am I the only one here who's going to cry and mourn for his soul?* I knew I wasn't, and maybe it was because I had his name, but I felt like it.

It wasn't that he was a bad person. He was close with Mom, and the two loved to share recipes and cooking secrets. And he was good at golf and how to shoot a bird—something I am still bad at despite years of duck hunting—and all sorts of different things. But I felt that I was the only person there truly mourning for him. Otherwise, he was just this guy up in Winnfield who drank and ended up with a failed business, and that was it. It just seemed so sad.

The finality of it struck me in an emotional way and I remember someone saying that it's not until we come face-to-face with death that we consider questions of eternity. If you are an alcoholic, you must do that every day. In fact, I feel like I have been to hell for a little peek of what it must be like.

By then I'd sat down with Pastor Davies and said, "Okay, I'm going to read the Bible, a chapter every day, the whole thing, from start to finish." And the experience was eye opening. Until you read *Genesis* to *Revelation* you don't get the whole story. What I started to see with greater clarity was that the truths taught to me by Poppy, Mom, Dad, and others as I grew up—the last shall be first, you must lose your life to keep it—all those things in the Scriptures are true.

In recovery you learn through experience that you had to lose to win, stop fighting, let go and let God, and be totally dependent on something greater than yourself. And as I studied reformed theology I started to understand the five points of Calvinism: *Total Depravity* (also known as Original Sin),

Unconditional Election, Limited Atonement, Irresistible Grace, and *Preservation of the Saints* (also known as *The Assurance of Grace*).

Presbyterians know this by its acronym TULIP. The first, *Total Depravity,* means that we are not as bad as we could be, but we are never going to be good enough to stand before a truly holy and righteous God. This always reminds me of something Lee says to the kids when they ask to be a "little bit" naughty. Just a little bit of sin won't hurt, right?

"I'll tell you what I'll do," she says. "I'll make a pan of brownies because I know you love brownies, but I'm going to put a little bit of chicken poop in them."

The kids go, "*Ewwww.*"

"But, it's just a little bit."

Sound familiar? Half measures availed us nothing?

And folks, let's just be frank (pun intended), we all have a little bit of chicken poop in our brownies. So we need God's help because on our own we are toast.

When I think of *Unconditional Election,* I think of the question, *Why me?* Of all the people God could have pulled from the oncoming bus, why me?

When I was a kid, there was a boy four years younger than me who lived across the street. I was sweet on his sister—she put up with my crush and seemed to think it was sweet—and he swam on the same swim team as me and so on. Years later, I ran into him at a meeting. I told him it was good to see him and that I'd run into some folks from the old neighborhood from time to time. We talked for a bit.

Not long after, he got lost again and drank himself to death in his parents' house. They'd given it to him because he couldn't take care of himself. He isn't the only person I've known who's done that. A friend from football died when he drove off I-55 after eating five Quaaludes. Meanwhile, I slid sideways down I-10 at three-thirty in the morning doing eighty miles per hour after the road crew just cut the grass so the clippings sprayed in through the open driver's side window, and I came to rest unhurt. Why did I not die? How did I manage to sidestep the freight train called cocaine when so many others were run over by it like a deer on the tracks?

Years after Vietnam, Mike the ex-Army Ranger and I went duck hunting and he told me he had been saved. I said, "That's funny, me too." We talked about coming to faith, and he told me the only story I ever heard from him about Vietnam.

He and a buddy were sitting on a log in the jungle facing opposite directions when they heard incoming mortar fire. Instinctively they both rolled over backward to take cover. His friend was killed. He wasn't. What pestered him for years until he got saved was the question *why?* Why him and not his buddy? He knew there had to be a reason, and he turned to God to find it.

There are more stories than I can even remember, but they all lead to the same question, *why me?* Only God knows.

Which leads to *Limited Atonement.* God doesn't save everybody. That is apparent. Just read your newspaper.

And then there's *Irresistible Grace.* Once God lays his fingers on you, there's not much you can do but go with it. This was how it was with me. I didn't want to go, then never wanted to go back.

Preservation of the Saints seems to be like what Paul Harvey used to say on the radio, "And that's the rest of the story." I'm still here thirty years after falling to my knees, and if you ask me how I did it, all I can say is, "There but for the grace of God go I."

And whenever I've felt lost, I walk outside and look up into the sky and ask God, "Okay, what do I do now?" I've found that if there's not a firm feeling the next morning, then the answer is don't do anything. Sometimes the best thing is to remain still and quiet. And wait. Or as they say nowadays, "Just wait for it!"

When Uncle Frank died and I stood at his funeral unable to sing with tears falling from my eyes, I was reminded how lucky I was. But, it wasn't luck. It was God's amazing grace, pure and simple. The restlessness I'd felt for so many years was gone. As Saint Augustine wrote, "Our heart is restless until it repose in Thee." [35] Whatever hole it was that I was trying to fill with drink and drugs was now filled by God.

#

One weeknight in 1995, it started raining and it picked up until it was an absolute downpour. It was about eight at night, and I was snoozing in the chair that Ganny gave me when I graduated from law school. Years of sitting in it smoking, drinking, watching football, and then bounced on by a growing number of boys left it beat up with cigarette burns, but I loved that chair. Nicholas was about fourteen, and he shook me awake. "Dad, there's water coming underneath the door."

I looked over at the kitchen, and I had water coming underneath the door.

"What the hell?"

Nicholas and I tried to put rolled up towels against the door jam, but it didn't do a thing to stop the water from coming in. "It's not supposed to flood here," I said, "we're the highest place in the Parish."

The water kept pouring in and we did what we could to stop it, but the level kept rising until I noticed a box of doughnuts on the counter. "Well, Nicholas, we might as well have a doughnut because there ain't a thing we can do about the water." We stood in the rising water and ate doughnuts.

Soon the water got near an electrical outlet and raised the hair on my leg. I looked at Nicholas. "I guess it might be a good idea if we went outside and turned the power off."

At this point, Lee came into the kitchen and said we should get things up off the floor so we started piling things on beds, but we lost a lot of stuff. All my albums were ruined—Humble Pie, The Who, Jethro Tull—and our wedding albums were soaked. Eventually, Lee took the kids to one of the neighbors whose house was built later and higher so that it didn't flood. I spent the rest of the night trying to save what I could and generally keeping an eye on things. Not sure why, but there I was, a suburban Noah.

The rain stopped during the night, and the next day I learned the flood was caused by a blocked drainage canal underneath Airline Highway. Apparently, a crew working on a bridge had put sheet pilings down so they could do the work, but they were covering the drains. If it rained someone was supposed to come and lift those pilings out with a crane, but no one showed up, and it rained nine inches that night.

The neighbors across the street were out of town, and their house was set lower than ours so the water was still up to their air conditioner. When it kicked on, it looked like an outboard motor with water shooting up into the air. I ran over and shut the electricity down so the air conditioner would stop.

Morning dawned, helicopters were flying overhead, and I realized the water was receding. I needed to open the doors to let the water out. I pushed the backdoor open and water flowed out carrying all sorts of things with it, so I grabbed my fishing net and caught Legos, plastic toys, and other debris as it floated out the door.

Once the water was out, I moved the furniture outside onto the driveway with Nicholas, which was a struggle since it was all soaked. Then we eyeballed rolling up the wet carpet with the padding. I didn't know how I was going to get the energy to drag it outside. By about ten that morning I was pretty punch drunk, standing in the den, looking at the water line left on the wall. How I was going to deal with the wet carpets, drywall, all our things that were ruined, where we would live, and all the rest of it? Tears welled in my eyes, and for the first time I felt a tinge of desperation. I looked up at the ceiling and offered an emotional prayer. "Help!"

Seconds later, two friends pulled up in the driveway. They'd been riding around in their truck and stopped to see if I needed any help. Boy, did I! They walked through the door smiling ear-to-ear. "Where do we start?"

They were the answer to my prayer.

We rolled the carpets, tied them to the back of the truck, and dragged them out the front window. Within an hour or so, all the wet carpet was out of the house. Then we took utility knives and cut out all the wet sheetrock and hauled that into a pile in the driveway. By the time it started to get dark, we had finished, and I admired the bare floors and studs four feet up throughout the entire three-bedroom house. It had been a long two days.

When Lee walked in, she started crying.

"Why are you crying?" I asked.

"Look at my house." Your house? My brain engaged. "Whoa, whoa, whoa, wait a minute. Remember, we have insurance, right?"

"Yeah."

"Didn't you want to move that fireplace?"

"Yes."

"And didn't you want to get rid of the breakfast nook and move that wall over?"

"Yes."

"And didn't you want tile flooring in here?"

"Yes."

"Well, now is your chance."

"You mean I can remodel now?"

"You bet." And her countenance changed.

I heard a speaker say once, "Everyone should lose everything at least once because it will reorient them as to what's important and meaningful and what isn't."

That lesson would come back to serve us again.

Chapter Ten

Playing with the Boys

I could clearly see that God had done things I never would have been able to do for myself. I don't believe in coincidences. There was simply no way that I could have moved from my dead-end job with a defense firm (no offense to defense lawyers) to a partnership in a plaintiff's firm without God working out the details. Just happenstance? Not hardly. So I tried to do God's will, as well as I could make it out, as a father, husband, lawyer, and in the things I enjoyed. Like coaching kids' football. Football is life, and life is football.

At the playgrounds with the other coaches, we always worked to help the kids become better people. To develop character. This meant making sure they got their school work done and made their grades. We taught them the value of teamwork and did our best to set good examples. And we prayed before games. No one objected. My wife homeschooled our boys, but they lined up and played football with all the other kids. I guess you could say that was how they developed "social skills."

My boys were raised color neutral. When they played with GI Joe's, I was happy to hear them ask for "that brown guy" over there. To them brown was just another color in the Crayola box. I knew that to cement it, they needed to play sports because the clock, the tape, the scoreboard, and the report card don't lie and don't care what color you are, nor do your teammates. We reinforced those lessons with biblical teachings, like *man looks at external appearances, but God looks at the heart*. It is disheartening to live in a world that constantly tries to undo what we have tried to teach. Have I been perfect? No, far from it. But I try, and we have never stopped trying.

I can think of playground players that I have had the pleasure to coach, who have gone on to play at colleges like Auburn, Michigan, Nebraska, and Mississippi State. Then there were others like our center and team captain who made straight A's and the President's List for achieving a 4.0 grade point average, even though his father was in prison. The year my quarterback's father died midseason and the other times I acted more as a child psychologist than a coach. Our tight end, who I admonished at practice one day, "You have to think, son!" to which he replied with a mischievous grin, "Coach, that could be dangerous!" And there have been all the others in between. After many practices, I would give rides home to four or five of these kids with their bikes piled into my truck. On the way home, we'd stop for fries and cheeseburgers. Those days were great.

I finally bought a bay boat to fish the south Louisiana marshes. And to teach my boys how to slalom ski and ride a tube. Clothed. I had my eye on an eighteen footer, but really wanted the twenty-one foot model and wanted to get Lee's approval. When I brought Lee in to see the boat, the salesman took her gently by the arm and asked, "How many boys do you have?"

"Four."

"Isn't it going to be nice when Frank takes all the boys fishing on Saturday, and you can go shopping by yourself?"

"Yeah, that will be great."

"Well then, this boat isn't big enough to do that. He needs this twenty-one footer over here."

She turned to me. "You need to buy that twenty-one footer over there." Man, that's what I call a salesman!

Raising boys, I came to say things that I never thought I would hear myself saying. Things like:

"That thing's not loaded is it?"

"Gee, that must have hurt!"

"Don't lock your brother in the dog kennel! How many times do I have to tell you!"

"I don't care who did it, all of you line up!"

"I told you that thing was sharp." (Or hot, or would shock you, etc., etc.)

And, "What is the lawnmower doing on the roof?"

There were some benefits. Like the emergency room at the local hospital knowing us so well that they could spot me and have my paperwork ready before I got up the driveway to the door.

At times it was funny. Like when Nicholas had his birthday party in fourth grade. My job was to wear out a bunch of eight year olds. The plan was a party at the house with squirt guns and Slip 'N Slides, then baseball, bowling, pizza, and all night movies.

As I stood on the driveway in my khaki shorts surveying the mayhem, I heard a squishing noise and looked down to find the worst kid in fourth grade going to town squirting a water gun at point blank range on my crotch. He looked me in the face, smiled, and tore off across the front yard screaming at the top of his lungs, "Nic's Dad peed on himself! Nic's Dad peed on himself!"

I wanted to kill him dead.

Then there was the Sunday night after Christmas and New Year's when we had a hard freeze, and a stomach virus ripped through the house. Normally that would not be a problem, as Mom would be on it. I had to work the next morning, and this time Mom fell victim too. I was on my own.

At 2:00 a.m., I heard retching and pulled one of the boys from his bed. As he hugged the porcelain throne I took the sheets out on the back deck and hosed them out into the yard. Then I went back in and got him situated on the floor with a handy bowl nearby.

As I headed back out to the deck, I thought, these sheets feel crunchy. They were frozen stiff. The temperature was in the low twenties after all. I turned toward the back door and hit the ice on the deck. *Zooop!* Down I went flat on my back. The stars were beautiful as I heard the back door swing shut and latch. Ah, the joys of parenthood.

One time after the birthday party, Nicholas was invited to dinner with his grandmother, aunt, and uncle. It was at a nice Italian place, coat and tie and all. Nic's Aunt turned to him. "Nicholas, would you like some calamari?"

"*Ewwww!* I'd rather have a vaginal yeast infection!"

Silence. You could have heard a pin drop.

Calmly, his grandmother inquired. "Nicholas, do you even know what that is?"

Of course fourth grade boys don't know what that is. They just saw it on TV.

"No ma'am! But you can cure it with Monistat 7!"

Our time raising the boys was perhaps the sweetest time of my life. I attended church on Wednesday nights, men's bible study Friday mornings, and Sunday services morning and evening.

Except maybe the time in the Sunday morning service called "A Time for Children" (it just invites disaster, doesn't it?) when the children come forward for a mini-sermon and prayer before being dismissed. During the prayer one Sunday, my son Sam scooted around behind the pastor who was seated on the carpeted steps and proudly flashed bunny ears behind his head. One of the deacon's wife sitting nearby looked as if flaming darts were about to shoot out of her eyes.

I met four year old Sam as he exited the back door, and seized his arm. He protested before he got spanked. "But we were praying! You were all supposed to have your eyes closed!"

One day, I was at the office when Lee called frantically. Fletcher was a year-old toddler in diapers.

"Fletcher is gone! I've looked everywhere! He must have gotten out of the house somehow! I am about to call the police!"

"Okay, I am on my way." Before I could leave the office my phone rang again.

"We found him. He and the Lab were asleep in the kennel."

I also forgot what real music was unless it was redone by Weird Al Yankovich. "Dare to Be Stupid!" is my favorite. It just fits somehow.

About that time I realized I was listening to talk radio. I had turned into my father! I was shocked listening to those old rock and roll songs I used to like so much. The lyrics are filthy! I can't believe we ever listened to that trash. I don't know why I never heard any of the words before. Then again, I thought REO Speed Wagon was singing a song about a Hispanic girl named *Inuletta*. Turns out the name of the song was "In Your Letter." Who knew?

It is impossible to summarize thirty years of raising seven boys. We did everything from fishing, hunting, swimming, football, baseball, you name it. And I had more fun than they did.

So, thanks guys, but I am not done yet.

#

The biggest issue Lee and I have had in our marriage, as I see it, was over the boys, and the single most important thing in our son's lives would be having a personal saving relationship with God through Jesus Christ. This is not surprising, is it? That two people in recovery would believe that the maintenance of one's spiritual condition is the only defense against sin, much less the first drink or drug?

We had found out that salvation through Jesus Christ was the only basis for any type of happy life. We live in a secular, godless world and I knew that without God in their lives, my sons would be at risk. I also knew that I had to trust God with everything and that included my children. I could not predetermine their path of faith and neither could she. After all, I was not God, was I? So, although this would be hard, we knew what was at stake. And if we disagreed and fought over how to be sure our boys knew Christ, at least we were both worried over the same thing.

Lee wanted to homeschool the kids. She rightly feels that it doesn't matter what each boy learned to do for a living; if he did not walk with God daily in a personal relationship of faith, what difference would it make how successful he was? I agree. However, I also agree that God calls a man to his work and that he must work to be happy. So he needs to learn to make his way in the world and be successful beginning with school. And although we could homeschool for a while, I knew there would come a point when we just couldn't teach what we didn't know. So in the back of my mind I figured that eventually they would have to go to school. More importantly, I knew that no matter whether they went to school or were homeschooled they would face the enemies of the world—the flesh and the devil—regardless. I was on the horns of a dilemma with no way to win but to trust God. And this was my call ultimately. I could not hide behind my wife.

One thing that Lee and I did agree on was that we would not raise our kids in a recovery program. God is bigger than that, and we did not want to fit them with a predetermined outcome destined to come true. When the age was right, I would let them know what was what. So we pulled Spencer from private school after first grade and became homeschoolers.

My appreciation of the depths of man's sinful nature, even in sanctification, has always been too shallow. I have seen in churches, schools, and other Christian organizations disputes and conflicts arise between the most godly men and women over the most mundane, trivial, and nonexistent matters that

I can only attribute to the depths of human pride, covetousness, or other unde-termined defects of human nature, if not the devil himself. So it was not too surprising that after a time at Grace Presbyterian Church, in God's providence, there was conflict.

The nature of the issue, as best as I can determine in hindsight, was over homeschooling, though its source, as it usually is, was human ego and fal-libility. Within the congregation there was a group who became dedicated to homeschooling as the proper way to ensure the spiritual education and upbringing of their children. They wanted to protect their children from the outside world filled with ungodly influences. There were others who were as meticulous about their children's spiritual training, but didn't mind if they went to school. Both views were valid, and in my estimation, each person had to do what they thought best for them. And with either, there were no guarantees.

Personally, I didn't have a problem with schooling, even though we were homeschooling Spencer, Sam, and Fletcher. The "issue" (which again to me was a "nonissue") put me, an elder, and a member of the Session in the middle. Fortunately, the friction would take some time before it became a fire.

After Jackson was born, life moved to its own rhythm and routine. We rebuilt the house after the '95 flood, and life remained centered on God, family, foot-ball, and church. Then in the summer of 2002, Lee said, "It's time for you to go back to Lamaze class." Ross "The Boss" was welcomed into the world on February 6, 2003.

In late June, Dad called to say he had been diagnosed with lung cancer in his left lower lobe, and he was going in for surgery. He was 79 years old but acted like it was well in hand, and this was just a bump in the road. Of course, he always had that attitude.

He'd retired years before, and he and Mom had moved back up to Win-nfield, which to me felt like they'd come full circle in their lives. They'd gone off to the city, raised a family, achieved financial security if not prosperity, and were more than deserving of a quiet and long retirement.

When they first moved back, they lived in their camp on Saline Lake while they waited for a house to be built on a slice of property off Highway 84, right across the street from Garden of Memories Cemetery. Poppy, Ganny, Grandpa and Grandma Shaw, and their ancestors were buried in the cemetery in town, which was now full. There would be no vacancies until Jesus's return, and who would want a plot then anyway, so those of my parents' generation moved out of town.

I remember walking with Dad during the house construction. "This is the last house I'm ever going to build. Then my last move will be across the road."

"Dad, don't talk like that." But I knew that was exactly the way he would talk. He didn't pull any punches. And I knew just what he meant, but I couldn't imagine it happening any time soon. He went in for the surgery, which went about as expected, but he never seemed to fully recover from it.

In the fall of 2002, I helped coach Spencer's football team to the Jefferson Parish East Bank Championship, and I was cajoled into coaching baseball the following spring for the first time. The Spaulding book, *Coaching Youth Baseball* by LSU Coach "Skip" Bertman had everything in it that I needed to know, plus I ended up with a good many of my players from football. We had fun and a good season, but as football approached, our line coach, who was to step in as head coach that year, bailed out just weeks before the season began, which left me as head coach. He said his wife didn't want him to coach "because I think about it, all the time." Okay, what else is new?

Truthfully, we had just lived at the park during baseball for the last several months having three boys playing, all in different leagues at different times. We had to split up at times for the games. So for me to coach the Minors, ages eleven and twelve, in football after that baseball season with no kids on the team, well Lee had to have the patience of Job. After that season, though, she put her foot down, and my playground coaching career was on sabbatical.

I prepared the team leading up to our opening Jamboree game. On the day of the game, Friday, September 5, 2003, Mom called. Dad's sodium was elevated, which had happened with him before. This could cause cardiac issues if untreated, so he was admitted to the local hospital in Winnfield. I talked to him on the phone.

"Look, you need me to come up? Because I want to be with you," I said to my dad.

"No, you go coach your football game and come on up tomorrow. I will be fine." I agonized over it, but finally did what I thought he would do. I stayed and coached.

I got my gear together, and that night my guys played really well against a

St. Bernard team, *The Storm*, but it wasn't enough. We lost by a single touchdown. Sad but proud, I went home and around one in the morning Mom called.

"Frank, your Dad's had a massive heart attack or seizure and he coded. They brought him back, but he is in bad shape"

She and Dad had talked about what to do if something like this happened, and they decided to place a do-not-resuscitate (DNR) order in his chart. But when he went into arrest, the code team didn't see the order and brought him back with a defibrillator after his heart had stopped for about five minutes. Once they had a rhythm back, they gave him steroids and other drugs to stabilize him, as well as a feeding and intubation tube because he had massive brain damage.

When I arrived at the ICU unit at Winn Parish Medical Center, I was nearly brought to my knees by what I saw. His body was pale and swollen, there were tubes running from his mouth and arms, his mouth was chapped and dry, and I could barely see his eyes from the swelling in his face. I leaned over him and his eyes widened a little bit.

"Dad, I love you." I looked up at Mom then back to him. "There's a better place in heaven for you, and I know that you're going to be there and that I'll see you again one day. It's going to be okay." Then I kissed him on the forehead.

His eyes never left me and he tried to say something, but the intubation tube that breathed for him meant he couldn't speak. In my mind, I knew he was saying, "Pull this damn thing out of my mouth and let me go."

All I could say was, "Okay, Dad, I love you."

Mom, Lee, Jack, and I stayed with Dad for as long as the ICU staff let us and then went to the house for the night. The next morning, we went back to the hospital, and while Dad looked about the same as the day before, I could tell he was uncomfortable and in pain.

A few minutes later, Dad's doctor came in and gave us an update. It did not look good. I glanced at Mom and could tell she was listening, but her mind was chewing on something. When the doctor finished, Mom asked if they could speak in the hallway.

When she came back in, it was about quarter-to-eleven and she said, "Okay, let's go eat."

I looked at her. It seemed a bit early, but I didn't protest.

The four of us went to a Chinese buffet just down the street. We chatted quietly and sort of tried to game out what would happen next. We finished about the time church was letting out so we went back to the hospital and up to the ICU.

When we got to the desk outside of the ICU there was a male nurse named Toby waiting for us. "I'm sorry, but he's gone."

"Gone?" I asked.

"Yes, somehow he managed to pull the breathing tube out and passed while you were gone."

Dad was a strong man, but I don't know if he could do that. I never asked Mom what she thought. It seemed best just to leave it alone. We went into the room where he lay. The quiet struck me. No beeps or alarms. No blinking lights. Everything was still and peaceful. Uncle John and Aunt Sarah came over straight from church. It was a sad time.

No matter how prepared you may think you are to lose a parent, you aren't. I was devastated, and though I believe your days are appointed and when it's your time, well, it's your time, it was hard for me to accept that he was gone. I do know that I will see him again, and I also know that when my day comes, he will greet me by asking, "Why didn't you pull that damn tube out when I told you to?"

Dad was clear in what he wanted after his death. He had a suit he liked and said would be comfortable enough for the occasion, and he'd always told me and Mom that he wanted to be buried in a simple pine box. "Dad," I said, "they don't make pine boxes anymore."

The day after he died, Mom, my sister Lee, and I went to the funeral home and told the director we needed a pine box.

"Really?"

"Yeah, really," I said.

This is the same man who helped bury Poppy, Ganny, Uncle Frank, and other family members, so he led us over to a basic brown casket made of southern pecan. "That's the one," I said. I'm not sure if that's what Mom and Lee had in mind, and it wasn't exactly what Dad had in mind, but it was a good compromise. Before Dad made his final journey to Garden of Memories, there was the visitation time in the funeral home. The time came to go to the church, and I was the last one at the casket before they closed it.

I learned my parenting techniques from my Dad. I mean just look how I turned out, right? I never drank or smoked around my kids, but like Dad, I felt it best to let them fight and figure out some things on their own. I worried that they needed to be tough enough to make it.

Dad and I had been through a lot with my drinking. He always had my back. As a father, that was his job, I suppose. He never complained, not once. And he never complained when he went to work, day in and day out, until he retired. I knew he did it for us; in essence he gave his life for us. He gave himself for us. And then it hit me! Fathers are called to be like Jesus and give their lives for their families. To set their faces like flint and just do it.

Then I remembered a hymn Dad liked. I liked it too. "Be Thou My Vision." I had been told the necessity of having a vision, a man without vision will perish. But for Jesus to be my vision? To empty myself, to give my life for my family? To be conformed to the image of Christ? That became my vision. And I formed one single concrete goal for my life. To die stone, cold sober. That's it.

I squeezed the casket lip and closed my eyes to talk to him one last time. Silently I said, "Dad, I'm going to make it." And I didn't hear him say anything. I don't believe in that stuff. But I felt him say, "I know you will." And that was good enough for me.

My brother had come up behind me and took my shoulder. "Come on, it's time to let go." I've always felt he misunderstood and thought I was grieving uncontrollably or refusing to let go. Actually, I was oddly happy.

Then we all made the trip to First Methodist Church for the service. As with every other funeral, tears flowed from my eyes, and I was unable to sing much less speak. Again, I was stopped by the overwhelming presence of God. The church was filled with people who knew, loved, and respected my Dad, and it was also filled with the presence of the Lord.

I coached football for the remainder of that year and that helped ease the pain of losing Dad, but as with all things I love, it was all or nothing. I never did anything halfway. As in seasons past, all I thought about was football. All the time. We had six kids, the law practice was booming, and Lee had had enough of feeling like a single parent.

"You need to lay off," she said to me as the season wound down. "We've had nothing but baseball and football all year long, and I'm putting my foot down. No more coaching."

Thinking back, she was right. Ross was still bouncing around in diapers, and here I was working and coaching football like a man possessed, but I still didn't like being told what to do by my wife. I suppose this was one of the little bits of chicken poop in my brownies. It still riled me to be told what to do. I didn't argue with her, at least not too much, and I did tell the other coaches to count me out for next year.

In the background, too, was the growing tension within the church between the more strident homeschooling faction and those who took a more open attitude to school. The friction between the two was starting to create some heat, but had not yet created a conflagration. And I was still in the middle of it all.

And within that, I couldn't help but reflect on the guidance and example set by Dad, his belief in education, and that school was important. It felt hard to say that our kids wouldn't go to school and would miss out on some of the educational opportunities I had as well as what they would get from a school setting. So, I put my foot down and enrolled Spencer into seventh grade.

Like I said, Lee's position was that she would rather have a kid who's going to go to heaven and be a plumber than a kid who's going to go to hell and be a nuclear physicist. I just felt I'd rather err on the side of being practical, understanding that a man should find his calling, which you do through school and education. I also wondered how much force we could apply on these kids to accept our faith before they started doing what I did as a kid. After all, salvation is of the Lord, is it not?

Lee wasn't happy about it, but taking things into my own hands, I enrolled Spencer in seventh grade at Crescent City Baptist. I knew other boys who went to school there, our Pastor's son and the son of a good friend who was a deacon, so I figured it must be a good school academically and spiritually. I had also heard they had a good baseball program and thought that would be something Spencer would enjoy, and it would be healthy for him.

Unfortunately, things didn't turn out that well.

There was one kid in particular who decided to bully Spencer and make his life hell. Spencer is left handed in most things. Since he was little, he just didn't know which hand to use to pick up and throw a baseball. I would roll the baseball to him and he'd pick it up and throw it back with his right hand. I'd roll it again and he'd pick it up with his left and throw it back.

"Spencer, I don't care which hand it is, but you have to decide which one you're going to throw with and which one you're going to catch with."

He went with his right, but there was always a kink in his motion that didn't look natural and took a bit off the ball. In the end, I bought him a right-handed and a left-handed glove and said use whichever one you want. He could switch hit, though, and I thought that would give him an advantage among the other kids. But he really didn't turn out to be a great baseball player. That was okay, I just thought he should play.

It didn't work. The baseball program at Crescent City is competitive because of its reputation, and the other kids picked on Spencer and gave him all kinds of grief on how he threw the ball and played the game. And they weren't Christian kids. Far from it. He asked if he could quit, but I thought that would set a bad example for him, you know, when the going gets tough, you don't quit. The result was the bullying didn't stop, and he even got into a fight, which for a gentle kid like Spencer was a big deal.

Lee wasn't happy about it either. "See, see," she said, "it's just a cesspool of fools, and he's going to sink to the lowest common denominator of all those fools."

The topper came when the pastor of the school and its associated church was accused of mismanaging the money for both. So yet again, another church I was associated with risked being torn apart by conflict. It got so bad that a suit was filed by some members of the congregation who wanted to oust the pastor and the board. A mediator was assigned after the pastor decided to fire the principal of the school. This set off a big ruckus, and I had put Spencer in the middle of it all.

One day a bunch of parents decided they would go to the school and pray for the principal. They met to pray in the circular drive in front of the school's entrance with the American flag flying on a pole right above them. And the pastor called the sheriff's department to remove the "protesters." Of course, the whole scene was on the news that night. *Ahhhhhhhh!*

It couldn't have blown up in my face any worse, so I agreed with Lee. He needed to be homeschooled. The effect of all this on Spencer was to turn him off big time to the church and God. I take heart that Spencer has kept an open mind toward faith and is the type of person to always seek out a spiritual path. I've also worked on apologizing to him for all that happened and to make the point that God is not small, that He is much larger than we can wrap our heads around. Surely He can work through these circumstances.

And then the friction between the strident homeschoolers and the open-to-school groups caught fire. This led to people leaving church, lingering bad feelings, and unresolved conflict. Again, what could have been a beautiful testament to the Lord got screwed up by human beings. The devil managed to get in the middle of people who didn't drink, didn't smoke, were dedicated husbands and wives, who loved our children, and sought to be of service to the Lord. All because of pride and sinfulness.

I was in shock that people could get as ugly as they did. It made me think that I don't mind putting myself under God, but I'm not going to put myself under man just for man's purposes. I also don't mind being submissive—for example, I happily consent to Walter's leadership and that he is my boss—but there's a limit.

At the same time, I'd pledged to act as an elder and member of the Session to this church. For good or bad, I'd given my word to God and others and now it was being tested. There were nights when I stood in our driveway looking up into the firmament and asked God again, "What should do?" Then I waited for His reply.

Hurricane Katrina wasn't the answer to anyone's prayers, but that's when it came along.

In the winter of 2004, Lee and I decided that we'd grown out of our house. We had it fixed up after the flood and were more than happy with it, but it was just too small. Lee was homeschooling the kids, so there was constant and frenetic activity in every available nook and cranny, and Lee wanted to have a couple of horses. Also, with my legal career and the practice doing well, we had the money to build something of our own.

We set about finding a piece of land near enough to New Orleans for me to commute to work but with enough acres to support the small farm Lee envisioned. We ended up buying a twenty-acre, plot just across the river. The land was undeveloped and was habitat to palmetto, swamp oaks, water moccasins, and various assorted other reptiles and mammals you'd expect to find in southern Louisiana. That includes our state bird, the mosquito.

There was a lot of timber, so I called in a guy from Mississippi and told him he could have the lumber if he cleared or burned the rest of the small trees and brush. Before he came in to cut, Lee and I decided we wanted to save some trees for shade, so I spent a day walking the property marking trees and getting hung up in banana spider webs. Banana spiders are about the size of your hand and their webs are huge.

While the logger started clearing the land, I called the State and Jefferson Parish to see if I needed a wetlands determination. They said no, the property was "fastland," land within a levee system that is being drained for development. I was reluctant, but I called the Army Corps of Engineers anyway. They said, "Oh yeah, you need a wetlands determination. There're wetlands here so you'll need a permit to build anything."

"How much of the property is wetlands? How is that determined?"

"You have plants that grow when the soil is wet." What a crock! It was within a levee system. But if it is covered with water a few times a year and certain plants grow, it is deemed "wetlands." And guess what, you don't really own it anymore. The federal government does. You can't do anything on it without a permit.

"Well, how much of it is wetlands?"

"All of it as far as we are concerned. Once we find the plants in one spot it is up to you to show if any of the tract is not wetlands."

"How do I do that?"

"Well, you need to have a botanist come out here and take a look."

Now I know what you do if you major in botany. You get hired by the Army Corps of Engineers to do wetland determinations, and then you retire and get other people to hire you to deal with the Army Corps of Engineers. A regular cottage industry that is the creature of statute.

I hired a botanist, who said out of twenty acres only two were wetlands. I applied for a permit with the Army Corps of Engineers to build my house and pay money to a "Mitigation Bank" for the "wetlands" I was about to "destroy." They said no, so I called them on the phone.

"We might decide that you don't need to build such a big house."

What? I almost fell out of my chair. I couldn't believe my ears.

Then I gathered myself. "Let me tell you something ..." I told him I would cut every tree to the stump with a rubber tire tractor—as I was legally able to do— mow it to the ground, and spray herbicide and pesticide killing every frog, ant, worm, crawfish, or minnow that may inhabit any seasonal puddle. "Or, you can take my remediation money and buy a duck habitat in Montana so I can have ducks to shoot in the fall." He saw it my way and they agreed to let me remediate the wetlands.

With that permit in hand, I found out the landfill at the end of the road had filed an application to double the size of their solid waste disposal facility.

Right to the end of my street. The application was filed on the Friday before Thanksgiving. Comments were due by the Friday after Christmas. The neighborhood had risen in protest at the initial solid waste permit application and filed a petition with about a thousand signatures on it but could not get itself organized over the holidays on such short notice.

That fall the Republicans had lost the governor's office to Democrat Kathleen Blanco. The night before she was sworn in, a Deputy Secretary of the Louisiana Department of Environmental Quality granted the permit to expand the solid waste facility—without the Environmental Impact Statement required by the statute as I read it. I sued to void the permit in East Baton Rouge Parish as required by the statute, which was just as well, as the owners were well connected in Jefferson Parish. It wasn't long before their lawyers got involved and I broached settlement.

Their eyes lit up. "What do you want?"

"Pay me for the land, the costs for clearing it and the Army Corps of Engineers permit and I'll leave." I wasn't trying to hold anyone up. I just didn't want to build my house by a landfill.

"Okay."

Within a week I had my money.

While touring the landfill with one of the owners before filing the case, I asked him where he would build if he wanted livestock. "I'd go down to Belle Chasse"—which was close to the Mississippi and south of New Orleans—"on River Road where they ride horses on the levee." Off I went.

We bought six acres on River Road that looked out over the river, cleared the land, and hired a local builder. We were finally on our way, moving into the City of New Orleans so we could be in the wide open spaces. A few weeks later on Saturday, August 27, 2005, we met with the builder on the property. There were flags in the ground marking the outlines of the house and barn, and he took us around to describe what it would look like and explain the building plan. "I've got your piling diagrams approved by the engineer, and I'll meet with you on Tuesday to sign the contract to build."

"Good," I said. There was a storm in the Gulf, nothing new to me, so I was headed to Hopedale to get my bay boat out of the shed and bring it to the house. Even in misses, the water rises down in the marsh. The builder said he was headed to Myrtle Grove to do the same and button up some condos he was building.

Tuesday never came. Hurricane Katrina made landfall on Monday, and the world changed. I remember well how Dad listened to the radio as Hurricane Betsy approached and how we had to get out. Subsequent storms and evacuations revealed a real traffic bottleneck on Interstate 10 as it crossed the Mississippi River in Baton Rouge and I-55 headed north. People were stuck in traffic for hours.

Back when Lee was pregnant with Jackson and getting close to her due date, Hurricane Georges was tracking right toward us for a few days. As it neared, it caused a drop in barometric pressure that gave Lee contractions, and I started to get nervous. We had a baby and a storm coming in what seemed to me to be a collision course. I called the hospital and asked, "If this hurricane hits and she goes into labor, can I bring her over there?"

The woman on the other side of the line said, "You can, but we don't know if we'll have a place for the rest of you. Also, if you go out in the storm and get stuck, we won't be able to send anyone to help you."

In the background, the news was reporting that traffic evacuating ahead of Hurricane Georges had backed up I-10 through Baton Rouge where the interstate crosses the Mississippi River, which was about eighty miles away from us. I had three small kids, a very pregnant wife, and a decision to make. Do we get out or not?

I woke up early the next morning and turned on the TV to see what Nash Roberts had to say. If you live in New Orleans, you know Nash Roberts. He was the ancient local meteorologist who trotted out to the news station any time a big storm got close. He was there before Betsy and every hurricane since and had a preternatural ability to predict hurricane paths. I turned on the TV, and there he was with his chart and grease pencil plotting the barometric pressure and whatever other variables he used to predict the hurricane's path. It's total old school, and he gets it right when the guys with all the doodads and devices don't.

"It's going to turn up just east of Biloxi. Being on the west side, we should be fine."

I turned to Lee. "Unpack. We're staying." Not only did Nash get it right, every other meteorologist got it wrong. And there were a lot of ticked off people who had spent a wasted day stuck in traffic.

When Hurricane Katrina came into the Gulf, it was travelling in a straight line off the tip of Florida going north-northwest which would take it right up the Mississippi River. It was huge—Category 5—and like a freight train, it wasn't going to stray from its course. Nash Roberts was an old man by now, and he had already bugged out of town. It was the first and only time he ever evacuated for a hurricane.

I had never left for any hurricane but Betsy. Katrina made the second. There was something about it. I just knew it would hit dead on. I spent those pre-dawn hours—and had been thinking about such a scenario for a long time—planning how I would get my family to safety, Winnfield, without getting stuck on I-10 in Baton Rouge. The model I had in mind was our family trips to visit Poppy and Ganny and the example I followed was Dad. We took to the back roads.

I looked at Lee. "Well, this is bad."

Walter had already decamped to Baton Rouge and that Friday I had told my paralegal, "This storm looks like it could be pretty bad. If they say get out, get out. And if you and your husband need a ride or something, you need to let me know. I'll come over and get you."

I liked her a lot. She was a heavyset African-American woman who'd received her undergraduate degree from Howard University. Originally, she was from Buffalo, New York, and though she was the sweetest woman, she had something of a New York attitude. She was also outstanding at her job. I'd give her something to do and whoosh she had it done. She'd say, "Here it is," and then go back to playing solitaire on her computer.

"What are you doing?" I'd say.

"Everything's caught up."

I would have picked her and Bob up. We had two cars and room for them, but she said she would let me know if they needed a ride. I never heard from them. Well, they didn't get out.

We waited until Sunday morning to leave. Baton Rouge is a little more than an hour north and as with Hurricane Georges, there was a lot of traffic stuck on I-10 and I-55, which skirts up between lakes Maurepas and Pontchartrain. But there were also a lot of people who either had nowhere to go, no way to get there, or didn't have the sense to leave. The day before when Spencer and I ran to Hopedale to get the boat, we passed back through the Ninth Ward and then down Saint Claude Avenue and saw groups of people at bus stops, traffic lights, and on the streets like nothing was wrong.

There was an evacuation order, but it wasn't mandatory, and these were the people who stayed. I guess they just had nowhere to go and no way to get there. "See those people, Spencer? All of them are going to end up in the Superdome, you watch." And sure enough, that's what happened.

We loaded up the car with our packed suitcases, a hedgehog, gerbils, two dogs, two cats, and a turtle. I felt like Noah. Lee drove the Ford Excursion and followed me in my pickup truck. Rain was starting to fall and the wind kicked up as we drove to Clearview Parkway, and instead of turning left toward I-10, I turned right and crossed the Mississippi River right there at the Huey P. Long Bridge. I had rehearsed it in my mind for years. We took River Road to Highway 3127 to LA Highway 1. That took us up through Donaldsonville to White Castle and then on to US 190 West then north on US 167 through LeBeau, where we used to stop at Stelly's when I was a kid, through Alexandria and on to Winnfield where we stayed with Mom. The whole trip took us five hours.

Meanwhile, my paralegal and her husband lived in a second-floor apartment in Lakeview. After the storm passed and the levee broke, the water started coming up and they had to get out. Lucky for them a neighbor had a canoe, so they loaded up with their little dog Pooch, and while they were paddling down their street, a photographer snapped a shot that made it on the cover of *Time* Magazine. They found dry land in The Marigny in the heart of the French Quarter and started walking to try to get to the Convention Center.

As this was going on, Walter—he was an Honorary Assistant Deputy Sheriff for Saint Bernard Parish—had come down from Baton Rouge to do what he could to help get people to safety. The only way to get into New Orleans was by boat on the River, and because he comes from a family of Bar Pilots, he was able to hitch a ride by boat into St. Bernard, which is south and east of New Orleans's Ninth Ward. Walter's house in St. Bernard was two stories, but it took eighteen feet of water. The sheriff's office did not fare much better.

At some point, Walter was on Poland Avenue on the Industrial Canal at the Army Corps of Engineers office when he dropped the leather wallet that held his sheriff's deputy badge. Later my paralegal, her husband, and Pooch found his badge. "Oh, dear God we've lost Walter!"

As this was playing out, I got a call in Winnfield from a friend, an LSU Law School classmate from Donaldsonville whom I duck hunt with. "Man, did you hear the news? The sheriff is calling for boats. All the levees broke in New Orleans and water's pouring in."

The wall of water rushed in so fast that at the St. Bernard Sheriff's Office, those brave souls who stayed and later evacuated vertically up to the third floor, conducted search and rescue missions using jet skis and whatever else they could find. Some who stayed took Sharpie pens and wrote their Social Security numbers on their leg and taped whatever else they had to their body with duct tape to assist in body identification. In the Ninth Ward, the levee holding the Industrial Canal burst open in three places.

But that wasn't the only levee to give way. Within the first twenty-four hours after the storm, there were twenty-eight levee failures of one type or another. Over the next few days, there were fifty more breaks and failures, which included the 17th Street Canal Levee, London Canal, and the Orleans Canal. The scope of the flooding is hard to capture in words. The city was drowning.

I told my law school friend that I'd get a generator to power up my house and come on down. I grabbed my shotgun, several five-gallon cans of gasoline, bought a generator, and left with Spencer. There was power down to Vacherie, a small town about fifty miles northwest of New Orleans, but after that, there was no power and everything was blown up by the storm. We came down through Donaldsonville on the West Bank, crossed the Mississippi River at Destrehan, and when we got to the Jefferson Parish line, there was a cop standing in the road.

"Where you going?" he asked.

I handed him my driver's license. "My house is two miles that way, like dead ahead, and I know it's not flooded because River Ridge doesn't flood."

"I'm sorry, but I can't let you in."

"What? Why can't you let me in? I have to go look after my property."

"Aaron Broussard"—Jefferson Parish President at the time and now paroled felon for bribery and theft on issues unrelated to Katrina—"has an order out that nobody can come back into the Parish."

"But I have a mud boat on my carport and they're calling for help to save people."

"I'm sorry."

I could have hit my house with a bottle rocket. I was ticked off, but what could I do? We turned around and went back to Winnfield.

My paralegal, her husband, and Pooch made it to the Convention Center, which was overcrowded and, in her words, they were mass deported to the equivalent of a refugee center in Bentonville, Arkansas. This is when she called me, and I explained that Walter was okay.

"Thank God for that," she said.

"How are you all over there?"

"Well, we're in a camp right across the street from a Walmart, but there's a bunch of Nazi Baptists up here running things, and all they'll let us do is go to Walmart two times a day. They think all the black people are criminals, running, and shooting guns in New Orleans and stuff."

"Do you want me to wire your salary to you, or what?"

"I've got to get out of here, but don't send me any money because somebody I'm in here with might steal it."

Her sister, a nun from Buffalo, arranged a plane ticket for her to go to North Carolina where she stayed until she could come back to New Orleans. When I saw her, I told her that I really would have come and got her before the storm. And then she told me she couldn't swim.

"Why in the world would you stay in the City of New Orleans, three feet below sea level and surrounded by a levee, with a major hurricane coming after they tell you to evacuate and you can't swim?"

She shrugged and said, "It's my home."

Four days after the storm passed, I was allowed back to my house. As Spencer and I entered my neighborhood, we saw crudely painted wooden signs, "No Looters! Drunks with Guns!" *Boy*, that made me feel safe.

We were lucky compared to many others. Walter's home was destroyed, but there was little damage to our house. A tree tore a hole in the roof, most of the roofing tiles were scarred by errant branches, a fence was damaged, and a Hackberry tree in the backyard fell over. And without electricity, the house sat for four days in hot, humid, fetid, post-hurricane air. Most everything in the freezer and refrigerator was ruined and rotting, and the whole house had a sort of humid dampness to it. Other than that, everything was fine.

We cleaned up as well as we could, and then went and cleaned up our neighbor's properties before they got back. We didn't have anything else to do. This went on for about three days without electricity except for the generator. I couldn't just let it run because getting gasoline was still a bit of a trick so we only used it at night and even then, turned it off when we went to sleep.

Not knowing when the power would be restored, we locked up and bugged out to my hunting buddy's trailer in Pierre Part on Belle River in the Atchafalaya swamp. Lee met us there, and the kids ran the river in the mud boat. I worked out of my friend's Donaldsonville office. But soon enough, we had to leave again when Hurricane Rita hit southwest Louisiana. The water came up and we were run out of there. I felt like we were being chased.

The folks in Belle River at the Baptist and Catholic Churches were cooking and providing clothes for us refugees. It was hard to refuse even though I had insurance, money, and clothes. Still, it was nice. The churches faced each other, and I was reminded of the story of the priest and the minister in front of their churches nailing up signs that said, "Turn Back, The End is Near!" Just then a fella in a convertible zoomed by and yelled, "You Bunch of Religious Nuts!" as he signaled that they were number one. He went around the curve and there came a sound of tires squealing and a loud Splash! The priest and the minister met in the middle of the road.

"Maybe we should change the signs to just say, 'The Bridge is Out!'"

Well, after Hurricanes Katrina and Rita all the bridges in South Louisiana were "out" and it didn't matter what church you were from as long as you came to help. We were let back into downtown New Orleans after a time and practiced law as well as we could. There was just the National Guard, utility trucks, and us. Two restaurants were serving lunch, and in a town famous for its food, it seemed odd that there was only one question, "Do you want cheese on that?"

Slowly, life started to come back to a sort of normal, and that fall I was sitting in the living room watching LSU play Alabama while a roofing crew worked to put a new roof on the house. It got dark, and they kept banging away. I stepped outside, "Hey, I'm trying to listen to the game down here. Y'all going to keep working?"

"Yeah," one of them said, "we're going to work all night till this thing is done."

"Well, you better be careful that you're nailing those shingles up right, because if you can't see and you get them up wrong the roof will leak."

"Don't worry, there's a full moon; we can see by moonlight." I guess you had to make hay while the sun was shining or, in this case, the moon.

Lee and I hemmed and hawed over what to do about building the new house. There were new challenges due to the hurricane—and we never signed the contract to build it. I called the builder and asked, "Are we going to build this house?"

"Well, all my guys are off doing repair work and we don't know how high the Corps of Engineers is going to make the new flood levels for the house. I also don't think there's a bank in the world that would loan you the money, and you'll never be able to get insurance."

"So the short answer is no?"

"Yeah."

I turned around to Lee and said, "We're going north of the Lake." Lee found a ten-acre property in Covington with an eight-stall horse barn, swimming pool, small pond in the back, and a house with room for the kids. Sure, it was all wood, exterior cedar, an odd shape, and painted turd brown. But it would do just fine.

After the move, we found our way to a small church where there were about seven or eight couples. Spencer played guitar, and they asked me to be an elder and serve on the Session. The next thing I knew, we were settled in the house, Lee bought three horses, the kids were busy with their homeschooling and various projects, and Lee came to me and said, "Time for you to go back to Lamaze class."

The hurricanes had picked us up like Dorothy in the *Wizard of Oz* and deposited us where we needed to be. Just another coincidence that worked out in our favor. *Right.*

#

The Governor asked Walter to head up the Road Home Program, which helped homeowners rebuild after the hurricane. Walter wanted to do it and it was a no-brainer. Of course, he should do it. There was an immediate need to rebuild our community and who were we to say no in such as time as this? He would be at the disposal of the Governor and work for free, but there would never be any other opportunity in our lifetime to make a difference. I was all for it, regardless of the cost.

I admire a lot about Walter. For one thing, he has always been meticulous about doing the right and ethical thing every time. He doesn't take shortcuts. He and I have always come back to the idea that if we just do the right thing, God will bless us and something good will come of it. We never knew how, and we never worried about it.

This was never truer than when Kenny came my way. He was working on an electrical panel on a barge unloader when it was accidentally charged, and forty-two kilowatts of electricity shot through him in an arc explosion. He shouldn't have survived, but he did, barely. He had third-degree burns from the waist up, as well as inhalation burns in his mouth, throat, and lungs.

He was in such critical condition that they couldn't do skin grafts because if they moved him from the ICU to a surgical unit, the surgeon was concerned that he would die on the way. At first, I worked with his wife Holly because he was in a semi-conscious state, and even after he stabilized, it was months before he left the hospital. On top of that, she found out after the accident that she was six weeks pregnant with their second child.

The specifics of the litigation get complicated, but because of the potential of a large degree of employer fault, winning this case was far from a sure thing. Enough that the defendants wouldn't settle, and we were heading toward a knock-down, drag-out trial. Just the fact that I was in the trenches for these clients was enough to get me up in the morning. I was born for fights like this. It is what God made me for. Put it on my tombstone.

In the first couple weeks after the accident, the doctor called Holly into the hospital twice saying that Kenny could go at any moment. She raced in and sat with him, praying this would not be their last moment together. He skimmed the void. There was a strength within Kenny that would not give up and, I believe, God still had a purpose for his young life.

When she found out that she was pregnant, she told me that she went straight to Kenny and whispered into his ear, "I just want you to know that I'm pregnant with your second child, so please don't go anywhere."

Like I've said, this was not my first rodeo. With Lee pregnant with our seventh child, I saw all that Kenny and Holly could lose. I threw myself into their case and faced a team of defense lawyers. Quite frankly, I tire of the David versus Goliath analogy for plaintiff's trial lawyers, so I won't use it to describe this case. Taking on a bunch of defense lawyers is the norm, not the exception.

As to my opponents, I don't believe that defense lawyers are bad people. I don't care for the little doodads on the shoes or the helicopter pilot sunglasses. But everyone is entitled to assert a defense, even Jeffrey Dahmer. I did believe that Kenny deserved compensation for all that he'd suffered, and it was their intention to deny him that, so it was game on.

After Katrina, I tried a medical malpractice case in north Louisiana. Slowly at first, and then more consistently, I noticed some tightness in my chest. When it didn't go away, I went to a cardiologist friend of mine from church who performed an angiogram. There weren't any blockages, my plumbing was clean, but he did see that I had a bicuspid aortic valve and said that I may need to have the valve replaced at some point.

I made an appointment with my general practitioner, and he said he had one, too. "We'll just echocardiogram it to keep an eye on it and if nothing happens, it's good."

"So, basically there's nothing I can do about it, but eventually I might have to have a valve replacement?"

"Yep."

"Hmm." I never told my wife or kids. Why worry them unnecessarily? Besides, I had life insurance and was worth more dead than alive. I just didn't want them to know that.

Lee was probably seven months pregnant, and though I'd aced Lamaze class once again and we were old pros at birthing, this baby wasn't going to be able to be born naturally. About a year before she became pregnant, Lee had a few uterine fibroid tumors removed. They weren't cancerous, but the surgery was like a C-section. The surgeon had used a vertical incision. This meant that during labor there is an increased risk of a uterine tear. She had to have a C-section.

Lee was also loyal to a fault to her OB/GYN, which I suppose makes sense since he'd delivered the last five of her pregnancies. With this next one, I think we set some sort of personal record for him, six boys. My worry was that we were now on the other side of Lake Pontchartrain with the twenty-four-mile-long bridge between us and the hospital.

I sat quietly in his office one day as he and Lee worked out when they should do the C-section. I was more than happy to let them discuss the details, but when it came to picking a date, I piped up to say, "Make sure you schedule it so I'm not on the bridge with a woman in active labor trying to figure out if I need to go one hundred miles per hour."

They looked at me and said, "No problem." They lied.

The night before she was supposed to go in, *guess what*?

"Frank, I think I'm in labor."

"You have got to be kidding me."

About twenty minutes later, I was timing contractions and trying to not crash while speeding across the bridge, which is exactly what everybody promised me would not happen. We made it, and on April 4, 2007, John Mason was literally pulled into this world.

With a new baby, Lee recovering from surgery, six boys doing their best to drive every adult insane, and now a heart condition to think of but not say anything about, I saw the tenuousness of life. I became that much more committed to Holly and Kenny's trial and worried if I could pull it off for them.

Over the next couple of months, things settled into a new routine at the house, and Lee was back up and at it. She is not one to remain inactive and is always on the hunt for a new project, which became turning our relatively new house into a home. It's not that we didn't like the house, but it had turd brown cedar paneling on the outside, leaky windows, and most of the interior was the same as when it was built in the 1970s.

By now it was 2008, the trial was scheduled for early 2009, and in August and September we'd had almost back-to-back hurricanes, Gustav and Ike. Neither was a direct hit, but we did lose power, so for each hurricane, I dug out the generator I bought during Katrina. I plugged it into the fuse box outside by the kitchen door and it ran the electricity in the whole house, except for the air conditioners.

On December 8, I woke up and it was snowing like hell, which only happens once in a blue moon in south Louisiana. Roads and bridges were iced up, so I called Walter and said I'd work from home. The boys were bouncing all over the house to get out in the snow—we got almost six inches—but it was a wet snow and suddenly, the lights went out. I went to the shed and dragged the generator out and set it up next to the garage by the kitchen door. But this time I swung it around facing the other way so I could hook up the ground wire that I had forgotten before. It pays to be safe. As I'm doing this, the boys were calling out, "Hey Dad, where are my boots" or "Hey, where are the neoprene duck hunting gloves" or yelling at each other.

I went back to the shed and got out all the gear they needed to play in the snow. Then I went back to the generator, made the connections and started it. I watched it for a minute and thought, *Anything wrong with this picture?* Nope.

Thirty minutes later the kids were outside, the house was quiet, I was standing in the kitchen with a cup of coffee, and the lights went out. "What the heck?" I opened the door to the garage and the garage was on fire! What I learned later was that because I was being safe and hooked up the ground wire, the exhaust from the generator pointed toward the exterior cedar paneling, and it caught fire from the heat. The fire spread quickly, and as soon it hit my workbench, where I had placed our painting drop cloths, the fire doubled in size.

"Fire!" I yelled and then called to Lee, "Grab the baby and get outside. The house is on fire."

We got outside with Mason, and the kids came and circled around when Lee said, "Where's Minnie?" our cat.

"I don't know. Last time I saw her she was in the garage." Oops!

I looked back to the house. Flames were coming out the garage door, and our van was parked right next to it. I pulled the van away as the side mirror was melting and thought to grab the hose to put some water on the fire, but when I turned it on, nothing happened. *Oh yeah, no power.* That was why I hooked up the generator to start with. "Lord, you must love me, or something."

The house was becoming more involved (don't you just love that expression for a fire, *involved*, like a romance that literally burns you to a crisp?) with more smoke pouring out of the garage, the front door, and anywhere else it could escape. That's when Lee ran into the house to get her laptop, purse, and some other stuff, and she found our other cat, Sarah. We also had another cat, but he had been missing for a few weeks. His name was Dawg. Yes, the boys had named the cat Dawg. Like, "Whassup *Dawg!*" I found what was left of him fishing leaves from the bottom of the pool that spring. I never told the kids and used a lot of chlorine that year.

I ran in too and got a few things, but the smoke was getting worse. I came out and saw Lee looking for Minnie, the kids half watching Mason and half gape-mouthed at the fire. We never did find Minnie.

Lee ran around the house looking for the cat and it seemed she might have wanted to go back into the house. "Sam, Fletcher," I said, "if she tries to go back in the house, put her on the ground and keep her on the ground." Both were good football players and strong, so they knew what I meant.

"Yes sir," they said.

The kids, Lee, and I stepped back from the house. I called our home-owner's insurer. In the distance, I could hear sirens.

"When did this fire happen?" the agent asked.

"I'm standing here right now waiting for the fire department, watching it burn." There was silence. I guess these things were usually reported after the fact, but I had nothing else to do. There wasn't anything else we could do.

The firefighters put out the fire before it destroyed the whole house. Later the insurance fire investigator called it "a good stop." It was just a few degrees from flashing over. We ended up losing the cat, as well as shotguns Dad and Uncle Frank owned, my bedroom furniture from the front room on Melody Drive, our Christmas ornaments and presents, and there was fire and smoke damage throughout the entire house. I had soot on my glasses that were still in their case in my bathroom medicine chest, which was on the opposite side of the house as the smoke. We couldn't salvage any of our clothes, and there was no way we could stay in the house.

The fire chief asked me to tell him what happened. I recounted setting up the generator and when I noticed the fire, then I told him we would need an electrical engineer because the fuse box arrangement had always made me nervous.

"Tell me how you set up the generator," he said. It lay there in a burned heap.

"Just like that. Look at it." I was getting annoyed.

"No, how did you set it up?"

"Just like that!"

"No, which way was the exhaust pointing?"

That's when it struck me. "Don't tell my wife!"Boooiiiinnngg! I couldn't help it. They were the first words out of my mouth.

A few minutes later she came around the corner of the house with tears in her eyes. I figured I would hit her while she was weak. "Honey, I'm sorry. It looks like I started the fire."

"Oh, that's okay." And we hugged. Later the firemen congratulated me for "manning up."

The fire chief said he would have to call the arson investigator.

"Oh yeah, right!" I said. "I carefully planned to wait until it snowed eight inches so the kids would be outside, and then I strategically placed the generator so the exhaust would light off the exterior of the garage. Really?"

He changed his mind.

I called a minister friend, father to Spencer's homeschool speech and debate partner, who had just taken a pastoral position in Humble, Texas, and had listed his house in Covington for sale. He said, "If y'all need a place to go, my house is open and the key is under the mat by the back door." We had a place to live. Then we went to Walmart and bought all the essentials—clothes, shoes, belts, toothbrushes, toothpaste, and so on. It's probably the only store where if you just lost everything, you can find everything you need.

But before we left the house for the night, Lee sniffled and tears rolled down her cheeks. Ever the optimist, I said, "Look, I wanted to basically tear this place down and build a new house. Don't tell the insurance company, but within a few hours I've demolished the house, arranged financing, and found us a new place to live while we rebuild. Look how far along we are. If it weren't for me, we wouldn't have made such rocket progress!"

I'm not sure what she was thinking, but it was probably along the lines of, "You idiot." But hey, might as well look at the bright side.

#

Lee began the work of cataloguing all our stuff for the insurance claim, which she dug into in an almost manic sort of way. Meanwhile, the kids were supposed to be homeschooling, but there wasn't enough time in the day to stay on top of that. Lee and I were stretched very thin.

To top it off, Spencer was the homeschooling equivalent of a senior and somehow the paperwork that would have allowed him to join a graduation ceremony with other homeschooled kids was never submitted, so he didn't have a ceremony. He also struggled with some of his math and though his SAT scores were good, the math portion was just low enough that he couldn't get into LSU. He was, however, admitted to Louisiana Tech. Though I felt bad about LSU I looked forward to seeing him spread his wings a little.

As this was playing out, I was also in final preparations for Holly and Kenny's trial. Early on I'd dealt mostly with Holly because Kenny was in the hospital undergoing one skin graft after another, something I'd never want to have to go through. But he's a strong man, and Holly was committed to him and remained by his side.

When he did finally come home, I decided to bring him into the conversations with Holly bit by bit and, over time, engage directly with him. This would not only let him know that he was his own man despite his injuries, but his contributions would be important for us to win at trial. And the stakes couldn't be higher. Not only was Kenny disabled for life, but he and Holly had $750,000 in medical expenses. Winning or losing this case would be life changing for them, and they'd already been through enough.

We were slated to present our case over five days, and I knew that the witness testimony on Wednesday would be our most important day. If things didn't go well, it could hurt our chances. As the plaintiffs, we presented our case first, and the following week the defense would take their turn to hack away at us. I had to make sure our presentation was strong enough to mitigate with the jury any counter punches they may land.

We selected a jury on Monday, and on Tuesday we started the show. Things went well, but it became even more obvious that if we didn't ace the testimony on Wednesday, we would be in trouble. It's an incredible thing to work on a case on which the lives of two people hung, and now it all came down to a single day. I was confident in the people I would call the next day, but there were enough unknowns that I couldn't be sure. That Tuesday night, I gamed out every possible scenario in my hotel room and reviewed each deposition and thought about how the defense could attack our position or undermine what I wanted the jury to walk away knowing. I think I fell asleep around midnight and then woke up at four-thirty in the morning to go over it all again.

Just after five in the morning, the phone rang.

"Frank, it's Kenny."

"Hey, Kenny, what are you doing calling me this early?"

"Well, I got up this early because the Holy Spirit told me to, and I was praying for you."

I've had clients who aren't of the character to pray, but Kenny was the genuine deal. "Well, thank you, Kenny."

"I'm just thanking God that you're my lawyer and that you're out there fighting for me."

Now that was a first. After he said that, I got this wonderful feeling of peace. Kenny wouldn't be there because he couldn't come out in the heat—this was the week before Easter—and his only appearance would be Good Friday when he testified. Before he hung up, he said, "Today is going to be a really good day, and I just wanted you to know that."

Of any trial I've ever had, that was the best day of testimony. Ever. It amazes me how God works. On Good Friday, I put Kenny on the stand. The visual of this severely scarred man, along with his heartfelt testimony of the accident, what he'd been through, and how it has changed his life was stunning. I projected a photo taken before the accident of him coming down a slide with his little girl. He was all buff and she was in water wings, and as I asked him questions, it was all I could do to keep from breaking down. But behind me at the counsel table, I could hear someone start to sob. It built in volume as I was asking questions, and I realized it was Walter crying as he watched this play out.

Then the jury started to cry. First it was one, then another, then three, and soon there wasn't a dry eye in the jury box. I turned to pick up a document, and the defense lawyers were wiping tears from their eyes. It was emotional. It was the truth.

We ended the testimony and the judge dismissed us for the Easter weekend. I already had a resurrection theme bouncing through my head for my closing argument. It was another good day, but the defense would get their turn. As I was walking out of court, the defense lawyers snagged me and said, "Hey, back to the courtroom. The judge wants to see us."

"You're full of baloney. I'm trying to get out of here. I don't know what you all are trying to pull."

"No, no, he wants to talk to us."

I sighed wondering what was up, and we went back to the courtroom. The judge walked out and asked, "What do you all want?"

I looked at the defense attorneys. "I knew you guys were lying."

"Wait," one of them said, "just hear us out. Look, we had two attempts at mediation in this case and the last number for a settlement the plaintiff gave us was (I will omit the amount), and we just want to tell the court that we'll pay it." Another first.

"Well, I will pass it on to my client, but at this point, I don't know if he will take it."

When they come and say they'll pay what you asked, though, it's hard to say no.

I called Kenny and he said just what I did, "I don't know if I want take it." I asked him to think about it. If he accepted this settlement, which I had recommended after all, within thirty to sixty days he would never have another worry or financial headache for the rest of his life. He wanted a minute to talk to Holly and hung up. A few minutes passed and my cell rang.

"Take the money," he said.

The jury had to come back that Monday to be formally discharged by the judge. I asked if I could speak with the jury afterward and the judge said only if they wanted to. On Monday I came to court. No one else did. After the jury was discharged I asked if they'd stay and let me ask some questions. They said okay and so I point blank asked them, "How were you all going to vote?"

I had to win nine out of the twelve, and on that Monday I only had seven. Two were undecided. We weren't home free, and they hadn't yet heard from the defense. I breathed a sigh of relief and couldn't help but think what I had been told years ago about doing plaintiff's work: "This business is not for the faint of heart." No truer words could be said. Still, I like the juice.

In the fall, Spencer headed off to Louisiana Tech, and while it's his story to tell, he struggled. Though much of his struggles were personal, his grades didn't reflect the intelligent kid that I knew him to be. At the end of the fall quarter, he'd earned a 2.8, which isn't horrendous considering some of the GPAs I saw during my freshman year, but it did make me think some other things might be going on.

During the winter quarter, the rest of the family was getting ready for Mardi Gras, and I called to let him know our plans, but there was no answer and he didn't call back. I texted him a few times and tried calling but got no response. I figured there had to be something wrong, so I drove up to Ruston to find him. When I got up there he was not well. It was clear he needed to come home.

As we drove, I said to him, "Look, I love you, but I think you need to figure some things out, so just sit out this next quarter. Once you've kind of gotten things together you can go back and get with it." He agreed.

A few weeks later on April 20, 2010, we got the first reports of the explosion and fire at BP's Deepwater Horizon oil platform in the Gulf. Then came the news that the well itself was expelling massive volumes of oil, which we watched in real-time via a live feed from the ocean floor. As with Katrina and its aftermath, the people in and around New Orleans could focus on little else. It would take until September 19 for the well to finally be capped.

That summer, Spencer took a couple courses at the local community college. He also met Hollyn, which I suppose was love at first sight, or at least I like to think so.

After seeing what Spencer went through as he applied for college, Sam became worried that he wouldn't be able to get into LSU. Sam is a smart kid, and by the time he finished his ninth-grade year as a homeschool student, he'd taken every math, biology, and chemistry course we could find.

He came to me and said, "I want to be sure that I am college ready. I want to go to high school. And I want to play football." He was running track at the time with a local AAU club.

I still believe when the kids are young, there is no reason not to homeschool them if you want. But at around seventh grade you get to more difficult material and they need to know how to perform in a classroom setting. As I looked at Sam and then Fletcher, both smart kids and good athletes, sending them to school was the right thing to do. I found a Christian school, I wouldn't have done it otherwise, and enrolled them both.

I was met by fierce resistance by Lee. "I don't know why you want to put our children in school with a bunch of other fools."

I'd done some research. It was common for homeschool kids to rebel and we'd already seen it happen with other families. I also know that salvation is in God's hands. The thought that you can raise a kid a certain way and expect him or her to come out the way you want isn't going to happen. Homeschool, Christian school, public school, or no school—they are independent people with their own thoughts and desires who will thwart even the best laid plans if it makes them unhappy. I also believe that children must be equipped with skills academically and otherwise when they go out into the world. I saw no other choice. To Lee's credit, she figured if I was going to enroll Sam, I might as well enroll Fletcher too.

It was also during this time that our new house was finally ready. I had taken what I thought was the best approach for the only new house I would build. I let Lee make every decision. Every one. That way I wouldn't ever hear any complaints, they would all be on her. And besides, it would all be invisible to me in about thirty days anyway.

I signed Sam up for football and went with him at seven in the morning to the first summer workout. Two guys in their workout gear—both good players—walked up and introduced themselves by shaking my hand and looking me in the eye. One of them said, "What can I do to help you, sir?"

"My son just signed up to play football, and he's here for workouts."

"Sounds great. We'd be happy to show him everything he needs to do."

I was impressed.

Later in the summer, the team went away for football camp. Sam went, although the decision was questioned by Lee. "You don't even know these coaches." But I had a feeling. When he got back, he was like a new kid, filled with energy, his eyes bright and full of light. Amazed by what I saw, I went to the coach, a man named Tony Agresta from Youngstown, Ohio, and asked, "How did camp go?"

He smiled and looked at me. "Camp was just great. We all got closer to Jesus."

I'd already come to respect Tony, but that was the last thing I expected to come from a football coach's mouth. My esteem has only grown and made me a lifelong fan of that man. He's the real deal.

Things only got better for Sam. In his sophomore year, he took Algebra II and Senior Anatomy & Physiology and aced both. By the time he was accepted to LSU he had placed out of Trigonometry, Physics, Chemistry, and English. He had something like sixteen credits on his first day of college. He also had a surgically repaired ACL, but that's life. Or football. Take your pick.

# # #

I picked up my first cigar when the Saints beat the Colts in the 2010 Super Bowl in Miami. We were on South Beach, and there were cigar girls everywhere. The Saints were in the Super Bowl so hell had already frozen over and pigs had flown. A cigar if they won wouldn't hurt. But let's just be rigorously honest here. Nicotine was my first drug addiction. It helped knock me out of high school football and led me down the path to other things. But due to the amount of time that had passed since I had quit, twenty-two years, I developed amnesia. I remember my Dad saying, "I never quit smoking cigarettes, I just haven't had one in thirty years." He had tried cigars too, but had to give them up after getting hooked on the nicotine again. I should have known better.

I found myself smoking on the lawn mower and slipping an inhale through the nose. Then I just inhaled. The buzz was awesome. Just like my friend's mom's Pall Malls. After being "caught" smoking one day behind the barn, Lee reminded me of "our deal."

"I thought we agreed before we got married that we weren't going to smoke?" Yeah, we did. But it was high time that I didn't do something she wanted. It was a matter of principle. I had an example to set. And besides, I was hooked again, big time.

Smoking gave me a way to act out on my resentment over the home-schooling wrestling match we kept going through and exert some control over my life. Kind of a stupid way to be—especially with my heart issue—but there was still some of that *if you want me to do something, tell me not to do it* attitude in me.

Despite Lee relenting on school with Sam and Fletcher, as Jackson approached high school, she was still angry that I intended on sending him to school. The cigar smoking didn't help either. She started sleeping in another room and wouldn't speak to me over the phone. Instead, she sent text messages to argue about sending Jackson to school and other issues. But I remained unmoved. At a certain point, the kids needed to go to school, and we should trust them, ourselves as parents, and God that they will find their way.

In the meantime I had to travel to Duluth, Minnesota, for a few days to take depositions related to a case. An eighteen-wheeler from Ashland, Wisconsin, turning off US 190 near Krotz Springs on a pipeline project, caught a Port-O-Let with my client inside, dragging it down the road and rolling it, and him, into a ditch. He injured his lower back and his pride. It was without a doubt the shittiest case I had ever had.

Krotz Springs was notorious for speed traps and it was on the route we had taken to go to Winnfield in the old days. Then to Cheneyville, Bunkie, and the last place of interest, Dry Prong. Uncle Frank claimed he knew a girl from Dry Prong with a last name of Dick. Her first name was Ima. Ima Dick, from Dry Prong.

I found myself up in Duluth wondering if I was being the dick, with Lee as mad at me as she'd ever been. And that was when I got a text saying, "I am really upset that you would not respect my wishes. I'm going to let Jackson go to school, but I might not be here when you get back." She'd never said anything like this to me before, and it cut me to my core. I don't think she understood how much she'd hurt me. But I didn't say anything and let it go. She was there when I got home, and I enrolled Jackson in school. But there was no resolution to our disagreement.

That Memorial Day weekend, I took Sam, Fletcher, and Jackson to Washington D.C. We visited museums by day and ate chocolate cake in bed at the hotel by night. That Sunday we donned coats and ties and went to the Episcopal Church in Arlington Virginia, where we were seated in the favorite pew of George Washington. Then we visited Arlington Cemetery, where a lone woman among a sea of white crosses made me cry. The last night, we again donned coats and ties and had dinner at a restaurant on the Potomac constructed from the remnants of Franklin D. Roosevelt's yacht. Each boy asked for a picture with Dad. It was a great trip.

It was also about this time that Fletcher began to unravel. Fletcher was tough, strong-willed, and walked to the beat of his own drum from the day he was born.

One day Sam and Fletcher were going somewhere in Sam's car and started arguing over something stupid. Fletcher's anger went from zero to sixty in about a second and reached such a point that Sam stopped the car just down the road from our house and ordered him out.

"I'm not gonna get out," Fletcher responded.

"Get out of my car."

"No."

Sam climbed out, opened Fletcher's door, and pulled him out of the car. Instead of just fighting, which I would have preferred, Fletcher pulled a knife on him to get him to leave him alone. Sam couldn't believe it, and got into the car and left him standing there. Sam nursed that grudge for years, and I couldn't blame him. To do that to your own brother was, well, disturbing.

This is what it was like with Fletcher. He had a manic-like energy that propelled him in all directions, usually in ways that were productive, but every now and again the cap came flying off. Lee and I knew that trying to force him in any one direction would send him skittering off in the opposite direction.

In the fall of 2012, Fletcher entered his junior year, and amongst the football and school work, he started spending more time with a new friend whom I didn't really like. This kid had trouble containing himself and behaving. But he and Fletcher hit it off. His friend got kicked off the football team and out of school. Then as the school year progressed, I noticed a change in Fletcher. He was lifting weights like crazy and had bulked his body up considerably, but with that his attitude went from fierce independence to angry and volatile.

One morning that spring, Fletcher was supposed to drive Jackson with him to school. Jackson is probably the gentlest kid I've ever met. He's the only one of my boys who never played football and hated athletics. If it involves sweat, he doesn't want anything to do with it. He just goes off and does something else, such as tinker in the shed, cut the grass on the riding mower, metal arts, and so on.

On this morning, Jackson was doing his normal plodding along, which made Fletcher mad. "I'm going to school," he yelled, "I'm leaving!"

I came out the door on my way to my car and said, "You just wait on him. You don't have to be such a knucklehead."

"I'm tired of waiting on him. He needs to be taught a lesson. I'm gonna leave."

"Well, you can't do whatever you want, because I own that truck."

"This is my truck." He knew he was pushing me.

I was angry now and walked toward him. "No, it isn't, and if I say you can't drive it, you can't drive it."

I reached in the truck window and slapped him. That was a huge mistake. Like putting a match to dynamite. He rolled the window up, put it in gear, and punched the gas.

I went inside and told Jackson that I'd give him a ride. Two minutes later Fletcher came screeching up the driveway. He jumped out of the truck with no shirt on, brass knuckles in his left hand and a knife in his right hand. Standing in the side yard he screamed at the top of his lungs, "Come fight me! Come fight me! I want you to come fight me!"

I went to the door. "What is the matter with you?"

"Come fight me now!" Fear gripped me. Fear never gripped Fletcher at least as much as I could tell. And I remembered my dad standing by his dresser as I stated that if he didn't like what I was doing that I would move out. Pay back is, well you know ...

Not in a million years was I going out there with a lunatic, seventeen-year-old, bulked up kid on God knows what with a knife and brass knuckles. I might be crazy, but I ain't stupid. "Just put the knife down."

He backed off and I went to Lee and said, "You better go out there and talk to him." I figured he wouldn't try anything with her.

There's a power that mothers have over their kids that is quite incredible. She went out and he dropped the knife and knuckles then got back in the truck and took off.

Lee and I worried he might do something to hurt himself, either by accident or on purpose, because of the rage-state he had flown into, but he came home a few hours later. We tried to talk with him, but he apologized and brushed it off. For the next few weeks I kept kind of quiet around him and didn't push things as I tried to figure out a way to get back into his heart. He went to counseling for a while at church. That seemed to help.

That April he and a friend had a nice stringer of bass from a pond across the road when he found a water moccasin. The kid liked to mess with snakes, and I can't count how many times I told him don't mess with water moccasins. They're poisonous and you don't ever want to get bit. And they are ornery as hell in the spring when they just wake up. Well, just like me, if you tell Fletcher not to do something, he's going to do it.

He pinned the moccasin down with a stick—the thing was about six feet long—and reached down to finish it off with a knife. The snake wasn't pinned as well as he thought, and it curled around and bit him. I wasn't home, so Lee had to deal with this one. He came running over to the house with his hand swollen and the poison making him sick. Two days later after thousands of dollars of anti-venom and the risk if losing his hand, he got out of the hospital. Even after that, he'd still mess with snakes. He really hated snakes after that.

In his senior year he turned into a fine football player—he was one of defensive coordinator, Mark Robert's, favorite kids playing nose guard, all one hundred sixty-five pounds of him, soaking wet—and on any given weekend the driveway would be filled with his friends' cars. Coach was also the school disciplinarian, so he knew Fletcher pretty well. The spring of his sophomore year, Fletcher wore blue jeans to Sam's graduation ceremony, which was expressly prohibited. Even though school was out, Coach had him report to school that Monday. He was handed a shovel and moved a pile of sand from point A to point B. Then he moved it back. In a suit. Fletcher listened to Coach Robert and did what he said. He also admired him as a genuine Christian man, one who loved him enough to punish him. Like his father.

As a football player, Fletcher had heart and worked as hard as anyone I've seen. After one particularly important game during his senior year when the team went undefeated in the regular season, he drove up to the house, stepped out of the truck, and sort of limped toward the house. I had been sitting on the front porch smoking my post-game cigar, each play tumbling through my head as I waited for him to get home.

"You hurt?" I asked.

"Yes."

"What hurts?"

"Everything."

What I didn't know was that he had a severely sprained wrist. He and Lee had kept it from me until Sunday, after Lee took him in for an x-ray. He knew if Coach Robert found out, he'd be benched, and since I was on the staff, he didn't want me to know either. When he did tell me, he made me promise not to tell Coach, a promise I kept. He played the next game with a wrist splint and the rest of the season on a wrist that must've hurt, but he played well and never complained. He said it didn't hurt as bad as being bit by a moccasin.

His tenacious and hardworking spirit when it came to football and his school work made me think that Fletcher would escape the issues that bogged me down in high school. I also thought he'd escape his own nature, which was to be fiercely independent and living life out just past the edge. But I was wrong.

Football ended and at the annual football banquet I presented him the Coach's Award for the player with the most heart. I was really proud of him. He did that all on his own. In fact, when he found out that I was going to help coach, he told me to never talk to him on the field and made me promise not to lift a finger in coach's meetings over film or elsewhere to help him. I did my best to never say a word for him. He earned it all himself. He graduated high school in the spring of 2014.

One of the ways Fletcher and I could connect was hunting. I shared a hunting camp with some guys from Donaldsonville in the Atchafalaya marsh a few miles from the Gulf. It was a two-hour drive, then an hour by boat. We'd shoot ducks, deer, and rabbits, and we fished. He loved to hunt rabbits, and we usually went every year the weekend before Mardi Gras. When he was ten years old, I handed him the twenty gauge as the beagles chased rabbits across the expanse of needle grass marsh. He took off across the marsh like a water bug wearing green knee boots and came back with eight rabbits. He was hooked. When I asked him if he wanted to go shoot rabbits the spring of his senior year, he said, "Sure."

On the drive, we got talking about how things were going for him, and though he didn't offer up too much, he listened. I told him that spiritually, you're not going to find anything in this world that's going to truly satisfy you, that will remove your restlessness, other than God.

I glanced at Fletcher again and he nodded.

His grades were more than good enough to get him into LSU for the fall semester. He was a math whiz and majored in electrical engineering. Again, Lee and I worried about him being on his own up in Baton Rouge, but with Sam up there too, we thought that might give Fletcher something of a touchstone as he worked through transitioning to college in much the same way my sister Ann helped me.

But I was worried about him. Heck, I worried about all of them. But Fletcher, he reminded me of, well, me. His initials "FGS" were the same as mine. He had already laid claim to everything I owned that had my initials on it when I passed on. But it wasn't just him.

I was used to people depending on me in my cases and at the law firm. That was the juice that made me get up in the morning. But I was starting to feel pulled, like a piece of taffy. And I kind of felt stuck, like a man standing with both feet firmly planted on either side of a ditch.

Maybe it was the tension with Lee over making the call about school, maybe it was being the father of seven distinctly unique sons, maybe it was a life of constant movement and needs placed on me. I couldn't help but feel that this had to be how Dad felt as he went to work day after day for us. That I was giving myself away. I was okay with that, I just wanted some respect for doing it.

One night just before Fletcher was to go off to LSU, I slipped outside to my rocking chair on the front porch to sit, think, and puff on a cigar. In that moment, I felt in my heart and soul what I put Mom and Dad through as a teenager and then as a stubborn, lost soul on his way to college for the first time. No wonder Dad's big advice when he dropped me off was, "Don't screw this up."

I had made a lot of closing arguments in my day. Yet I couldn't come up with the words that I thought would have the impact on Fletcher that I wanted. The best I could think of was tell him, "I love you and I've always got your back." I suppose that's the one thing I always knew. Dad had my back, and I wanted Fletcher and all my boys to know that I had theirs.

Football season was right around the corner. I faced four months of coaching Ross on the fifth and sixth grade team and offensive line for the high school varsity. I would be in the office by 7 a.m., work through lunch until 3:30 p.m., head to two practices, get off the field around 7 p.m. and go back to the office for a while if need be. Of course, I would deal with discipline issues, homework, keeping Lee happy, church, and being the head of this sorry outfit. Lee had suggested that I back off. I didn't want to. Sometimes I wished I could call Dad and ask what he'd do.

I stepped out onto the driveway and looked up into the sky. It was a mass of swirling clouds and a light rain fell. I knew I would have to wait for my answer.

Chapter Eleven

Letting Go

And He walks with me, and He talks with me,
And He tells me I am His own;
And the joy we share as we tarry there,
None other has ever known.[36]

—"In the Garden," Charles Austin Miles

Fletcher made it through his first semester at LSU with a healthy GPA. He was still fearless. In the student section at an LSU game that fall, a frat pledge told him he had to move because the seats were saved. No one was there when Fletcher and his buddy sat down, so he said no. "Come on man, I don't want to fight you!"

"You want to fight? Let's go. Right here, right now." He was ready and he wasn't moving. (This is just me, but I would have told the dude, "I wouldn't do that if I were you." Just sayin.) The frat kid backed down.

Fletcher didn't pledge Sam's fraternity. It seemed like he wanted to set himself against the establishment as he saw it. Funny thing though, his buddy he hung out with, pledged. He did okay his first semester, and it was good to see him and Sam for Christmas. With the New Year coming, we were only a few months away from Spencer and Hollyn's wedding date of April 11, 2015.

With so much going on, one would think that the tension between Lee and me would have been old news, but it wasn't. I smoked cigars, which I knew Lee didn't like, but I was hooked and rebelling in a real juvenile sort of way.

Smoking was a form of protest. But that wasn't all. The fact is that women go through menopause. Men don't. I should have never said it, but I did: "If I wanted to be broke *and* celibate I wouldn't have gotten married. I would have joined the Catholic priesthood." The smoking surely did not help.

And as time went by, I felt something else that took me a while to put my finger on. I felt a longing for that old emotional and romantic roller coaster feeling of being in love that I had fought so hard to escape when I got sober. Warning sirens should have been going off. I had a bad nagging feeling about it but kept it to myself. After all, that was my job as husband and father, as I saw it. The buck stops here. Besides wasn't I supposed to pour myself out for others just as Jesus poured himself out for me? That is what love is all about right? An action, not a feeling. I kept my mouth shut. Well, most of the time, except when I got angry and couldn't really say what I was angry about.

In all honesty, all the moving parts of our world weren't helping. Here we were with these seven sons, each a universe unto himself, out in the world spinning away with friends, dreams, hopes, problems, challenges, and all the things that make us human. And we are their parents each moment of each day, no matter how old they get, existing within this constant state of movement and low-level chaos. And on top of it, Lee and I were in this control battle that showed no signs of letting up because we are both "type A" personalities and just too damn stubborn to give in. Oh, we would say we were giving in when we traversed into the other's sphere, but like good humans, a little resistance was reserved and you never knew when it would show up.

How in God's creation could two people find the space and energy to maintain intimacy, affection, and an emotional connection to sustain our relationship? The answer to that, I guessed at the time, was to just keep muddling through and find a quiet moment when you can. The friction between us just made me sad, like depressed sad. And my thoughts kept going back to, "I may not be here when you get back." But I shook that off too and just kept my mouth shut.

I really have to give Lee credit for putting up with me during this time. She is a great wife, and it is a good thing that she considered love to be an action and not a feeling. Sure, she complained about the cigars. I would sit out on the porch and smoke and she would come out and ask, "Why don't you want to be with the rest of the family?" Because I was hooked on nicotine, that's why. I flat out gave up and told her that. I had only quit for one woman. Her. And now I had to do it again.

So, I smoked cigars, which is the equivalent—especially with my age and a bicuspid aortic valve —of putting a gun to your head and pulling the trigger until either things changed or there's a bullet in the chamber. I realized what I was doing to myself and the risk I was putting my family in should they lose me to a smoking addiction that I maintained out of spite.

But this is a way of life for an addict. It's the knowledge that the addiction is just a form of slow suicide mixed with the desire to quit and the inability to do so. You get stuck in this cycle of fear for what you are doing and then self-loathing for the fact that you can't end it. I knew all too well the spiral of events in my life that began with the drug nicotine. And so, around that Christmas it became clear to me that despite the overwhelming urge to do that one thing my wife didn't want me to do just to prove a point, (funny how that scenario keeps popping up, huh? And rather stupid too) I decided that in order to live as long as I could to support and raise my kids and be a good example to my sons, I had to quit. And I wanted my wife back.

For Christmas that year, I got Coach Agresta two tickets to the Sugar Bowl so he could see his beloved Ohio State Buckeyes take on the Crimson Tide of Alabama. Coach is like no other football coach I have ever known. We pray together as a team before and after everything we do. He leads it. We have our priorities posted on the locker room wall, and they have never changed. God first, family second, school third, and football fourth (you can really fill in the blank here with any "other" passion). These priorities remain the same through life. I measure most everything I do by these priorities, just substitute work for school. And like I tell anyone who will listen, our three enemies are the world, the flesh, and the devil. Welcome to the war, gentlemen.

Anyway, Coach was excited when I brought him the tickets on Christmas Eve. I mean, I had to do it. Ohio State just couldn't be playing in the quarter-final game for the National Championship right in New Orleans and Coach Agresta not be there. And I doubt that it was really the "best" Christmas present he "ever" got but I thought it was pretty awesome.

I probably should have prayed about how I could quit smoking and straighten out some of the internals that had developed in my marriage. I had not been to an AA meeting for several years. Although I prayed daily, I had not been back through my life for an updated, thorough, and rigorously honest personal inventory in twenty-nine years. If I had done that, I would have seen how those small remaining seeds of self-seeking had sprouted in the form of my failure to be truly grateful for all that God had given, all that he had taken away, and all that was left. I had learned those lessons well in the material realm, now it was time to apply it to the rest of me. God was about to deal with me. Again.

I made an appointment with my doctor.

"I'm going through a mid-life crisis."

"You're fifty-eight years old. Shouldn't that have happened already?"

"Yeah, but it's a young fifty-eight. My youngest boy is just eight years old. I'm a late bloomer."

The year before, we were in Florida and I was heading from the beach to the pool with Mason. I was holding his hand as always. Three squeezes means, "I love you." Two squeezes back means, "How much?" When I crush his hand it means, "This much!"

We met a young lady on the sidewalk in a string bikini that I tried hard not to notice and did the "Excuse me, pardon me" dance on the sidewalk. She smiled at me and I went into suspended animation. Then she said, "My, what a beautiful grandson you have!"

I burst out laughing. "Actually, he is my youngest."

She ducked her head and headed off embarrassed. And I realized that I was over the hill, and picking up speed.

"Okay, what are you doing?"

"I started smoking cigars after the Saints won the Super Bowl, and now I'm hooked again on nicotine."

He actually laughed. Audibly. "I have seen guys get hair implants, hair removal, liposuction, buy sporty convertibles, divorce their wives, leave their kids, and spend all their money on young women. And that's it? You started smoking cigars?"

My feelings were hurt. And I wasn't happy he had just put all those ideas into my head. I didn't need to think about any of that stuff. I have all my hair thank you, I work out, drive a fast car, listen to loud rock and roll, and would never leave my wife or kids. I would be an idiot to even think about messing that up.

But I had an innate feeling that returning to my first addiction might, just might, be a start down a slippery slope. And I didn't want that. It just felt like I was having a slip after all these years.

"Look," I said, "I want to quit smoking, but I'm hooked. I have an eight year old, a twelve year old, and a junior in high school, and my other boys need me and, well, I need to quit for Lee, again, so can you give me a prescription?"

He said, "Sure," and gave me a prescription for Chantix.

In hindsight, that wasn't the best thing for an overwhelmed guy in an emotional state.

#

By Mid-January of 2015, Fletcher and Sam were back up at LSU, the other kids were back to their routine, work was busy and the wedding was approaching, quickly. I had also started the Chantix, which was beginning to elevate my moods, make me absent-minded, and fall off into elaborate daydreams. I didn't realize it was the Chantix at the time; I had a cold and figured it was that or whatever it was I took for it.

By about the third week in January, things had reached a bit of a holding pattern when the wedding plans were set and work had calmed down. I knew it wouldn't last, so I decided to head out to the camp for the last weekend of deer and duck season. I packed up my winter hunting gear, and as I headed out the door, I grabbed a couple of cigars thinking if this was my last weekend of calm, at least I could smoke a last cigar or two in peace. Again, this is the thinking of an addict: *I must quit; I'll die if I don't, but I can wait until later.* I was waffling, no doubt. Slipping and sliding all over the place.

Lee wanted a deer roast. I hadn't killed a deer that year. Sunday found me sitting in a deer stand on a cold morning sniffling and coughing while trying to be quiet. I lamented not being in church, and then my phone beeped and it was a text from Lee with a photo of an eight-point buck standing out behind the house by our pond. I could have shot him from the back porch. I wanted to scream, but instead I climbed down from the stand, packed up, and left for home in disgust. The hunting camp is at the mouth of the Atchafalaya basin, forty-five minutes by water from the camp to the boat launch and an hour by car from there. I guess the deer had gotten smart, hiding right outside my back door.

I pulled the mud boat out, loaded my gear into the truck, climbed in, and called Lee to let her know I'd be home sooner as opposed to later.

"Did Spencer tell you about Fletcher?"

"No. What happened?"

"Well, Fletcher and his college friend came here this weekend—"

"Yeah?"

"—and they had a bunch of acid. I think Fletcher took about ten hits."

I wiped my face with my hand. "And?"

"He got to the point that he was running around in the yard like he'd lost his mind. Spencer was here, and he tried to talk him down, but Fletcher started screaming that he was the devil and hit Spencer in the arm with a piece of firewood." That sounded vaguely familiar.

"Was he hurt?"

"Spencer thought it might be broken, and Fletcher kept racing around like a lunatic, so I called Sam."

"Is Sam there, too?"

"No, he's still in Baton Rouge, but I thought maybe if he spoke to Fletcher maybe he could calm him down."

"Did it work?"

"No, and meanwhile of course Mason and Ross were scared to death and had no idea what was happening and why Fletcher was running around threatening to do I don't know what all, but he was just gone."

"Did he run off or something? Where is he?"

"Well, Fletcher finally wore himself out, and I got him inside and settled down in front of the TV, but I had to sit with him all night."

"You have got to be kidding me."

I heard real fear in Lee's voice so I raced home to see what I could do, but Fletcher and his friend had left. All I could do was try to comfort Ross and Mason.

I waited a day to let Fletcher settle down before I called him. He gave me the low down.

"I'm sorry Dad." He went on to say that he was failing a Calculus 3 class and that the professor was terrible. That wasn't like him at all being a math whiz.

"Well, why don't you drop the class and add on an elective so you get the credits you need for the semester? You can shore up your GPA and live to fight another day. And you can retake it with another professor. It's not the end of the world."

He seemed relieved that I had a solution. That's what he did. And he ended his "friendship" through which he got the acid. I told him how I felt about it, about the bad trip up on the mountain when I was in high school, how disappointed I was that it had happened. He seemed really shook.

That summer Fletcher re-took Calculus 3 and in his words "raped it." He made a ninety-eight in the course. Good thing he didn't make a one hundred, it might have gone to his head.

#

In February, I walked into our bedroom and Lee was folding some clothes on the bed as she watched TV. (Why do they always end up on my bed?) I glanced at it for a second and paused. "What show is that?"

"I don't know, *Everybody Loves Raymond* or something."

"Huh." I watched for a bit and there was something about the woman who played Ray's wife Debra. I thought I'd always liked her as an actress and I asked Lee, "That's Susan Lucci, right?" I have no idea where I got that name.

She looked at me and screwed up her face a little. "No. That's not Susan Lucci."

"Well, yeah, it's someone." I could sense a disagreement brewing.

A few minutes later I passed back through the room. "Her name is Patricia Heaton." Ha, she had to wait for the credits.

"Patricia Heaton? Never heard of her." I always liked Ray's wife though. I paid it no mind and left the room.

#

It was about two weeks from the wedding on a Friday night. I was in Baton Rouge at a board retreat for the school's board of directors. The headmaster ran the meetings, and I stood in awe of the other board members. One was a doctor who had served for many years, two were financial advisors, and then businessmen, all of whom were not only successful but known to be good Christian men. I was honored to be asked to be a part this group. By just doing what I could for the school and keeping my head low, I thought I could sidestep this duty. I had served on sessions and boards in the past. I tried to lay low but somehow, they found me.

I had a deposition that held me up, so I met up with the group in the late afternoon at a hotel in Baton Rouge where we met to discuss fundraising goals and strategies and then tour another flourishing Christian school. It was after the tour and around 10 p.m. as we were just beginning to start the meeting, when my phone rang—actually, vibrated in my pocket—but I let it go to voicemail while the headmaster spoke. I did notice, though, that the call was from my sister, which concerned me. Mom had moved from Winnfield to live with her in Texas and she'd not been feeling well.

When a break came, I excused myself and stepped into the hall to return the call.

"Hey, what's up? You called?"

"We are on our way to a hospital in Houston. They're airlifting Mother by helicopter and we are meeting her there."

"What's wrong?"

"She's not been eating well, has had this pneumonia, and today her primary doctor told us to bring her to the hospital. They ran an abdominal CT scan and found an aortic aneurism. The doctor said it could rupture anytime so they put her on a helicopter to Houston where they can address something like this."

"Will she have to go to surgery?"

"We don't know yet. I guess we'll find out when we get there."

"Okay, let me know as soon as you find anything out."

I ended the call and stood there stunned.

When I reentered the conference room and sat down, the pain and disbelief that I felt was clear to the other people in the room.

"What's wrong?" asked the doctor.

"That was my sister in Houston. My mother, who is eighty-four years old, has an abdominal aortic aneurism and is being transferred to a downtown Houston hospital for treatment. I don't know much about aneurisms other than if they rupture they can be fatal. Right now, I don't know what to do."

There was compassion in the doctor's eyes. "You need to leave right now and go be with your mother." There was no doubt in his voice.

The other men voiced their agreement and then the headmaster said, "Let's pray for Frank and his mom." Each man came forward and placed a hand upon me and then the doctor led a prayer. His words are lost to me because my heart and mind were filled to overflowing with worry and grief. In my thoughts, I asked God for His mercy and grace. My mind flashed back to the verse, "My grace is sufficient for you" that I had prayed so fervently for my dad as he passed through the veil. I prayed that now for my mom. And for God to do no more than help me get to the next step, to the next minute.

I gathered my belongings and hustled out to my car. The night sky was clear and the weather warm for that time of year. I called my sister to tell her I was on my way, then put the address for the hospital into my GPS. Then I called Lee and told her what was going on.

"Frank, I'm sorry."

"Thanks."

"I love you."

"Love you, too."

My Acura came to life, and I guided it toward the interstate and immediately my Chantix softened mind began to wander. I knew that God was trying to show me something; He always is. I castigated myself for not having called Mom when I had the chance. Truthfully, I could not recall the last time we had spoken, and I was ashamed to admit it. She'd stayed with us for Thanksgiving, and I know we spoke at Christmas. She had sent the kids cards for the second year in a row having bought chickens, goats, and livestock, I think maybe a cow, for poor folks in third world countries struck by famine and adversities. She had done this through World Vision, and I knew the boys had been sponsoring a young man in the Philippines for several years, also through World Vision. She wrote a long card, always the one to teach a life lesson to the boys.

That's the way she was. I remember as a boy meeting a couple and their family from Jordan at Aunt Sarah's house in Winnfield. They had been displaced by the Seven Day War. You just never knew who you might meet in Winnfield. I had talked to Mom on the phone a few times since Christmas, but then life got in the way.

I hit I-10 heading west toward Houston, let the car just run, and turned on the radio. My foot got heavy. Somewhere west of Lake Charles, the first few bars of "Panama" by Van Halen came on, and in those notes I was a teenager again, on the road, nothing in front of me but life. *Better than love ...* I glanced down at the speedometer, and I was doing over 100 miles per hour. I eased her back a bit. I couldn't help think about how many times my '68 Camaro had trumped girls. I poured every dollar I made into that car, ordering from the factory new coil springs, motor mounts, wiring harness, the actual 396-cubic inch block, you name it.

My eyes fixed on the night sky again remembering the flat black Camaro. I had to leave it at home when I went up to LSU. At age eighteen, I could not afford the insurance on a sports car. I asked Mom to start it at least once a week.

Nervous that she'd forget, I called her from school the first Friday afternoon after class. "Did you remember to start my Camaro?"

"Yes, I took it to the grocery store."

She did her grocery shopping on Fridays. One Thursday my brother and I were starving after swim practice and the pickings were slim. I made a ketchup and onion sandwich. I asked J.R. what he ate. "I heated up that half can of hash." Hash? Mom never bought hash. But Dad fed the dog Alpo, half a can at a time. He put the other half in the fridge and many times the paper label fell off.

"Uh, I think that was Alpo, man."

"Really!? Man, I can't believe we are feeding stuff that tastes that good to the dog!"

Perspective is everything.

"Is the car running all right?"

She laughed. "Yep, and when the bagboy came out with the groceries he asked what I had under the hood. I told him a 396. He wanted to look so I said that was fine. He just whistled kind of slow. Must've thought I was something."

I called again on Friday the next week.

"Of course, I remembered."

"Thanks."

"And as a matter of fact, as I was coming back from the grocery store some knuckleheads in a jacked-up Mustang with wide tires, the works, pulled up at a stop light and yelled over at me, 'Hey lady, wanna race?' Then they all laughed."

I had to smile. I kind of knew the answer, but I asked anyway, "What did you do Mom?"

"I blew them away, what do you think? When the light turned green, I smoked 'em. At the next red light, they yelled over, 'Good Lord, lady, what ya got in that thing?' I yelled over, 'I got a 396 with duel exhausts and a Hurst four-speed.' Then I dusted 'em again."

"Mom, you didn't."

"Sure did."

That's the kind of mom I had. She had played basketball at Louisiana Tech, helped me win the fishing tournament when I was eight years old taking a saltwater catfish barb in the foot through a tennis shoe, and could shoot a squirrel through the head with a .22 rifle, no scope. She taught me what was important in life, and I didn't want to lose her, not yet.

It was around 4 a.m. when I pulled into the hospital and wended my way—as suggested—around the hospital to its parking garage. It was something of a maze inside the building to get to the vascular surgery area where Mom was in a nearby ICU. "Park in the garage and walk to the left and there will be a set of elevators, which will bring you to a crossover," etc. etc. "and to ICU."

Well, I parked, walked left and ended up going all the way out and around to the front of the hospital. At that hour, the place was deserted and there was one drunk sleeping on the lawn. I kept walking all the way around the hospital and back to the parking garage where I realized the elevator was about fifty feet to the right of my car. I'd walked around the entire outside of the hospital only to end up where I started. *Crap!*

I went through the maze and finally reached the ICU. I will never forget walking into her room. "Hi, Mom, how are you doing?"

Her eyes searched out the source of the voice, and she recognized who I was. I sat with her for as long as the ICU staff would let me and then found a hotel room near the hospital. I was still caving on cigars, now smoking cigarillos from gas stations. It was hard to find plain cigars without any weird grape or peach flavors. Fletcher said I was probably the only person in the world who actually smoked them, whatever that means. So, I smoked for a nicotine hit before I crashed.

The next morning, I returned and met the surgeon assigned to Mom. I made it a point to be there when he came.

"We need to perform surgery to repair the aneurism, but we can't do that until her condition is stabilized. Right now, she's having issues with her stomach and GI tract—nausea, pain, bloating—in part, because she hasn't had a bowel movement in quite some time and is impacted."

This was Saturday and my nephew and his wife had also arrived late Friday from Austin, TX. It was a hard day. Mom had moments when she was somewhat lucid, but mostly she was asleep or lost to her own internal world. The doctor and nurses did what they could to make her comfortable and gave her medication to help her move her bowels, which seemed to them to be the big problem. The challenge was, they didn't want to move too aggressively and risk rupturing the aneurism.

We sat with her until evening, but there was little change. My nephew offered to spend the night so we could get some rest and he'd call if anything changed. I said goodnight then walked out of the hospital and straight to a shop where I could buy a couple cigars.

The Chantix was fighting with my brain. I was emotional, moody, and easily drifted off into daydreams and other reveries. I sat out at the hotel, smoked, and daydreamed. It wasn't an easy night for Mom. She was in pain, her body bloated, and she threw up a few times and aspirated.

The next morning the doctor didn't want to risk waiting for her condition to improve. A nurse supervisor came in. "You have to have a bowel movement so we're going to see if we can help get things going, okay?" Then she looked at us. "Everybody, out."

I kissed Mom on the forehead and took a last look as I left the room. She was lethargic, not quite coherent, and the pain in her eyes was obvious.

I'm not sure exactly what they did to her, but when they let us back into her room in the early afternoon, she looked up and said, "Hi, how are you all doing?" It was like she was sitting at her kitchen table, perfectly fine. It would be an understatement to say that we were relieved.

The doctor came in and explained she still had to gain more strength and get her white cell count down, (there was a staph infection near the aneurysm), before he could do the surgery, and they would have to see how things went over the next few days. Each day her strength came back a little bit, but by Wednesday there still wasn't a determination on when they could do the surgery. I did research on surgically repairing aortic aneurysms in octogenarians. It was a brutal surgery. Basically, the conclusion of the medical literature was if there was no other condition that would result in morbidity then do the surgery. In other words, the rupture of the aorta was fatal, so if she was up for it, go for it. The doctor recommended it. We discussed it with her, talked about all the options. There really weren't any. She decided to do it. No hesitation. I still had nagging doubts. After all she was eighty-four years old.

With Easter coming that weekend, followed by Spencer and Hollyn's wedding the following weekend and some work piling up, Mom said, "You need to be home for Easter." I said okay and came home. Fletcher and Sam came down from LSU and we had a good Easter Sunday with all the kids around our table for the first time since Christmas.

I also noticed a bit of a change in Fletcher. I couldn't quite put my finger on it, but his eyes were brighter and he seemed lighter, as if some weight was lifted from him. I asked how things were going and he said fine, but I didn't want to get in his way, so I didn't push.

The next morning, just before I left to go to the office, my sister called me. "They're going to do the surgery tomorrow."

The surgery was to take place on Tuesday, the rehearsal dinner on Thursday—I have no idea why on Thursday for a Saturday wedding—and the wedding Saturday. I could handle it. I was a bit stressed that so much was happening so fast and all at the same time. The Chantix made things worse, but I didn't realize at the time the whole effect it was having on me. Actually, being the screwball that I am, I kind of liked it. It was a mood elevator, and I was doing my best to stay positive. I swung by the office, buttoned up some things, and drove to Houston arriving that evening.

Mom had really been looking forward to going to Spencer's wedding. I mean Ganny and Poppy came down for all our graduations, weddings, grandkids, you know. Mom really wanted to be there, and you never knew what could happen.

She had bought her dress and everything. We talked about it and I said that Spencer and Hollyn really understood. It couldn't be helped. Mom hesitated, then teared up. "I don't want to die on Spencer's wedding day. It should be a happy day for him." She was crying. I was stunned and it broke my heart, but the hard tail in me took over. "Then don't! I can't believe you just said that!"

She laughed. "Neither can I! I was just saying what I was thinking."

"I know. But that's up to God, not us. Think positive." *My grace is sufficient for you* kept rolling through my head.

I was at the hospital early the next morning. We went into the pre-op room, and I watched as Lee said that we'd be praying for her. Mom smiled.

I kissed her forehead, and said, "I'm not going to tell you goodbye. You know that. No matter what happens, I'll see you later." She knew that this referred to our discussions of heaven at the kitchen table and John 14 after I came to faith. I knew, come what may, that I would see her again.

The surgeon said the surgery would last four hours, but after an hour and a half a nurse came out and said the doctor wanted to meet with us. I thought Mom must have died on the table or something, but he marched into the room beaming. "Everything went fine! As I said, I'm the fastest knife in Baghdad." He drew me a picture of what he had done, and because she was so old he'd done it fast. I was really amazed and grateful.

She came out of the recovery room back into the ICU, and considering what she'd been through, she looked about as good as I could have hoped. If you haven't guessed by now I don't believe in coincidences. Providence yes, coincidences no.

I purposed to stay in the ICU with Mom after surgery. Everything in the room was whirring or going *beep, beep, beep*. She was holding my hand and squeezing it. I didn't dare move or let go of her hand, and I don't know how many times I looked out the window and counted the number of floors of the building across the way and then the number of windows and anything else to occupy my mind, but I wasn't going to let go of her hand.

At eleven that night, another ICU nurse came on duty, a big black guy in scrubs. "I'm on until seven in the morning, so it looks like you and me will be here together. Let me know if there are any problems. He checked the drains and IV and everything and then said, "Are we going to be good?"

I said, "Well, we'll be good as long as I know one thing."

"What's that?"

"You're not an Alabama fan."

He smiled. "Oh no, I went to Ohio State."

"No kidding."

That night was calm, but the next day they had to put her through hell. The respiratory therapist suctioned her throat and lungs by sticking a tube down her throat, and I saw Mom's eyes narrow in pain. Then they had to do an x-ray, which required lifting her to slide the plates under, and that was painful, too. It was just one thing after another.

That was Wednesday.

After the surgery, she couldn't speak but she knew where she was and she knew the wedding was coming in a few days. On Thursday, I told her I had to go and her eyes said all she needed to say. "I'll be sure to take a video of the wedding and everything for you, okay?"

She nodded and I kissed her one last time. "I love you, Mom."

Then I left for the mad dash home to the rehearsal dinner. I made it with moments to spare, gave my toast, and then went home with Lee and the boys. The next day I worked for a bit, and that night I walked by Mason as he was watching TV.

"What ya watchin'?" I asked.

"The Middle."

"That's the name of the show?"

"Yeah."

I sat with him for a moment and then recognized that Patricia Heaton played the mom in that show. Huh, I thought, and watched through to the end.

The next morning was tuxedo mayhem, *rain*, the race to the wedding, *rain*, Chantix inspired daydreams and elevated moods, *rain*—why is it always rain?—and Spencer's most beautiful wedding.

# # #

That night, in the calm that followed the storm, I stepped out beneath clearing, cloud-swept skies and felt the absence of a cigar between my fingers. Meanwhile I was worried about Fletcher; I also didn't want to neglect work; Mom was in pain and suffering; and with the boys it felt there were ceaseless appeals for more of me and from me.

What am I not seeing or hearing? I wondered.

The next thought led back to the question I'd pondered up to December of 1986, *Is this all there is?* Of course the meaning had changed. In my past, I'd wondered if there was more to life than what I saw or experienced that would give it meaning. In my faith and acceptance of the Lord into my heart, I'd found the answer to both questions. Now I was asking God, *Is this all You have planned for me because I want something more, to serve You better and to feel at peace again.*

The restlessness had returned, maybe it never left, and I was back to wrestling, in one form or another, with something written by Os Guinness: "Inevitably and inescapably, then, all who will not hear the signals of transcendence, and all who hear them but refuse to follow them, condemn themselves to be restless." [37]

I looked up to the sky once more. "Okay God, what do You want me to do? I need an answer here."

Silence.

Waiting for me inside was a mess of cummerbunds and other tuxedo paraphernalia, and the next week looked like an endless series of office work, depositions all over the state, phone calls to Mom, worrying about Mom, and wondering what in the heck it all was supposed to be telling me. I was well beyond overwhelmed and wished I could just turn my brain off for a while and let the world coast for a bit without me.

Monday came and I checked in with Mom and worked, but when I came home, Mason was in the TV room watching that show *The Middle* again. "Hey, is that show on every night? Or what?"

"Nah, I DVR it."

"Huh?"

"You know, DVR, it lets you watch shows whenever you want."

I sat down with him. "You mean you have more than just this episode?"

"Yeah, I think we've got like more than fifty."

"Huh."

"Yeah."

"Show me how to use that thing, will ya?"

"Okay."

By Thursday of that week, I'd watched fifty-some episodes of *The Middle* and developed a bit of an interest in Patricia Heaton. One night as I sat watching one episode after another, I used my phone to look at Twitter and noticed she had an account. I sort of picked through her Tweets and so on and found out that she is the same age as me and that she was born in Cleveland, Ohio. Then I Googled her and learned that she was one of the few conservative Christians in Hollywood, is also prolife, and that she has four boys. I'd sort of hoped to find out that she was some sort of bad ass chick, but no such dice, she was just like my wife. "That's weird."

My Chantix mind wondered what would happen if I got caught Googling someone. It just sounded bad. I actually daydreamed about meeting her one day and having to explain, "I'm real sorry, but I Googled you." It sounds like invasion of someone's personal space or something. I was embarrassed that I had even done it.

Friday morning I woke up early with an urge to drive to Los Angeles. I had no idea what I'd do when I got there, I just felt it was something I should do. I gnawed on it like a dog with a bone and as I drove to see Mom in Houston, I could not let go of the thought that at age fifty-eight, my life can't be over, this just can't be it. Tears welled in my eyes, and I felt nothing but helpless and run down by life.

A song came on the radio, "I just want you to know who I am."[38] Traffic broke me from my thoughts and I looked at the speedometer. I was doing over one hundred again. For the last however many minutes, or longer, I wasn't even aware I was driving. I pulled over, tears were now streaming from my eyes, and I paced up and down the shoulder of the interstate.

"Okay God, what do I do with the next twenty-two years of my life, if that's what you give me? What do You want me to do because I'm telling You, this can't be it?"

I kept pacing as cars sped by, the hot wind kicked as they passed and tossed my tie like a little flag. I found myself reliving my youth and talking to myself, probably not a good idea considering all the things I had done. "I've water skied naked underneath cypress trees grabbing moss, that's on film somewhere. I've jumped off drilling rigs into the Gulf. At LSU we did road trips off the cuff all the time. I've done crazier stuff than this before. Getting back into that car and driving to Los Angeles wouldn't be that big of a thing." I know. I was bonkers.

In the past, I've justified decisions I've made by explaining, "It seemed like a good idea at the time." And I would say most of those were done either stoned, drunk, or both. And this time there was a definite chemical component. I wasn't hallucinating or psychotic or anything else like that. I was, let's say, in a very elevated mood from the Chantix.

Either way, God remained silent. That or I couldn't see or hear what he was trying to tell me, probably the latter. I paced some more, which calmed me, and then I got back in the car, cranked the radio, and pulled out onto the road.

When I got to Houston and Mom's room she looked better, not quite like the mom I knew, but better. I spent the weekend chatting with her and listening to what the doctor had to say. I talked with her nurse—the fella from Ohio State—about football and how he ended up in Texas, and then it was time to come home. On the drive, my thoughts ran from the kids, to Mom, to Lee and our troubles, but always came back to Patricia Heaton and driving to Los Angeles. I didn't know what it all meant, but I let my thoughts wander wherever they wanted to go.

Over the next couple weeks, these thoughts wouldn't go away and they wound me up tighter and tighter until I thought I would burst! Los Angeles felt like some mythic destination where I'd find answers, to what questions I had no idea. I also had no idea what I'd do once I got there. Even if I met Patricia Heaton, I had no idea what I would say. Actually, I had no idea why I wanted to meet her. I just had questions.

Like, do you know anybody who went to Viet Nam? Anyone killed in Viet Nam? Have you ever been to the Rock and Roll Hall of Fame in Cleveland? Did you go to a Catholic school? What did you guys used to do for fun? Then the Fifth Amendment questions—ones you could either refuse to answer and take the Fifth, or give me a one dollar bill and hire me so I'd be bound by the attorney client privilege to keep my mouth shut—like did you guys smoke pot or do drugs in high school?

I had a friend as a kid. He was a few years younger than me and looked just like Brad Pitt. Hanging around with John was a real kick. There was no telling what we could dream up, from spoofing the life guards to messing with the girls. But he was my friend. Famous people have to just have friends, don't they? I've always wondered who these people were deep down in their souls. I guessed I would never know.

If I ever met Patricia Heaton what would I say? You know, "Hi, you don't know me, but I binge watched fifty-some-odd episodes of your show while I was on Chantix. I'm a fifty-eight-year-old married lawyer with seven boys, and I'd like to find out what makes you tick." Really?

I swear to the reader and my wife that there was not one shred of a romantic overtone in my fixations at all. Absolutely none. It was all part and parcel of some unidentified call to a higher, nobler, heroic purpose that I used to pine for in all my relationships before I got sober. I recognized it. It was not person specific, but emotional in nature. I had been warned in recovery to watch out for what can only be termed as emotional slips, usually relationship-oriented and unhealthy. They were in my case. And once God had set me right, I was able to fall in love, get married, have kids, the whole bit. All my dreams had come true. And now I was having this midlife, emotional, Chantix-induced emotional slip that would have made Walter Middy proud all because my wife didn't like cigars. And I knew it! I just couldn't do anything about it. And I hate to say it, but Patricia Heaton was fixated in my mind in the middle of it all. Weird, huh?

I'm sure God's signals were flashing red, but I wasn't picking them up.

By Friday, May eighth—the Friday before Mother's Day—I'd reached some sort of boiling point. The urge to say *to hell with everything* and drive to Los Angeles was overwhelming, and I kept picking at it like a scab.

I've done crazier things than this, I thought. *When I was young, I'd have done it. I've got money and I can stay in any hotel I want. I could just get in the car and go. Why not?* I'll tell you why not. I had no idea what I would do once I got there and I didn't want to get arrested like some lunatic fan.

I was possessed by a deep, visceral need and thoughts that life, my life, had to be far more than it was. I walked into Walter's office. "Walter, the BP thing is going to be over at some point this year, and it's been our way to wait for the next disaster to come along and trust that God would show us what to do and everything, but we need to start thinking further down the line. I don't know what we are going to do next, but I want to do something really big! Really great!"

He sat back. "What in the world are you talking about?"

"Look, you're sixty-three and I'm fifty-eight, and I think God wants us to do something great. I'm not sure what. I don't know, maybe it's this medication I've been taking, but something needs to change and we need to do something big."

Walter was silent for a moment. "Frank, I know you get emotional when you get inspired, but you're too inspired. You need to stop taking that crap."

"I want to do something to affect the world, and I really mean it."

"I know you mean it, but look at you, you gotta stop taking that medication."

"Yeah, you've probably got a point."

But I wasn't done yet.

That week, Mom was well enough to leave the hospital and move into a long term acute care hospital nearer to her home. After my meltdown with Walter, I worked for a few hours, and late that afternoon I pointed the Acura back toward the interstate and Houston. As usual, my mind wandered, but this time I went back to growing up on James Drive when we were all together and the many Christmases we had. I remembered Mr. Bingle and riding in the back of Dad's car as he eased down St. Charles Avenue to look at the houses that were lit up for the holiday.

And I remembered standing by the piano singing as my sister played, "To Dream the Impossible Dream." I dialed that song up on iTunes with my phone and listened to the lyrics.

> *To dream the impossible dream*
> *To fight the unbeatable foe*
> *To bear with unbearable sorrow*
> *To run where the brave dare not go* [39]

To be honest, the Chantix really had me kind of whacked out. But I had loved those lyrics my whole life. And then came my verse, the one that I had grabbed hold of early on in my life and never let go. *To right the unrightable wrong ... To fight for the right without question or pause.*[40] That was me.

But I started to think about the whole song. *That the world will be better for this, that one man scorned and covered with scars, still strove with his last ounce of courage, ... to reach the unreachable star.* [41] And for the umpteenth time I realized that I had it "bass ackwards," all wrong.

In fact, the name of the song was all wrong. It should be "The Possible Dream," that we will never be totally victorious on this earth, that we will only see in a mirror dimly, but if we have that attitude to keep trying, to never give up despite the disappointments, despite the defeats, despite the scars, that God will see us through. And though we will die, covered with scars, the victory will be ours. It was why I had cried my eyes out on the floor of my apartment in December of 1986 only to rise to my feet with my obsession with alcohol lifted. Because Jesus had given all and I had to follow Him.

My thoughts went back to the day I pulled over to the side of the road with tears falling from my eyes. I wanted to know what I was supposed to do with the rest of my life. I was saying I wanted to hang glide in California, and I wanted to go to Nepal and bring relief to the victims of the recent earthquake there. I remembered, too, as I paced up and down the side of the road, that I'd stupidly said I wanted to fall in love again and have the feeling I got when I had a crush on someone one more time. Of course, God was listening, and in His own inimitable way, granted my wish as disconnected from reality and truth as it was. Be careful what you ask for. You might get it. God has to have a sense of humor. And at that moment He must have laughed long and hard.

I laughed at myself as well. At age fifty-eight what had I learned? I was still capable of being a fool. As it always does, it comes back to being right with God and being in love with God before it is possible to love another person.

"I shouldn't have said that," I prayed. "I'm sorry, God. You have indeed granted to me every desire of my heart, and I am truly grateful."

When I walked into the acute care hospital that Saturday before Mother's Day, Mom still had a nasal cannula for oxygen, but she looked nothing like the frail figure laboring for each breath when I was last with her. The skin on her hands was thin and clear, the tops discolored and blue from IV needles that at her age would take a while to heal. She was asleep, and I reached out and stroked the side of her cheek with the back of my hand.

Her eyes fluttered open. She wasn't startled or scared. Her eyes, alive and shining with a touch of mischief, drifted up to mine and a slight smile broke across her lips. I'd seen that face my entire life, checking me out, gauging my mood or disposition, but not to scrutinize, it was in a loving way. I wanted to give her my heart just like when I was a small child.

"Hello there." Her voice was soft, gentle, sleepy.

"Hello, yourself. Your voice sounds stronger and I've heard your swallowing is better."

She paused to search for a thought. "Yep, I'm doing better."

"I came to see my mom on Mother's Day."

"I'm glad you did."

We had a good visit.

"Okay." I bent and kissed her. "See you in the morning."

"Yep, see you in the morning."

I was glad she was out of the ICU. We had a nice Mother's Day visit and once again, I was humbled by her love and the woman that she was. She was as close to perfect as I believed any person could get and I wanted the world to know it. I wanted every person to know what we were perhaps on the verge of losing.

I said goodbye on Sunday afternoon and wheeled my car out of the parking lot toward I-10. I stopped at a red light, and in front of me was a choice. To the right was New Orleans, home, Lee, the boys, work, my life. To the left was Los Angeles and an ideal, a fantasy, a dream. I'd stopped taking the Chantix, but I was still prone to daydreams, and for a moment I saw myself on the Tonight Show with Jimmy Fallon. I was talking about my story of coming to faith and this whole Patricia Heaton thing when he says, "Well, we've got a surprise for you, and it's somebody you never thought you would meet, and here she is, Ms. Patricia Heaton!"

And then, with the audience applauding, after waiting all this time just speak to her, I say the dumbest thing ever, something that I've said a thousand times, something that never worked or went over well. "I'm sorry, I was on drugs."

I shook my head. "This really is a midlife crisis."

The light turned green and I turned right, thinking, *I want to be in love with a woman who's in her fifties, grew up when I did, has a few stretch marks, and will, if I'm lucky, have sex with me.*

"I know exactly where to find her."

Led Zeppelin's "Rock & Roll" started playing on the radio, "It's been a long time." [42] I hit the gas and headed home.

#

Sometime that spring, Lee called me. "Have you heard what Fletcher's been up to?"

"Will it never end?"

"No, it's good. He's been going to a Bible study group with his friend up at LSU."

"Well, I'll be."

"Yeah, I know."

This was Fletcher's friend from high school. Lee was excited that Fletcher had accepted Jesus. "I couldn't believe it," she said.

Fletcher came home that weekend, and when I asked him about it, he said, "Yeah, I had that bad trip, and God told me to get my act together and that He was going to save me. He revealed himself to me."

"I don't know about all that, but I know you needed to get your life together."

I thought about it. When he was in high school he wouldn't listen to anybody. So, what better person could God have on a college campus than someone who didn't care what anyone thought?

Frogging season opened Memorial Day weekend and I called Fletcher to go to the camp. As we drove, I started out saying, "You know, this is what happened to me," and I told him how I was in high school and college and how my drugs and drinking got out of hand so much that I started thinking if this is all there is, I want out. Then I told him about December of 1986 and how I got on my knees and gave myself over to God, and afterward it felt like He lifted a rock off me and I haven't had a serious urge to drink since then.

"The whole point is that you're not going to find true happiness or meaning in life from what you can take from it, but instead it is by what you give to it; by wanting to serve rather than be served. None of the things in this world are going to make you happy. Your worth is what you can give this life, not what you can get out of it."

"Dad, I get it. I'm good with it. I believe that Jesus died for my sins. That Jesus loves me, 'this I know for the Bible tells me so.'" I looked him in the eye. He meant it. That is important to me now. "I have accepted Jesus as my Lord and Savior, and I know He has forgiven me for my sins. But I don't want to get into any debates about baptism, dunking or sprinkling, or anything else. Can we just go get some frogs?"

"Yeah, I'm good with that."

In late June, Mom was moved to a skilled nursing facility with a feeding tube but otherwise was stable. We decided to do the Fourth of July in Katy with Sister Lee and Jack because there was no way Mom could make the drive up home to Winnfield. It was a nice time with all the family and like all family gatherings, there was a lot of love and a little conflict, but nothing serious. I mean, we had to get fireworks and "someone" had to throw a skyrocket backward into the area where everyone was sitting. I was still off and on with the cigars. 2015 wasn't over yet, and I said I would quit in 2015. I just didn't say when, so I was doing the hokey-pokey.

I lit a cigarillo and stepped out with my sister who had quit smoking years before, but said, "Give me a drag off that." Just like the old days around the horse barn with Picayune cigarettes.

That first day, a group of six or eight of us went to visit Mom. She was in bed, a feeding tube snaking beneath the covers and the cannula beneath her nose feeding her pure oxygen. She looked better than I'd seen her, but still frail, not the spry and energetic woman I'd known my whole life. Some of us filtered into the room, while others lingered near the dividing curtain looking in.

"Mom, how you doing?"

"I'm doing all right."

"Yeah? That's good to hear. Hey, I brought someone for you to see."

Fletcher was standing behind me, sort of leaning against the door frame and like his usual self, he was wearing a workout shirt, slides, shorts, and a headband. He came into the room with a broad grin on his face. It was his trademark. I looked at Mom and she got that glint in her eye and broad smile that used to always be there, rain or shine, and she said, "How are you doing, boy?"

"I'm good Nana. How are you?"

And there they were, the two brightest, completely connected things in that room. It was uncanny. There were about five people in the room around her bed and another three or so standing watching, but when Fletcher and Mom saw each other, none of us existed. He just lit her up. He walked over to her side and held her hand as they chatted and laughed, and it was as if they both knew something that no one else did, a little secret between them.

Fletcher kissed her cheek and said he'd see her later. She smiled at him. "Now you be good, boy, ya hear?"

He smiled, too. "Yeah, I hear you." Then he walked back into the hallway and the halo of light that connected them dimmed.

We all chatted some more with Mom, but she tired and I lingered behind as the others left and walked outside. I leaned down and gave her a gentle kiss on her forehead, but before I lifted my head she placed one hand on my shoulder and whispered, "You and your sister are in charge here, aren't you?"

"Yes ma'am." She had a medical will that put us in charge of decisions over her care. She had worried that if she left it up to anybody else who was a softie that they wouldn't follow her wishes. She knew we would call it like we saw it.

"I've had enough. I'm ready to go home."

"Okay."

Then she looked at me in a way that was uniquely hers. "You know what to do." It was a statement, not a question.

"Okay."

I spoke with my sister later and we both agreed, it was time to bring Mom home with hospice care looking in on her. She'd be with all the things in the world that held meaning to her. There were all the photos from the years we'd grown up and of Dad when he flew in World War II, her rocking chair and some furniture that had traveled with her throughout her life. It was those pieces of her life that made up what people are all about, the memories. We went through that surgery so she could get home, and we'd be darned if we were to go through all that and not let her come home.

Before we left, I went to visit her. "You know you're going to go home. You can wake up and look out the window and everything else."

"Oh, okay, that would be fine."

And so, we left.

Later that month in July, I was running around the house getting ready for varsity football camp and football with Ross who was starting seventh grade. It was his time to go to school, but Lee was giving me the usual pushback, though the pushback seemed more pro forma this time.

I had plans to go back to Texas in about a week, but then I got a call from my brother-in-law on Sunday night. "Your Mom's not doing so good."

"Should I get in the car and come over?"

"No, just stay by the phone. We'll let you know."

"Well, I'm coming tomorrow morning, but let me know if things get worse."

The next morning at daybreak, I had my bags in the car and I was waiting for Lee to come up from the back pasture to say goodbye when my sister called. Somehow, I knew. "We lost her."

The first thought that went through my mind was how it is that people say they lost somebody like they misplaced the person. But I knew exactly what she meant.

"She died last night in her sleep."

I don't care how prepared you think you are, you're never ready when it happens. I learned that with Dad. It was no different with Mom.

#

Because of all the people she had come to know in Texas, we decided to hold a funeral service in Katy at the Methodist church and then bring her to Winnfield where we'd have another service and then place her in the Garden of Memories next to Dad. In Katy, my sister and the minister asked me what verses I thought would be appropriate, and I gave him John 14:1-3.

> Let not your hearts be troubled. Believe in God; believe also in me. In my Father's house are many rooms. If it were not so, would I have told you that I go to prepare a place for you? And if I go and prepare a place for you, I will come again and will take you to myself, that where I am you may be also.

It was what we had talked about at her kitchen table, the same table that had witnessed everything from moon walks to Viet Nam and all arguments and discussions that go along with raising four children.

It asks the fundamental question, "Do you believe in God?" That is where we started. A first cause of the universe of necessity must be eternal. Why? *Ex nihilo, nihil fit,* out of nothing, nothing comes. Put another way, if there ever was a time that there was nothing, what could there possibly be today? Nothing. Like the song says, "Nothing from nothing leaves nothing ..."

God gave us the ability to think rationally. It is one of His attributes. And nothing can exist and not exist at the same time. Things cannot create themselves. So, if there is something today—the world and all its people—it means that something had to create it and that something couldn't have created itself. That something, God, must be eternal.

And then question number two: "Believe also in me." Why? Because Jesus did those things only God with His ex nihilo power could do. Jesus commanded nature by calming the seas, walking on water, and changing water into wine. He commanded demons and healed the sick, blind, and lame. And He conquered death by raising Lazarus from the dead, among others. And He rose from the grave.

Of course, at the Katy service when the congregation sang her favorite hymns, "Morning Has Broken" and "In the Garden," I could do no more than weep.

Before the service in Winnfield, I had a meeting with a client up in Jena. I called Fletcher and said I'd pick him up at LSU the night before. We'd stay at a hotel in Vidalia and then head on up to Winnfield the next day after my meeting. We drove from Baton Rouge to Vidalia and on the way up Fletcher said, "Pick me up a six-pack of beer."

I didn't appreciate how he asked and started to tell him, when he interrupted. "Either that, or I'll use my fake ID." He was still headstrong if only nineteen.

"Okay."

We got to our room, which was on the first floor and had a little porch outside, and I told Fletcher I was heading outside to smoke, which, yeah, I know, I hadn't yet quit.

He came out with me and drank his beer while I smoked and from where we were, we could see the Mississippi River moving slow and easy. The lights of the Natchez-Vidalia Mississippi River Bridge shone in the night. Fletcher was buzzed when he started talking about how much he loved Nana and missed her. Tears welled. Then he got serious and looked me dead in the eyes. "You need to quit smoking."

I stayed silent.

He started to cry in earnest. "I don't know what I'd do if anything happened to you. It's bad enough losing Nana."

I thought for a moment. "Well, that's reason enough, Fletcher, for me to quit, because I love you and I've been through a lot with you. So, okay, I said I would quit this year and I do as I say, so I'll quit." He was more of a squeaky wheel than any of the boys, so I was touched and knew it was time to stop screwing around with tobacco.

I met with my client, and then we went up to Winnfield and the funeral. The kids all had to wear suits, which was a production. Fletcher was so buffed up from weight lifting that a suitcoat wouldn't fit over his shoulders so he just wore a shirt and tie. The boys were pallbearers.

Once again, feeling the presence of God in that place, I cried. I started when the congregation started into "Holy, Holy, Holy." Tears rolled down my cheeks. I was in the presence of God, and I was good with it.

Chapter 12

God Has His Way

In June of 2015, leading into the Fourth of July, the federal judge in the BP case assigned the U. S. Magistrate, a former Director of the FBI and former Mississippi Attorney General to assist in negotiating a settlement of the Clean Water Act and government claims. This included claims of local governments.

The negotiations were sensitive and ultra-secret. Once a person even became aware that they were taking place, that person was subject to a federal court order, which I will attempt to summarize: Do not divulge anything to anyone under penalty of extreme prejudice.

As a result, Walter was enlisted to assist in resolving the local governmental claims, which was a time consuming and ponderous process that often went well into the night. As he left to attend one such late-night meeting, his wife asked where he was going.

"I am under a Federal Court Order not to tell you," he replied.

"Yeah, right, that's a good one."

Later I found out that my wife didn't believe it either.

I won't get into the specifics of how this went down, but the government claims, of which we represented many local government entities, were settled. As a side note, many of the local governments we represented were those that Walter worked with through the Road Home Program after Hurricane Katrina, which he did *pro bono*. Funny how God works these things out when you just try to do the right thing, isn't it?

The long and short of it was that we made a few coins. The money was disbursed at the end of October, which left me with some decisions to make, not the least of which was my tithing. There were the usual churches and charities I'd supported through the years. As I was thinking on this, we received a piece of mail from World Vision. For years, we had sponsored a young boy named Jerry in the Philippines through World Vision. As I read through the letter they'd sent, I called out to Lee, "How long have we sponsored Jerry?"

"Since he was nine years old, I guess," she replied.

That was back when Ross was little, so this young man must be a teenager by now.

I read through the little report they sent, and I think my eyes just about bugged out of my head. The official spokesperson for World Vision that year was Patricia Heaton. No doubt about it, I was being haunted. It seemed like every time I went into the den, there'd be Mason watching his favorite show, *The Middle*. I would literally look away. Then over the next few days, we started getting more and more mail from World Vision and all of it had a picture of Patricia Heaton on it. I would treat the mail like hot lava and was getting a little spooked.

When I sat down to write year end checks, I gave a donation to World Vision thinking this was a chance for me to affect someone in the world and do something great. I mean that's what I wanted to do after all. Then I included in the cover letter:

> *Last, but not least I would like to meet your spokesperson, Patricia Heaton. I did not know who she was as 2015 began. Yet through the year she kept popping up and World Vision was there as well. Hence, this donation. I guess God works in mysterious ways. It's not the first time, and hopefully not the last.*

Then I took that paragraph out of the letter. And put it back. Then took it out. And put it back again and sealed the envelope and mailed it.

In January of 2016, I got a call from the area director at World Vision. She said they were having their annual conference in San Diego in March and invited me to come.

"We got your letter with your donation, and the speaker this year is going to be Patricia Heaton. You could have lunch with her if you want," she added.

"Wow. Okay, we'll be there." Mason was thrilled. Lee gave me an odd look, like she might be concerned for my mental health, but she was up for it.

I booked the flight to San Diego for Mason, Jackson, Ross, Lee, and myself. We got there on a Friday and stayed at the Ulysses S. Grant Hotel. Not my favorite Yankee General. In fact, I have no favorite Yankee generals. And then we had fun. We took the boys to the aircraft carrier MIDWAY and on the hanger deck were the airplanes my Dad flew during World War II. Hellcats, Corsairs, dive and torpedo bombers. It was awesome. I had a hard time getting them to leave, and we were almost late for the dinner that night.

The next day we were to meet Patricia Heaton for lunch. Of course, nothing can be easy. A few days before we left for San Diego, Jackson came to me and said, "Can we meet my friend Cesar? He lives in Riverside, California, which is near San Diego."

"How do you know Cesar?"

"Oh, from playing online videogames."

"Come on. You have got to be kidding me."

Skip to that Saturday morning when Jackson came to me and said, "Cesar is coming down from Riverside; his mother is bringing him and he'll be here in ten minutes."

Ugh. I'd totally forgotten.

"Jackson, we are supposed to meet a TV star for lunch, and you invited this friend of yours that you've never met except for over the Internet, and he'll be here in ten minutes? I mean, are you really telling me this?"

"Well, yeah. That's what I said."

Double ugh!

"How do you know he isn't a pimp or some kind of drug dealer or something like that?"

"Oh no, when we play I can hear his dad fussing at him in the background. He's a junior in high school and a nice guy."

Triple ugh.

"Okay."

Cesar showed up and, yeah, he was a nice kid who seemed like he was normal and everything. He and Jackson scooted out the hotel door to the MIDWAY with me calling after them, "Be on time for lunch!"

They managed to show up, and at the appointed time, we were all led to a room in the conference center where World Vision was holding their meeting. The woman who guided us said Patricia Heaton was going to bring her lunch to sit with us and have a visit.

I looked at Cesar. "Today's your lucky day. I never met you before, but you're about to meet a TV star."

"Okay, sounds good to me." He seemed unimpressed. *Kids.*

Patricia Heaton came in, and as we sat and chatted it was clear she wasn't her character from the show. She is friendly with a good heart. Not that Frankie Heck isn't of course.

"Frank, what kind of a lawyer are you?" she asked.

My pat response to that question is, "A real good one." But instead of something funny or even coherent, I said, "Maritime, Admiralty, I mean, Admiralty and Maritime law." Talk about the driest most boring thing to say. And in retrospect not totally honest being that I am a plaintiff's trial lawyer.

She didn't fall dead asleep or run from the room, and we talked for a while longer. She was sitting next to me, and at one point I thought I'd turn the conversation to why we were there.

"Actually, you're pretty much the reason we're here."

"That's what I heard. Tell me about that."

"Well, it's kind of strange." I told her about the Saints winning the Super Bowl just to be sure that we were clear that miracles can happen. Then I talked about the cigars, Chantix, the surgery, Spencer's wedding, losing Mom, and watching *The Middle.* I mentioned that at first I thought she was Susan Lucci and described almost everything that had gone on the past few months, including how she haunted me into my donation to World Vision.

Most importantly, I told how I knew God had orchestrated it all because this wasn't the first time something like this had happened to me. After Hurricane Katrina and the house fire, we were invited to a New Orleans meeting of Desire Street Ministries on August 29, 2009. As was my custom, I read a chapter of the Bible each day, and at that time had gotten stuck on the book of Haggai. This was also around the time I was trying to decide how to rebuild our house. The words of the prophet about living in paneled houses while God's house lay in utter ruins were stuck in my head, as was the admonition to "consider your ways." [43] I didn't want to put money into a bag full of holes.

At the dinner, Danny Wuerffel—executive director of Desire Street Ministries as well as the 1996 Heisman Trophy winner and former NFL player—had gotten up to talk. He started on chapter one of the book of Haggai, which reads, "In the second year of Darius the king, in the sixth month, on the first day of the month, the word of the Lord came by the hand of Haggai the prophet ..."

Then he pointed out that the footnotes in study Bibles, including mine, have that date as August 29, the date of Hurricane Katrina. Danny, Lee, and I looked at each other in amazement. Look, I'm no page-flipping, superstitious Christian, but I can feel God in something when He is there. I can't tell you how God worked things out in my life better than I ever could. Just look, *for crying out loud.* This was just another instance.

Then I talked to Patricia Heaton about my conversion and coming to God. How the worst thing that could happen to me turned out to be the best thing that had happened to me. How I'd fallen to my knees, and in that moment God removed the urge to drink, and after that I'd met the love of my life and now had seven sons and more trouble than I knew what to do with.

I ended with the goal that I had set at the side of Dad's casket. "It really seems like I'm pulling something over, but I'm not. I just think that people might laugh if they knew that my only goal in life is to die sober. The rest of this is all just gravy."

It was a total brain-dump and by the time I finished, took a breath, and looked back up at her, I thought she'd be running for the door.

Instead, she said, "You know, that's funny. I came to Los Angeles and it just wasn't happening for me as an actress and I tried different auditions and got some small parts, but I was frustrated and at the end of my rope. I remember getting on my knees in my sister's crummy apartment in West Hollywood with shag carpeting and crying and just saying, 'Okay, I've had enough. I'm tired of fighting this and I'm going to turn it over to you, God. What am I supposed to do?' And that's when everything started happening."

"I guess everything happens for a reason. That same force brought us here today, and isn't that weird?"

"Yeah, that's really something."

"Yep."

I know that I should not think of God's Providence as weird. It's just that God is so much greater, larger, huger, more powerful than us that it sometimes just blows my mind. And that was one of those times when everything just seemed to fit. Just trust God. That's it.

The simple is profound. The profound is simple.

#

After lunch, I found out that Cesar's dad had Stage 4 prostate cancer and the prognosis was not good. He, Jackson, and I locked hands and prayed for his dad.

He seemed a bit uncomfortable, but went with it. We talked, and it looked like they did not attend church too regularly. I made a mental note.

#

I hadn't been to California since 1986 when I took that convertible ride down Sunset Boulevard that I can't remember. But after the trip to San Diego, we were invited to the premiere of the movie, "God's Not Dead 2" in West Hollywood. Just Lee and I went, and we had a blast. The premiere wasn't until Monday night, but we arrived Saturday so we could have dinner at a fancy Beverly Hills restaurant. I couldn't help but ask the waiter if Jed, Ellie Mae, and Jethro ate there often? I just got a blank stare. Don't these people watch TV Land? And we also came Saturday so that the next morning we could sit in the third row at Grace Church to listen to John MacArthur preach. We were warmly received as visitors by a local realtor, went to Sunday School, and ate lunch at In-N-Out Burger. The premiere was great and the after party was better. Only God could get me to Hollywood and *boy*, did He deliver.

That spring we nailed the bass in the marsh on the spawn. Fletcher hung white spinner baits from the sun visor of his black Silverado. Everything seemed copasetic.

#

In June, I had to do some depositions in Huntington Beach, California. Fletcher was out of school, and so I said, "Why don't you come along?" He did and each day we'd get up early and surf. He did okay, I wasn't so good. After surfing, I'd head out and do the depositions. We'd go out at night for dinner and to just cruise around and see what we could find.

When the depositions were done, we took a car up the Pacific Coast Highway and ate at a Brazilian steak house. Fletcher may have put down the drugs and gotten saved, but he still drank on occasion, and when he did he got drunk pretty much like I did when I was his age. I talked to him about not being able to stop once he got started and all that.

Fletcher was, how can I put this ... cool? He had two "X's" carved on his chest from back when he was cutting himself in high school. He trained like a fiend on the weights, was a math whiz, and didn't take anything from anyone. He was fearless and had the biggest heart on earth. He would fight for someone who was weak at the drop of a hat and had a grin that shone. He was over age eighteen so he didn't have to listen to me, but he did. I told him all of what happened to me, how I found God, and how he reminded me so much of, well, me. And for that reason, I really feared for him.

The next day I took his picture at Griffith Park Observatory with the Hollywood sign in the background and we ate at In-N-Out Burgers on Sunset Boulevard. You would've thought they were giving something away as it was more crowded than Popeye's at Mardi Gras. We took the Warner Brothers studio tour, a cruise through Muscle Beach and UCLA, and on Sunday we packed up and headed out to make our flight home. At the airport, we heard that Huntington Beach had been closed because of the sighting of five Great Whites. They never messed with us; professional courtesy I guess.

Uncle John turned ninety that summer, and the Fourth of July family reunion was held in Winnfield at the Methodist Church because the camp on Saline Lake had flooded from torrential rains. Uncle John had moved into town, and Fletcher, Jackson, Mason, and I stayed with him. I noticed a needle-point he had in his bedroom from the camp.

> God grant me the serenity to accept the things that I cannot change,
> Courage to change the things that I can,
> And wisdom to know the difference.

I like the long version which keeps on,
> Living one day at a time,
> Enjoying one moment at a time,
> Accepting hardship as the pathway to peace,
> Taking, as Jesus did,
> This sinful world as it is,
> Not as I would have it,
> Trusting that You will make all things right,
> If I surrender to Your will,
> So that I may be reasonably happy in this life,
> And supremely happy with You forever in the next.
> Amen [44]

"Where did that needlepoint come from Uncle John?"

"That was Daddy's." My Poppy. Maybe there was more of a reason why I never saw him drink? One day I'll find out, I guess.

For the upcoming school year at LSU, I bought a condo for all the boys to stay in as they rolled through college. Seemed like a good investment because separate apartments for Fletcher and Sam were killing me.

Sam graduated in the spring of 2016 with a degree in Biology, passed on medical school, and while waiting on publication of a paper he'd written to apply for graduate school, began interviewing. He was hired by a worldwide Japanese corporation out of thirty-plus candidates, mostly engineering majors. He lamented that he should have just majored in Physics. Who knew? After five weeks of training in Chicago he designs, installs, and sells laser quality control systems to manufacturing concerns and has responsibility for the state of Florida. He makes more money than I ever dreamed of graduating in Accounting in 1979. Even with inflation.

We rolled into August and September preparing for Jackson's senior year in high school. I could not resist agreeing to help coaches Agresta and Robert by coaching offensive line, which felt like it put everything on track. The only issue was a call in late August that Fletcher made to Lee. He told her he'd been out with some guys and blacked out. He couldn't remember anything from that weekend. I spoke with him, too. To me, it seemed like the handwriting on the wall. He needed to deal with his drinking. He said he would take it under advisement. All I could do was hold my breath.

I told Lee, "School's starting and the friend he was running with is at another school, so that should get better because they won't be hanging out together." But I wondered.

With the start of school I saw Fletcher for some football games. He seemed to be doing all right. At least that is what he told me. But the week before the Ole Miss game, Lee said, "I'm worried about Fletcher."

"How come?"

"Oh, he's just depressed and I don't think he's doing too good."

"What do you mean?"

"I don't know, he's just not doing well, I think."

Hearing this from Lee worried me, so I texted Fletcher late that Wednesday night and asked how he was doing. He responded, "Well, it's not that bad. I don't feel like dying."

I took that to be good and replied, "Well, that's good, it's Wednesday."

"Yeah, this week is awful. I can't wait for it to end."

"This, too, shall pass."

"Okay."

I made plans to come up and go to the game with him that Saturday and told him I was coming. I would bring Ross and Mason and meet Fletcher at the condo and go to the game. That Saturday morning I called him around 11 a.m. "Hey, when do you want us to come up?"

"You can come whenever you want to. I'll go down and move my truck." He had to angle his truck to block off the two parking spaces that I had at the condo or else someone would sneak in and park and I would have to get them towed.

The game wasn't until eight that night, so around noon I texted him to say we were on our way. I got no response. We dropped by Ross's friend's house to get some gizmo, and then we stopped for beef jerky and drinks. At about seven minutes after two, I texted Fletcher that we needed the code to get into the condo complex. He didn't respond, which wasn't that unusual. Fortunately, Ross remembered the code so he hopped out and opened the gate for us. Fletcher's truck was angled into both parking spaces so he expected us.

"Ross, would you hop out and get Fletcher to come down and move his truck so I can park?"

Ross got out and I watched him walk up to the door and knock. He waited a bit then knocked again and waited. Nothing. He came back and said nobody's answering.

I walked up to the door with Ross and knocked, but didn't hear a thing. I started to get a panicked feeling so I opened the door with my key and walked in. To my left, I could see Fletcher in his bedroom kneeling at the side of his low bed with his upper body lying across the bed face down and his arms spread open. His dog Baxter was sitting on the bed next to him. Fletcher looked like he had been dropped in his tracks, and it didn't escape me that his arms were stretched out wide as if on a cross.

I called out as I crossed to his bedroom door, "Fletcher, get up man. What are you doing?"

No response.

Panic started to rise in my chest.

I yelled back to Ross. "Go outside and dial 9-1-1." I pulled Fletcher's head up. His face was blue like he had been in a freezer. He was just wearing workout shorts, no shirt, his upper torso was also blue, and he wasn't breathing.

I reached down to Fletcher and shook him, "Fletcher, get up. Fletcher."

I rolled him to the side off the bed and he just fell over backwards. I pulled his leg up. He was totally nonresponsive.

"Fletcher, Fletcher!"

I started chest compressions and at the same time I tried to dial 9-1-1 on my cellphone. I recommend that you practice this one handed and panicked because I screwed it up three times before I finally got through and put the phone on speaker. A lady come on the line and I told her, "I'm here with my son. I just got here, he's unresponsive."

"Do you know CPR?"

"Yeah, I'm doing it and I'm pushing and it's going squish, squish, squish."

"How many chest compressions have you done?"

"I don't know, about ten."

"Give him a hard blow."

I did. It sounded like a sponge as the air went in and then out again. "He's got fluid in his lungs and he's blue! I can't believe it, he's blue!"

"Keep going, I've got help on the way. Do you feel a pulse?"

"No." His eyes were open like little slits and his mustache scratched against my mouth as I breathed into him.

I pushed on his chest a few times then breathed for him in the rhythm I was taught for CPR. Some color returned to his face. I told the lady on the phone. "Well, keep going, it looks like it is having some effect."

The entire scene seems so surreal in my mind to this day. Outside it was the most beautiful, sunshiny festive day. Young college football fans drank and celebrated. But inside this small apartment, in the middle of all that goodness, a nightmare.

Ross tried to come back in but I ran him out. "Stay outside! Do you hear me! Stay outside!"

In minutes that seemed like hours, the paramedics arrived. "We'll take over, we'll take over," and they stepped in. "Okay, we have to drag him out to the middle of the floor so we have more room to work on him." They took his arms and drug him from the bedroom to the den shoving a pool table out of the way.

They looked into his lungs, they bagged him, they gave him CPR, they gave him injections, he never flinched as they stabbed him with needles, and they had an emergency room doctor on the phone.

They hooked him up to a heart monitor, but he never had a pulse. I stood and watched the outstretched body of my blonde-haired son on the floor. Fear gripped me, but I choked it down.

Baxter started to get testy so I locked him in the other bedroom as they worked. I watched. I prayed. I cried out silently. I screamed silently.

One of the paramedics looked up to me. "We've reported all the conditions and everything to the doctor. He's on the phone line at the hospital, and he said we should discontinue efforts."

This was after about twenty minutes. I didn't move. Each of the paramedics looked at me with an expression that acknowledged that they knew their words could never express what I felt. One by one they passed. "I am very sorry for your loss."

He had orange socks that were halfway on his feet and a pair of shorts that he lifted weights in. There was a lighter on the bed and his wallet on the night stand with his health insurance card out next to it. In the dresser behind us were six packets of syringes and two spots of black tar on the bottom of the dresser drawer. There was an ice cream scoop with burn marks on the bottom. And there was a bag of Xanax in the drawer in the bathroom.

The police arrived and asked me to wait outside while they processed the scene. I felt glad to get out. I found Ross, age thirteen, downstairs behind the building. Poor kid had been out there all that time watching people pass on the way to the Ole Miss/LSU game gawking at the police cars, EMS, and the lights.

He looked into my eyes and he just knew.

"Fletcher is dead." I didn't know how else to put it.

The coroner's office van arrived and I couldn't put it off any longer. Mason, age nine, had sat in the back seat of the car the whole time. He was crying.

"Do you know what is going on?" I asked.

"Something bad has happened to Fletcher." He started crying more. He was dressed as Batman and had come up ready to play games. Now I had to tell him.

"Something bad has happened all right. Fletcher is gone. He's dead." Later he needed to pee and I led him to the side of the building. The bright day and passing people now were just a blur.

It seemed like it took forever to get the scene processed. Then they all left. Just like that. The detective said it looked like a heroin and Xanax overdose. He said there were no signs of foul play. I could not find his truck keys and as the condo door was locked, I wondered if someone had been present and left. I told the detective. He took a note. Then, as if he didn't know what else to say and with a pained grimace on his face he said, "We are getting four to five heroin overdoses a week just here in East Baton Rouge Parish."

One patrolman waited as I had to call a Baton Rouge funeral home and arrange for transport of the body back to our home. Somehow, I remembered the name of the funeral home that had buried my great uncle Nub Jackson. And I knew of a cemetery on the way to our church in Covington, so I called them. Coach Robert arrived before they did.

It took three of them to move the gurney down the stairs from the second floor. Drunk college students pulled up short when they saw the hearse, gawking like it was some sort of a joke. I wished it was and wanted to scream at them. But what?

I wanted to get home before I melted. Coach Robert offered to drive Ross. Mason and Baxter rode with me. Baxter is a big white Great Pyrenees. He's like a big stuffed animal from the fair, and Fletcher slept with him. And I had looked into his eyes as I gave CPR to my dead son. God, I wish that dog could talk.

I don't think Fletcher knew what he was doing. It was just like when he got bit by that water moccasin when he was out fishing. It was a bigger thing than he knew, and it bit him.

He was only twenty years old.

I made Mason ride in the front seat with me so I could squeeze his hand and tell him that I loved him. "Are you okay?"

He frowned in tears. "This is going to take some time to process."

And a voice in my head said, both to him and me, "You look a little green there, son."

I could not sleep.

The first thing I did was to start reading the book of Job and got thorough chapter one. "Naked I came from my mother's womb, and naked I shall return. … Blessed be the name of the Lord." [45] I grabbed that. If that could just be my response it was good enough for now.

The funeral home attendant found his truck keys in his pocket when he arrived that Sunday morning. I was there when he got there. I wanted to see him again. They let Lee and the boys see him the next morning after he was cleaned up. They were all racked by grief. He looked a lot better to me then, but I didn't want to say how he had looked before. None of them was there and I could spare them that.

I had to buy a funeral plot. It was something that I had never considered doing. Lee suggested that I buy two. One for him, and one for me. I was ready so I bought two.

We buried Fletcher that Wednesday. I put him in a pair of my blue jeans and one of my nice blue shirts and a fishing tie that Sam gave him for Christmas. He wore the steel toed boots Lee had bought him. I was going to bury him with his boots on.

The funeral was here in Covington. My sister Lee, Jack and family, and John Robert were there, as was the entire Northlake football team. I hugged each one. Caleb Sampson, all six-feet-five-inches and two hundred sixty-five-pounds of him, who started as a freshman and earned the nickname Godzilla when Fletcher was a senior, passed me a letter he wrote about how Fletcher had encouraged him as a youngster. I could see the defensive huddle, two giants and Fletcher in the middle holding hands. Coach Tony was there as well as Coach Robert and the other coaches who had worked with Fletcher through his life. My Fiji brothers showed up, people I'd drank with, streaked with, and more, some of whom I hadn't seen in years. Lawyers I'd worked for and against came and paid their respects. All our friends from Grace Presbyterian, Three Rivers Presbyterian, and First Baptist churches and the guys Fletcher grew up with came. And, of course, the family from Winnfield was there. These were people I knew my entire life. Thank God they were there for us then.

When I looked up, tears streaming down my face and my soul laid bare before the awesome beauty, love, and power of God, the church was filled, and people were edged in the doorway looking in. That evening, I walked out onto the driveway and looked up into the sky. It was filled with stars. I asked that old familiar question, "What am I supposed to do now, God?"

Chapter 13

Daniel my brother, you are older than me
Do you still feel the pain, of the scars that won't heal? [46]
    —"DANIEL," ELTON JOHN

The Thursday after Fletcher's funeral, I went to football practice. I missed my guys on the offensive line and, as it turns out, they missed me. We had a game that Friday against the team that we beat Fletcher's senior year at their place after coming from behind in the second half. Fletcher had recovered a crucial fumble late in the third quarter. I remember our defensive end picking him up over his head with the ball held high. Then he ran to our sideline and spiked their ball. I held my breath for a flag that thankfully never came. Two days after Fletcher's funeral, I really wanted to win this game. I just didn't want to tell the guys and put unfair pressure on them. I mean, what if they did their best, as they always did, but lost? It happens.

They were thinking the same thing, wanting to win the game for Coach but wary not to say it, just in case. We won 34-14 after the O-line coach got his head out of his butt and figured out how to block their defensive scheme. Good thing too as they gave me the game ball and a special moment. It is signed by the coaches and the team and sits on the shelf in my office.

On the way home after the funeral, I looked at Sam. "I know the Bible says that for those who love God all things work together for good, but for the life of me I can't see any good coming out of this." I just couldn't. Winning that game was, in my mind, the first thing that I could do to balance things out and put something good on the other side of the scale after Fletcher died. And I felt the need to take the lead and set the example to keep on keeping on. So I did.

#

The next Saturday at 2:07 p.m. was hard. I awoke every day before dawn and could only sleep if I took two extra strength acetaminophen with a sleep aid that Mama had left at the house. That Saturday I was at the gravesite when 2:07 p.m. came and ran through the entire scene again in my mind. And I have questioned myself time and again. Why didn't I call 911 before I left? Why did I make those stops? Why didn't I go up earlier? What had I done wrong raising this boy? Was I too lenient? Too chummy? The buck stops with me after all. In the final analysis, this was my fault.

I wondered if a day would ever pass by that I didn't run through the events of that day in my mind. And if it did, how I would be able to live with myself. I kept reading Job.

#

We were in church on Sunday as always. I insisted on that. It was hard on us all. The boys got back to school that Monday and I went back to work. I also went to AA meetings. Fletcher had sat in one of those chairs, I saw to that. He knew where to go if he wanted.

#

Mason wanted to go trick-or-treating on Halloween so I took him in the neighborhood where we had just dropped Ross off for a party at his friend's house. They must have been running short on trick-or-treaters because we mopped up on the candy.

A few days later I was upstairs and Mason was sitting on his bed with Baxter crying. He had Elton John's song "Daniel" playing on his iPad. I went in.

"You okay? Why are you sitting up here by yourself?"

"No, I'm really sad. But I don't want to bother you or Mom and upset you."

I went to Ross's room. He was hiding out too.

"Come to Mason's room. We have to talk."

When we sat together in Mason's room I said, "Look guys, if there is a big gaping hole in the floor, we are not going to walk around and pretend that there isn't a hole in the floor. We have to let it out and tell how we feel."

We had a good group cry and that seemed to help.

#

My crying mostly took place in my bathroom where I could be alone. I would feel it coming and head back that way. It came in waves and, like the ocean, I could do nothing to stop it. So I would just go with it. Then I would be angry.

One time as I was alone, I could not help recalling crying like this on the floor of my apartment when I got sober over Romans 5:8. "God shows his love for us in that while we were still sinners, Christ died for us." It stopped me in my tracks again. For all these years I had no appreciation of how much God loved me. He had given His only Son, and I too had just lost a son. And it hurts. It hurts really bad, so bad that I had no idea how much God must love me. More balance.

Then Jackson, who was to have his older brother for a roommate the next year, had his senior retreat. For each retreat, each parent writes a letter to their senior giving them private words of love and encouragement. Fletcher had kept his letters from Lee and me close by. I found them that Monday when I went back up to clean up the condo. I didn't want anyone finding the trash the paramedics had left on the floor. I had finished reading the book of Job again. Where was I when God created all of this indeed? Here is the letter that I wrote to Jackson.

> There once was a man that God saved by his sovereign grace alone. He blessed the man with seven sons.

> The first fell victim to the temptations of the flesh, the devil and the world though the man loved him dearly and tried as best he knew how to do all in his earthly power to save and help him and tell him that true happiness with God would never come from such things. The man still tries to get this son to listen and not just hear.

> The second son too heard God's word and God hardened his heart. He too fell victim to the temptations of the flesh, the devil and the world rejecting God. Again the man did all in his earthly power to save and help him and tell him that true happiness with God would never come from such things. This son too fell hard and as a result turned and rejected worldly things but continues to wrestle with God. The man still points to signals of transcendence all around and prays that God too changes this son's heart.

The third son too heard God's word. It pierced his heart so he rejected the ways of man but still battles temptations of the flesh, the devil and the world. This son accepted the man's entreaties that true happiness with God would never come from such things. The man prays for his soul and lifts him up daily.

The fourth son too heard God's word. It by all appearances pierced his heart so he rejected the ways of man but still battled temptations of the flesh, the devil and the world. This son accepted the man's entreaties that true happiness with God would never come from such things. But he fell back into worldly things. God would not have it and took him from the man causing him great pain and distress leaving the man only with the comfort that he had heard the man's message and believed and that God had promised that not one who believes will be snatched from his hand.

The man now has three sons left to raise and see if they will hear God's word.

The man then bowed his knee to God as he once did when God saved him as he cried for help. And as he had done many times he again cried for God's help. And by not answering God answered.

And he thanked God for blessing him and entrusting him with such suffering as losing a son. For God had shown his love for the man that while he was yet a sinner God sent his only begotten son to die for the man so that he might be saved. And the man greater knew the love of God by what had happened to the man's son. And the man then understood that men are born, suffer, grow old and die so that they may know God's love for them.

And the man purposed to take up his cross and show God's love by imitating his Heavenly Father to his remaining sons. And the man's heart was glad.

#

I had agreed to be the speaker and tell my story at an open AA speaker's meeting before Fletcher died and didn't think that I should welch on my commitment. You've read as much of my story as I've been willing to tell, but maybe not this.

"It was like light and darkness. I was the light and I was surrounded by darkness. I had that so 'back-asswards,' it wasn't even funny, okay. The truth is, I'm the one that's in the dark. I was the one that was lost. I was the one that was searching and I'm surrounded by light. And the more I work and the more I try to get out of this, the more light, you know, that I come to see."

I was still fighting my way out of the darkness to the light.

#

We made it through Thanksgiving, staring at Fletcher's empty place setting. I started to breathe a sigh of relief, then realized that shortly I would get down the Christmas decorations along with his stocking. The opening day of the second split of duck season, I thought to take Jackson and Ross to the camp for a hunt, just to get our minds off things. Lee said, "Sure, go ahead and go. I will just go get the Christmas tree by myself." No way. I can hunt next year.

We went to take the yearly Santa picture that we take every Christmas before looking at the lights. This year Fletcher was not there, so I filled in. I had stopped shaving after the funeral, so I had a beard. On Christmas Day, Lee put something of Fletcher's in each of our son's stockings and filled Fletcher's with crazy stuff like he would have bought for them. I guess we will keep that going.

I read Peter Kreeft's book, *Making Sense Out of Suffering*. I have many books, but could only handle one. After reading Romans 8:28, I should have kept reading to verse 29 to realize that the working by God of all things together for good has a purpose, so that I might "be conformed to the image of his Son." One day over Christmas alone in my bathroom, I was racked with grief and felt like God had just left me all alone. *Why?* I had to ask the question that appears over and over in the Psalms. Why did this have to happen? I could see no answer. Job had taught me that. The answer was that there would be no answer. *But why?* So I cried. And cried. And when I could stand it no more these words came to my trembling lips: "My God, my God, why have you forsaken me?" (Psalm 22:1). And the world stopped.

Jesus took our sufferings on the cross and shares in those sufferings as we are conformed to His image. Before Fletcher died, I had no real appreciation of the word *grief*. It was just a cute word Charlie Brown said was somehow good. The word *grief* does not cover it. The word is too small. But Jesus is somehow there with us in this. "Surely he has borne our griefs and carried our sorrows" (Isaiah 53:4). Notice the plural and the addition of "carried our sorrows," which is past tense. I will accept the purpose of this as bringing me closer to Christ. And I will be sure someone good wears #53 on the offensive line next season.

#

Cesar bought a plane ticket and stayed with us over Christmas break. He and Jackson spent the week together. His Dad's prostate cancer is in complete remission.

#

I was asked to give a lunch address to the faculty at the school. Not knowing what to say, I borrowed heavily from the learned men I listen to on the radio like R. C. Sproul, Derek Thomas, Alistair Begg, Albert Mohler, and John MacArthur just to name a few. And as God would have it, the doctrine of providence came up. Over and over. Here is a portion of the newsletter to parents of the boys' school that I wrote before the talk.

January Newsletter

We hope that you had a very Merry Christmas and an enjoyable time off with family and friends. As we head into 2017 and we pause and reflect on how God is working in our lives we are overcome with a sense of gratitude and comfort as to how God sovereignly provides for us and will into the coming New Year.

The doctrine of providence gives us strength, courage and focus as we rest on the assurance that God is in charge. He holds the whole world in his hand. In the words of John Calvin "The Lord is everywhere at work ..." [47] He knows every hair on our head. Not a sparrow falls from the sky without his ordaining that it come to pass. (Matt. 10:29-30) He is the

God of all creation (Ps. 104:24-30) who never slumbers (Ps. 121:3-4) and will see his plans for us through (Ps. 33:10) because his hand delivers. (Ps. 138:8). He turns hearts where he wills. (Prov. 21:1) He is the God of life and death. All of our days are written in his book. (Ps. 139:16). No one will snatch a single sheep from his hand. (John 10:29) Life is not random. The Lord will fulfill his purpose for you.

So what does this mean for us? It means that at Christmas time and all the year we can rejoice in the blessings that God has given. And for those of us who haven't had such a great year but have been met with loss and adversity we should take great comfort knowing that God is in control of all things and upholds all things by his providence.

Let us not cling too tightly to this world. In the words of John Calvin "[w]e must learn to live like birds on a branch." That is, we must be ready to fly away at a moment's notice. God "works all things according to the counsel of his will." (Eph. 1:11) "And we know that for those that love God all things work together for good ..." (Ro. 8:28). Not some things. All things. Not just the things we like, but all things, particularly those we don't like. Things that are hard. Things that we do not understand. Keeping in mind God's purpose for our lives, that we "be conformed to the image of his Son" (Ro. 8:29).

At Christmas we only need look at God's plan for our salvation in Jesus Christ to see that he orders all things. Consider the prophecies of the coming of Christ that were fulfilled in his birth, life, death and resurrection. There is no doubt that God is in control and we will be with him in the end. Or in the words of Billy Graham "I've read the last page of the Bible, it's all going to turn out all right." [48]

So here's to a Merry Christmas and the excitement of what God has in store for us in the New Year to come.

I wrote that more for me than for them. Psalm 139:16 got my particular attention. If God has written in His book all of our days, why at funerals do we hear expressions like "she suffered too long" or what I wrote in Fletcher's obituary, "He died entirely too young"? I should be horse whipped. Everyone dies exactly when they are supposed to.

Not being able to sleep, I read *The Brothers Karamazov*, by Fyodor Dostoyevsky. It is only a few thousand pages long. I believe that I will make it required reading for offensive linemen. Here are some quotes that struck me.

"Christ is with you. Do not abandon Him and He will not abandon you. You will see great sorrow, and in that sorrow you will be happy." [49]

"Love cannot be created from nothing: only God can create something from nothing." [50]

And this one perhaps the most when the young monk Alyosha Karamazov's mentor dies: "The great grief in his heart swallowed up every sensation that might have been aroused, and, if only he could have thought clearly at that moment, he would have realized that he had now the strongest armor to protect him from every lust and temptation." [51]

Shortly after Thanksgiving, my oldest sister called to tell me that she had throat cancer. She has now successfully undergone radiation and chemotherapy and has been deemed cancer free, but the treatment was brutal. I liken this grief to cancer treatments in a way. It kills me from the inside out yet destroys the enemy within. I had never considered that grief would become my strongest armor in my sanctification battle for the mortification of the flesh.

It has been just over five months since Fletcher died. But who is counting? Mardi Gras is over. I went to Phoenix the Thursday before on business, then to the World Vision Annual Conference in Carlsbad, California, near San Diego to plan a trip to Zambia. Lee started a memorial fund for Fletcher to drill water wells to combat poverty. We hope to be there when a well comes in. I met up with Lee and the boys at Copper Mountain, Colorado, to get away from the Mardi Gras madness. Lee hurt her knee skiing. Skiing has too many risks for me and reminds me of what Bear Bryant said about the forward pass. Three things can happen and two of them are bad.

Fletcher hated snow skiing. One time he told me that the first time he felt alone and abandoned was the first time we went skiing and left him in ski school. He wondered whether we were ever coming back. I can't help but think if he didn't have one of those soul-altering events like I had as a small child.

While in Copper Mountain, I went to work out, and while benching remembered Fletcher spotting me in the very same gym a few years earlier. And while waiting on our bags at the airport, I could see him walking right up to then Saints defensive coordinator Rob Ryan for a photo.

#

At 3:45 a. m. I am looking to the east for the sun to rise. I can feel it. Again.

I can't see it. I can't touch it. I can't hear it. I can't taste it. But I know it's out there. And I can almost see it. I can almost touch it. I can almost hear it. I can almost taste it.

I want to go there. I want to be with Dad and Mom. I want to be with my son. Is that so wrong?

Now I am crying. Again.

#

On Palm Sunday, I brought Sam to the airport for an early flight and was crossing back over the lake at dawn. *Coast to Coast* was talking about near death experiences and people coming back from a warm cozy "light." I then tuned to Martin Lloyd Jones preaching on the Resurrection of Jesus, the subject of the movie released that weekend entitled *The Case for Christ*. I had a thought of Fletcher and I being together soon. It was a happy warm feeling. I felt like I had started to turn a corner. It was a good Easter.

I had been venting my anger and despair in the weight room but it was getting to me. One Saturday in early May at 4 a.m., I awoke sad and scared. This had been brewing for a while. I was under attack. The choice was presented to me. Take the advice of Job's wife, "Curse God and die," [52] and for me to drink again even if to temporarily stop the pain would be to surely die. I was not sure how long I could continue. I went to a meeting and spoke to some old timers in recovery. Their advice was to not keep it bottled up. To let it all out.

I went home, got on my knees, and began to cry. These weren't tears of grief but tears of despair like the tears years before. I had been touched before and changed. I did not want to go back. Hebrews 11:6 says that "without faith it is impossible to please him, for whoever would draw near to God must believe that he exists and that he rewards those that seek him." I pleaded for the gift of faith. I knew that God existed. That is why I wrote this book, so I could see it yet again. I wanted to feel God's love and peace again.

I never understood God. I don't understand God. I have experienced God, and I wanted to experience Him again. In John 6:67-69 after telling the disciples that they must eat of his flesh and drink his blood, something the disciples clearly did not understand, all left but the twelve. "So Jesus said to the twelve, 'Do you want to go away as well?' Simon Peter answered him, 'Lord, to whom shall we go? You have the words of eternal life, and we have believed, and have come to know, that you are the Holy One of God.'" I have told my sons, my players, and all who would listen that the single most important thing in their lives was whether Jesus Christ was their Lord and Savior. The vision was crystal clear. I was nothing without Jesus. I wasn't damaged, redeemed goods. I wasn't a human in the process of sanctification. I was absolutely nothing. Smitten, afflicted, and despised. I cried out to Jesus yet again to save me. Thankfully yet again the tears and my being silenced were evidence that God was there.

When I got up I didn't see, touch, hear, or taste it. I felt it deep within my soul. "It's all right. It hurts, just like when they nailed Me to the cross, but it's all right."

God is not done with me yet. I have to live life one day at a time and help save as many as I can.

From the Big Book of *Alcoholics Anonymous:* "Abandon yourself to God as you understand God. Admit your faults to Him and to your fellows. Clear away the wreckage of your past. Give freely of what you find and join us. We shall be with you in the Fellowship of the Spirit, and you will surely meet some of us as you trudge the Road of Happy Destiny. May God bless you and keep you—until then." [53]

Epilogue

I have not included in this book all the wrong that I have done. Just enough to see that any change in me was wrought only by the unmerited grace of God. I have also tried to stay away from heavy diatribes into either theology or philosophy. The omission is purposeful. For what use is there to refer to these sources, such as philosophical thought or the Bible, if the truths revealed are not reflected in real life and in the world?

I always had this feeling that this world just wasn't all that there was. I got signals along the way. Perhaps you have too. Does this scenario sound familiar to you?

Assume there is a man who has tried everything in this material world to find happiness. Wine, women, and song. Sex, drugs, and rock and roll. But happiness eludes him. He has a nagging feeling that there must be something more, but what? And then his pleasures do him in. He becomes a slave to those pleasures, but knows nothing else. Time and again he tries to find happiness, but his idols fail to produce. He sinks deeper and deeper. Getting fired and being given a first last chance don't do it. Then he comes to the end of his rope. He crashes and burns.

You would say this man is insane, would you not? He thinks and feels that there must be something more, but he can do nothing to save himself as hard as he may try. At the end of his rope, he is finally ready to quit. Ready to give up. His pain finally outweighs the pleasure he is seeking. He comes to his senses. In desperation, he says, "God, if this is it, if this is all that there is, you might as well take me out of this world because I have had it. If not, I am ready to admit total defeat, to lay aside all pride and self-sufficiency." He realizes that it is impossible to save both face and his ass at the same time. He is powerless and hopeless. The thought that he must save himself in his own power is terrifying. He cries out for God to reveal Himself! And He does. The man has a spiritual awakening. And he never wants to go back to the way he was. He is changed.

And in response, he prays and meditates every day. He rejoices in the goodness of just being normal. He fearlessly examines his life, confesses his faults and misdeeds to God and to another human being, asks God to help him remove his defects of character, does his best to make amends for all the wrongs and havoc he has caused.

This man knows the depth of his shortcomings. He continues to examine himself, take personal inventory, and when he is wrong, admits it and fixes it as soon as he can. Each day he abandons himself to God and seeks only His will for his life. And when he rests his head on the pillow each night, he goes over his actions, confesses to God where he was wrong, and asks forgiveness. He stops fighting anything and anybody. He lives life one day at a time, developing an intuitive sense of how to handle any situation that arises. He gives over his will for God's will. One day he suddenly realizes that God is doing for him what he cannot do for himself. He has indeed been reborn.

This is what happened to me. I live the way I live because I want to. And I have become convinced that such a man, one who is not self-deceived, is on a narrow road.

Early in my sobriety someone gave me a book by a man named M. Scott Peck entitled *The Road Less Traveled*. I read the first sentence, "Life is difficult"[54] and thought, *No joke, Sherlock!* I tossed the book aside and have never read it. I am sure that it is a fine book, don't get me wrong. But I know now that each person's path, each person's road, each person's journey is different. My path intersects with the paths of others daily, and it is my hope that by sharing the details of my journey, it will be of help to fellow travelers. I am just passing through this life. This isn't all there is. I am a spiritual being undergoing a human experience, not a human being undergoing a spiritual experience. And I cannot take any credit for the good things that have happened in my life. I stopped believing in coincidences long ago.

Are you on the narrow road? Maybe you should consider your ways. For those who are convinced that all is well, perhaps they should consider the parables of the wheat and the tares, the sheep and the goats, the narrow and broad roads, and Jesus's dismissal of those who did all those things for Him with the words that should strike fear and trembling, "I never knew you!"

I heard a young man say years ago, "If you are not looking the Devil dead in the eye every day, you must be walking down the same road he is." What road are you on, and isn't it time to get it straight?

Just sayin'.

The Last Signal

It was 2:30 a.m. in Lasaka, Zambia, and I could not sleep.
The hotel room was as dark as pitch, and Lee was snoring, exhausted from jet lag. Tomorrow we were to travel to a nearby village to dedicate a bore hole for fresh water in memory of Fletcher. My mind drifted to the question I had pondered many times and had posed to the family before we began the journey to Africa, "What do I want to get from this trip?"

The question was in God's hands; I had no clue. I just knew that for some reason my wife and family were inexorably drawn to making this trip. There had to be a reason.

I did not want to light up my phone's Bible App and disturb Lee so I tried to remember a piece of scripture that would help me understand why I was here. I fixed on Psalm 23. I know, it is frequently read at funerals. I recited it in my mind and looked for God's promises.

I have a shepherd. "I shall not want." He "restores my soul." Lights went off. That's what I wanted out of this trip. My soul restored! I repeated it over and over in my mind.

"He restores my soul."

"He restores my soul."

I kept on reciting the entire Psalm in my head. I had wondered at times how long I could go on like this. And *why? Why let God lead me down this path? Why?* "For His name's sake." That's why. So that victory over my difficulties would bear witness to His power and love. A familiar feeling began to settle in. I had been through these rodeos before.

And I will fear no evil, "For thou art with me."

I drifted off to sleep.

#

We traveled by car to the World Vision Area Development Project office the next morning for a devotional time with the team before we struck out to dedicate the well. After a few hymns, it was time for the devotional reading. World Vision's work throughout the world is difficult, arduous, poses seemingly insurmountable obstacles, and may even be dangerous. The scripture reading selected was fitting:

"The Lord is my shepherd ..."

Notes

1   C. S. Lewis, *Mere Christianity* (HarperCollins e-books, 2009) p. 278.

2   Philippians 4:6-7.

3   Peter L. Berger, *A Rumor of Angels: Modern Society and the Rediscovery of the Super-natural*, Copyright 1969, (Open Road Integrated Media, e-book, 2011) pp. 140, 141, 165, 171, 191, 208, 216, 218, 224, 249, and 250.

4   Os Guinness, *Fool's Talk: Recovering the Art of Christian Persuasion* (InterVarsity Press, 2015) e-Book, p. 299.

5   Creedence Clearwater Revival. "Born on the Bayou." By John Cameron Fogerty. *Bayou Country*. Fantasy, 1969.

6   Author unknown.

7   The Byrds. "Turn! Turn! Turn! (To Everything There Is a Season)." *Turn! Turn! Turn!* Columbia, 1965.

8   Luke 19:1-10.

9   Homer & Jethro. "After the Hangover's Over." By Vaughn Horton and Sammy Mysels. *Fractured Folk Songs*. RCA, 1964.

10   Robert Goulet. "The Impossible Dream (The Quest)." By Mitch Leigh (melody) and Joe Darion (lyrics).

11   *Ibid.*

12   The Fireballs. "Bottle of Wine." Words and Music by Tom Paxton. *Bottle of Wine*. Atco, 1967.

13   The Beatles. "I Want You (She's So Heavy)." Words and Music by John Lennon and Paul McCartney. *Abbey Road*. Apple, 1969.

14   Creedence Clearwater Revival. "Run Through the Jungle." By John Fogerty. *Cosmo's Factory*. Fantasy, 1970.

15   Gilbert O'Sullivan. "Alone Again (Naturally)." By Raymond O'Sullivan. *Back to Front*. MAM, 1972. BMG Rights Management UK / Grand Upright Music Ltd.

16   Five Man Electrical Band. "Signs." By Les Emmerson. *Goodbyes and Butterflies*. Lionel, 1971.

17   Jethro Tull. "Wind-Up." By Ian Scott Anderson. *Aqualung*. Reprise, 1971.

18   Charlie Daniels. "Long Haired Country Boy." By Charlie Daniels. *Fire on the Mountain*. Sony, 1975.

19   Jethro Tull. "Wind-Up." By Ian Scott Anderson. *Aqualung*. Reprise, 1971.

20 "Holy, Holy, Holy!" By Reginald Heber (lyrics) and John Bacchus Dykes (melody, "Nicaea"). 1861.

21 The Bangles. "Walk Like an Egyptian." By Liam Hillard Sternberg. *Different Light*. Columbia/Bangle-a-Lang, 1986.

22 Steve Winwood. "Higher Love." By Stephen Lawrence Winwood and Will Jennings. *Back in the High Life*. Island, 1986.

23 August & the Spur of the Moment Band. "I 95 Song." By Frederick "August" Campbell. Pantera, 1983.

24 Bill W. [William G. Wilson], *Alcoholics Anonymous: The Story of How Many Thousands of Men and Women Have Recovered from Alcoholism*, [The "Big Book"] 4th ed. (New York City, Alcoholic Anonymous World Services, Inc., 1976) p. 58-60.

25 *Ibid.*, p. 21.

26 The Who. "Who Are You?" By Peter Townshend. *Who Are You*. Polydor/MCA, 1978.

27 Bill W., *Id.*, p. 1.

28 *Ibid.*, p. 39.

29 *Ibid.*, p. 23.

30 *Ibid.*, p. 55.

31 *Ibid.*, p. 57.

32 *Ibid.*, p. 63.

33 Bill W., *Id.*, p. 44.

34 Lewis, *Id.*

35 Saint Augustine of Hippo, *The Confessions*. AD 401, Translated by Edward Bouverie Pusey, e-Book, p. 2.

36 Charles Austin Miles. "In the Garden." 1912.

37 Guinness, *Id.*, p. 139.

38 Goo Goo Dolls. "Iris." Words and Music by John Rzeznik. *City of Angels: Music from the Motion Picture*. Warner Bros., 1998.

39 Robert Goulet. "The Impossible Dream (The Quest)." By Mitch Leigh (melody) and Joe Darion (lyrics). *On Broadway, Volume 2*. Columbia, 1967.

40 *Ibid.*

41 *Ibid.*

(Notes continued)

42   Led Zeppelin. "Rock and Roll." Words and Music by Jimmy Page, Robert Plant, John Paul Jones, and John Bonham. *Led Zeppelin IV.* Atlantic, 1972.

43   Haggai 1:5.

44   Reinhold Niebuhr. "The Serenity Prayer."

45   Job 1:21.

46   Elton John. "Daniel." Words and Music by Elton John and Bernie Taupin. *Don't Shoot Me I'm Only the Piano Player.* DJM/MCA, 1973.

47   John Calvin, *Institutes of the Christian Religion*, 2 vols., ed. John T. McNeill, trans. Ford Lewis Battles (Philadelphia: Westminster, 1960) Vol. I, p. 224.

48   Billy Graham. Twitter @BillyGraham, April 4, 2015, 12:10 pm, available at https://twitter.com/billygraham/status/584432845600468995?lang=en (last visited August 1, 2017).

49   Fyodor Dostoyevsky, *The Brothers Karamazov*, trans. Constance Garnett (New York: Lowell, 1912) p. 91.

50   *Ibid.*, p. 965.

51   *Ibid.*, p. 443.

52   Job 2:9.

53   Bill W. *Id.*, p. 164.

54   M. Scott Peck. M.D. *The Road Less Traveled.* (New York: Simon & Schuster, 1978) e-Book, p. 31.

About the Author

FRANK SHAW is a practicing trial attorney, husband, father, coach, LSU football fan, and sportsman who studies theology in his spare time. He is a recovering alcoholic who "knows that he knows" he was saved by God as surely as if plucked from the path of a speeding bus. The rest he is still figuring out.

Donations to the Fletcher Shaw Memorial Fund
with World Vision can be made online
by searching
World Vision Fletcher Shaw Memorial Fund
in your internet browser,
or,
at https://mycause.worldvision.org
Type Fletcher Shaw in the Fundraiser search box on top left
then click on Amy Thompson Sponsoring Fletcher Shaw

Thank you

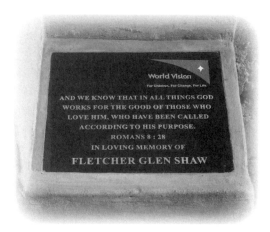